W9-ACX-069

HOLY

ROMAN

EMPIRE

Bologna

Orvieto
Viterbo • Rieti
Rome

Gaeta
Naples

KINGDOM
OF THE
TWO
SICILIES

Trapani
Palermo

ARMENIA
Lajazzo

CYPRUS

St. Jean d'Acre

Jerusalem

DA 229
C5

A Knight of Great Renown

THE LIFE AND TIMES
OF OTHON DE GRANDSON

By Esther Rowland Clifford

THE UNIVERSITY OF CHICAGO PRESS

102095

DEC 1965

*With this book
the author pays tribute
to Vassar College
on the occasion of its Centennial*

Library of Congress Catalog Number: 60-14361

The University of Chicago Press, Chicago 37
The University of Toronto Press, Toronto 5, Canada

© *1961 by The University of Chicago*
Published 1961. Composed and printed
by The University of Chicago Press
Chicago, Illinois, U.S.A.

TO HENRY

For if heaven be on this earth, or ease to any soul,
It is in cloister or in school, by many skills I find.
For in cloister cometh no man to chide nor to fight,
But all is buxomness there, and books to read
and to learn;
And great love and liking.

WILLIAM LANGLAND

Be good, sweet maid, and let who will be clever.

CHARLES KINGSLEY

Acknowledgments

If the study of the Middle Ages needs any excuse, the juxta-position of these two quotations should afford it; it is clear that the medieval clerk was far more understanding than the modern cleric. Having lost touch with the academic life during the almost twenty years that intervened between my under-graduate days and my return to the cloister to take up the studies of which this work is the fruit, I had forgotten that so much goodness exists in the world as I found among the learned. If I were to attempt to make a list of everyone whom I should like to thank, it would be endless.

But although endless, it does have a most definite beginning; though I spoke with the tongues of men and of angels, I could never express my gratitude to Professor George Cuttino, the parallel lines of whose learning and kindness meet only in an infinity of patient and inspiring helpfulness.

v i i

I owe so much to so many librarians that I can mention only the institutions at which they work: Bryn Mawr and Haverford Colleges, the University of Pennsylvania, the New York Public Library, the Library of Congress, the Manuscript Room of the British Museum, and the Bibliothèque Cantonale in Lausanne. But I must single out Mrs. S. M. Campbell, who transcribed documents for me in the Public Record Office, London.

My researches took me along strange bypaths: I should like to thank M. Ollivier Dessemontet of the Archives Cantonales Vaudoises for information on the early history of the Grandsons; Professor Berthe Marti of Bryn Mawr for her help in translating medieval, and especially papal, Latin; Dr. Michael Stettler, director of the Bern Historical Museum, for supplying facts on thirteenth-century embroidery; Evelyn Sandberg-Vavalà of Florence for supplementing these from her boundless knowledge of contemporary painting; Professor Henry Savage of Princeton for information on heraldry; and Tobias Wagner, Esq., of Philadelphia, for setting me right on recondite questions of falconry.

I am also grateful to M. de Jongh of Lausanne for his excellent photograph of the effigy.

And only by keeping silent can I make up to my husband and sons for the exemplary patience with which they endured the years in which Othon seemed to have become a permanent member of the family.

*And because it is an ability not common to write a good
history, as may well appear by the small number of
them; yet if particularity of actions memorable were
but tolerably reported as they pass, the compiling
of a complete history of times might be the better
expected, when a writer should arise that were fit for it;
for the collection of such relations might be as a
nursery garden, whereby to plant a fair and stately
garden, when time should serve.*

FRANCIS BACON, *The Advancement of Learning*

Foreword

In the first half of the eighteenth century, when they opened
the vault under Othon de Grandson's effigy in the cathedral of
Lausanne, they found the armed skeleton of a knight with his
golden spurs at his heels and his lance and shield by his side.
So he had lain for four hundred years, and so he was still to lie
until another two centuries should usher in the progressive age
that demolished the useless tomb in order to cut a doorway
though which tourists could more easily pass to visit the exca-
vations in the crypt. People who open graves even for the most
scientific of reasons are never wholly admirable, and those who
wantonly destroy them are even less so, but since starting my
researches into Othon's life and times I have come to the con-

clusion that for sheer ghoulish effrontery grave robbers and even body snatchers must yield to biographers.

It is such a shameless proceeding, this unsolicited interference with the dead, from the moment when we first start to sink a shaft into the valley of dry bones until our tools no longer grate on skulls and vertebrae and we spread our pathetic finds in the unaccustomed light of the sun and try to assemble the complete skeleton. Still if we were content with this, if the bones, arranged to the best of our ability, were put on display in some museum, the experts who visit such places could form their own conclusions. They would be quick to see all the mistakes that we had made in selecting and arranging our finds; they would point out how wildly inaccurate some of our guesses had been when we had to fill out missing parts of the original; above all, they would not be misled into thinking that our reconstruction was anything more than a skeleton, and they would warn the casual sightseer never to mistake it for the real man. If this were all, no great harm would have been done to the dead. But we must go further and drag our skeleton from the dim shadows of a museum into the glare of the footlights, where we string it together on the tenuous wires of chronology, cover it with scraps of steel and velvet picked up Heaven knows where, and as a last indignity set our makeshift marionette jigging to our own twentieth-century "Variations on a Thirteenth-Century Theme."

A Sicilian puppet-master, at the end of the performance, will lower his enormous flesh-and-blood hands onto the stage to show his blinking audience that Orlando was only a cardboard paladin after all and unshattered Durindana, four inches of shiny tin. It is in an effort to imitate his honesty that I should like to mention some of the reasons for Othon's never becoming anything more than a puppet.

The problems that confront a biographer vary for different writers at different periods; in this case there were three principal difficulties. The first is purely chronological; Othon died over six hundred years ago. The mere passage of time does not in itself build an ever higher barrier between the centuries and, so far as great movements go, certain ages have an affinity with others that have preceded them, irrespective of the years that lie between. But when it comes to portraying an individual, time does make a difference, for although human nature may not change, or the change may be so slow so as to be imperceptible, circumstances undergo a constant alteration. To take a minor example, Othon walking armed through Westminster moved differently from a man in a gray flannel suit walking along Madison Avenue, and now that modern science has requalified the substance of so many old wives' tales by the dignified adjective "psychosomatic," we know that these different movements produce different mental as well as physical reactions. Just as it is always easy to give a photographic description of a stranger, so it is possible to say, after looking at Othon's effigy, that he had a short, determined nose, a long upper lip, and a firm chin. But that is not the way we describe people whom we know well; usually, the better we know them the harder it is to remember exactly what they look like, and when we visualize them it is far more likely to be as a complex of gestures and intonations than as a collection of features. After six centuries of changing circumstances it is impossible to recapture the idiosyncrasies by which Othon's friends recognized him.

The second difficulty is lack of material. It is partly connected with the first, just because so much has crumbled away and disappeared during the intervening years, but it is also due to one of the intrinsic characteristics of the Middle Ages. I have no intention of joining the innumerable battles over medieval personality as such and am perfectly willing to be convinced that thirteenth-century men went into as much anguished soul-searching as did any heroine of a "Gothic" novel, but the fact remains that they left behind them very few of those unimportant but revealing documents that are the delight of the gossip-writer and the biographer. Nor is it necessary to spin long-drawn-out theories to explain why; it is simply because most of them were illiterate and writing materials were bad and expensive. It is one thing for a man who knows how to write to jot down passing thoughts at a well-stocked desk, but when it means calling in a secretary and waiting on his whims and on those of a goose-quill pen and oak-gall ink and perhaps wasting a good piece of vellum into the bargain, such spontaneous outpourings are the exception rather than the rule. Certainly Othon could not write with any facility; possibly he could not write at all; probably he never even wanted to, and this brings up the final difficulty. He was a man of action, and such men are usually inarticulate and as different as possible from their bookworm biographers who, sitting in libraries, set out to chronicle lives passed in courts and camps and think nothing of ascribing motives that they can barely comprehend to explain deeds that they never could have performed.

Even in the case of a contemporary, where the first two difficulties would no longer exist, this last consideration would make me pause before attempting to write anything about such a man, and certainly I should not dare trust any of my findings until I had submitted them for his approval. But death has robbed Othon of all his defenses. I can scarcely criticize the workmen who shoveled his bones out of what should have been their final resting-place when I am proposing to dig up anything that I can find about his long and active life; in defense of my behavior I can plead only one excuse.

To most people the knight is the typical figure of the Middle Ages, and Othon, by his birth, which placed him almost squarely in the center of the feudal hierarchy, was, to use a term that he would have found incomprehensible, the typical knight, the real-life counterpart of such imaginary nobles as William Stearns Davis' Baron of St. Aliquis. But in addition he was gifted with rare and valuable qualities that made him the friend and confidant of both the spiritual and temporal rulers of his time, and for this reason his career is so well documented that I can think of no one of his social equals in all of medieval Europe for whom we have such a mass of references.

Most of the books on chivalry as such leave the reader with the impression that a knight's life was divided between warfare, with its corollary the chase, and love-making, but although these activities were all carried on according to the most tedious and time-consuming rules, fighting was then, as hunting still is, a seasonal pursuit, and no one except a Don Juan can have spent all the intervening time in making love. What else did a knight do?

Because he is so frequently mentioned, we know at least what Othon de Grandson did. This is an attempt to tell his story.

ABBREVIATIONS

A.C. . . . . .Ancient Correspondence.

A.C.V. . . . . .Archives Cantonales Vaudoises.

A.S.T. . . . . .Archivio di Stato, Turin.

C.C.R. . . . .*Calendar of the Close Rolls.*

C.C.W. . . . .*Calendar of Chancery Warrants.*

C. Ch. R. . . . .*Calendar of the Charter Rolls.*

C. Chanc. R., Var. . . . . .*Calendar of Various Chancery Rolls.*

C.D.I. . . . .*Calendar of Documents Relating to Ireland.*

C.F.R. . . . .*Calendar of the Fine Rolls.*

C.P.R. . . . .*Calendar of the Patent Rolls.*

C. Pap. R. . . . .*Calendar of Entries in the Papal Registers.*

D.K.R. . . . .*Deputy Keeper of the Public Records.*

R.G. . . . .*Rôles Gascons.*

Rymer . . . .*Foedera.*

Contents

Illustrations

i. Setting the Stage

The Chinese, as expert in malediction as in all other forms of artistic endeavor, can think of no more baneful curse to lay on an enemy than "May you live in interesting times!" The only thing that weakens its force is its universality; the stagnant, peaceful periods, although they may not have been the golden ages that we fondly imagine, are still so rare and of such short duration that most of us miss them altogether, even though, like Othon, we live for ninety years. Moreover, the "interesting" ones vary among themselves, for there are some that even in retrospect remain merely periods of turmoil, of confused marking time in the dark, while during others the line of events seems so clearly drawn that future ages profess to see in them a special significance. Such was the period that included the end of the thirteenth and beginning of the fourteenth centuries and that saw the most active part of Othon's career, the fifty-six years between the accession of Edward I of England in 1272 and his own death in 1328.

Exactly at its halfway mark, as though to focus all that had gone before and much that was to come after, he witnessed the event that more than any other symbolized the fact that history had reached one of its many turning points. In 1300 he was in Rome as Edward's emissary to Boniface VIII. It was the year of the Great Jubilee, and to the observers it must have looked as though the century that had opened under the pontificate of Innocent III, most powerful if not greatest of medieval popes, was closing under very much the same auspices. No other pope had ever made greater claims or thundered anathemas with more reiterated conviction than Boniface; for centuries none had felt safer from attack, now that the emperor had confirmed the Papacy in all its Italian territories and the Two Sicilies was ruled, at least nominally, by a creature of the Church; certainly none had ever given such visible evidence of his power as did Boniface during the months of the Jubilee, when pilgrims from all Europe were flocking to Rome to acknowledge his supremacy and incidentally to throw their money into the papal coffers. But in fact, the medieval Papacy was as obsolete as the medieval Empire; within a short five years Boniface was to meet imprisonment and death and his successors had left Rome for seventy years of exile in Avignon. The world into which Othon had been born sixty years earlier, in which there was still hope that pope and emperor, enthroned side by side, might rule Christendom in harmony, no longer existed.

It had been beautifully and hierarchically planned, that ideal world of the scholastic philosophers, but as incapable of realization as the vaulting of Beauvais Cathedral, which fell and fell again as the architects attempted an impossible perfection. The very foundations had never been properly laid, and the edifice had always tilted dangerously from one side to the other, as its weight shifted now toward the Empire, now toward the Papacy. However, as the thirteenth century opened it had seemed definitely to have settled in favor of the latter, and it took sharper eyes even than those of the great Innocent III (1198–1216) to discern the cracks by which the strain had already breached the weakened fabric. The Empire, which had been so troublesome to his predecessors under Frederick Barbarossa (1154–1190) and the latter's short-lived son, Henry VI (1190–1197), was now torn and power-less: in Germany, a civil war was raging between the two rivals for the empty throne, Otto of Brunswick and Henry's brother, Philip of Swabia, and this meant that in Italy the Ghibellines, the Imperial faction, could look for little help from beyond the Alps, so that the pope, freed from pressure on his northern frontier, could turn his energies to consolidating his power within the narrow limits of the Patrimony of Peter. He could also look southward with equanimity, the first pontiff to be able to do so since the marriage of the future Henry VI to Constance, heiress of the Norman kingdom of Sicily, had troubled the papal sleep with nightmares of what would hap-pen to the temporal sovereignty should the Imperial and Sicil-ian crowns ever be united. It is true that as the years passed by and the Empress Constance, who had been over thirty when she married, produced no children, these apprehensions were lulled, but the awakening was all the more bitter when, at the age of forty, she bore a son and, so that there should be no doubt cast on his claim at least to her Sicilian kingdom, suckled him under an open pavilion within sight of the inter-ested citizens of Jesi.

The popes had endeavored to safeguard their position by exacting promises that the king of Sicily should never be emperor as well, and once again their minds were set at rest, for Henry died when his son was only three and obviously not a possible candidate for election, while Constance, dying a year later, left the baby Frederick to the guardianship of the pope. Innocent fulfilled his duties so conscientiously, keeping law and order among the turbulent Sicilians during the minor-ity of his ward, that he seems to have expected an equal conscientiousness on the part of the young king. When papal support first of Philip of Swabia and then of Otto of Brunswick still failed to restore peace between the Germans themselves or between the Empire and the Papacy, he obtained the Imperial election for Frederick, being careful, however, to make him repeat the promise that the Empire and the Sicilian kingdom should never both descend to his son.

But neither docility nor gratitude nor respect for his pledged word were among the varied and contradictory qualities that still make Frederick II one of the most controversial figures in history, the *Stupor Mundi* who by the combination of his Hohenstaufen brilliance and ruthless charm with the hardheaded characteristics that he inherited from his Norman ancestors alternately enchanted and outraged not only all Christendom but his Saracen enemies as well. However, until the death of Innocent's successor, Honorius III, who had been Frederick's tutor and was fond of him, relations between the Empire and the Papacy remained more or less friendly: it was only after the election of Gregory IX (1227–1241), a fiery and firm old Roman, that there came the open breach that involved Frederick in a series of Italian wars lasting until his death in 1250.

Gregory and his successors turned first to their old allies, those trading towns of the Lombard League and Tuscany that had never failed to put up a fight whenever the emperors had shown signs of making their claims over them anything more than nominal, and when even their united strength proved insufficient, the popes went farther afield for help. Innocent IV (1243–1254), the most bitter of Frederick's antagonists, offered the crown of Sicily to Edmund, the younger son of Henry III of England, and when this failed to produce the desired results and the struggle was continued even after Frederick's death, first by his legitimate son, the Emperor Conrad IV (1250–1254), and then by his bastard, Manfred, Pope Urban IV (1261–1264) offered the kingdom to Charles

4

of Anjou, the brother of Louis IX of France. It took Charles only four years to establish himself in Sicily; Manfred was killed at Benevento (1266); his even more unfortunate nephew Conradin, the fifteen-year-old son of Conrad IV, was captured at Tagliacozzo and beheaded at Naples—for Charles was as ruthless as any of the Hohenstaufen, although completely lacking their charm; and Enzio, the only one of Frederick's sons to survive, was already in the Bolognese prison where he was to live out the rest of his life, for no help could reach him from Germany, which was to remain without an emperor for almost twenty years. During the Great Interregnum, the Imperial crown was disputed by two more rival claimants, Richard of Cornwall, the younger brother of Henry III, whose Cornish tin-mines made him one of the richest men in Europe, and Alfonso X, the learned king of Castile. It was only the election of the first Habsburg emperor, Rudolf I, in 1273 that brought an end to the struggle.

This election was favored by Pope Gregory X (1271–1276), who was more than ready to make peace with the ancient enemies of the Papacy, for it had become apparent soon after Charles's invasion of Italy that there was little to choose between French and Imperial encirclement of the Patrimony. Indeed, the Angevin little finger promised to be thicker than the Hohenstaufen loins, for while the power of the Empire had been declining, that of France had been steadily rising ever since the accession of Hugh Capet in 987. For two hundred years his cautious successors slowly consolidated and extended their domain; their queens secured the succession by bringing forth an uninterrupted line of heirs male; then, under such gifted administrators as Philip Augustus (1180–1223) and his grandson, Louis IX (1226–1270), both the organization of the government and the position of the monarchy were immeasurably strengthened. Since the Capetians had far too much sense ever to indulge in family quarrels, this meant that the Angevin rulers of Sicily could count on efficient and instantaneous support from the sister kingdom of France. Even in the days of Frederick II's greatest power his southern kingdom and disrupted northern empire had never been able to play into one another's hands in this fashion and, moreover, the popes had always had the backing of the Guelph cities of Italy in their struggles with the emperors. But now even this support was denied to them, for Charles of Anjou had come by papal invitation and was thus theoretically leader of the Guelph party.

In this double game, while France and Sicily had been mutually helpful, the expansion of French power was also furthered by the weakened position of England during most of the thirteenth century. Just as it is impossible to study the medieval Papacy apart from the medieval Empire, so it is impossible to separate France from England. "Each to mould the other's fate as he wrought his own," the two countries had been closely linked from the beginnings of their history, and the links had been forged into the meshes of the feudal contract when Duke William of Normandy, the vassal of the king of France, had made himself king of England in 1066. His great-grandson, Henry II (1154–1189), more than doubled the continental possessions of his ancestors. Count of Anjou, Maine, and Touraine through his father, duke of Normandy and Brittany as well as king of England through his mother, in 1152 he married Eleanor of Aquitaine, the divorced wife of Louis VII of France, who brought to him all her broad possessions, which stretched from Poitou to the Pyrenees and from the Bay of Biscay to the far side of the Auvergne, at which point only a narrow corridor of French land separated his holdings from the boundaries of the Empire. Through the misfortune of King John (1199–1216) in being pitted against the formidable Philip Augustus, the northern half of these territories was lost and the southern declared forfeit in 1204, and John's son, Henry III (1216–1272), had too many troubles during his reign to be able to make more than a couple of abortive attempts to recover his lost fiefs. Some of these troubles were not his fault—he could not be held responsible for the civil war that was raging when he ascended the throne at the age of nine; but his very virtues, when possessed by a man who lacked any strength of character, were sources of weakness in themselves. He loved God and he loved his fellow man, but the piety that led him to rebuild Westminster Abbey rendered him helpless before the demands of the popes and of the legates whom they sent to England and caused him to acquiesce in the harebrained and expensive scheme of trying to secure the crown of Sicily for his son Edmund. His more human affections placed him at the mercy of his Poitevin and Savoyard relatives. The former came into England after his widowed mother, Isabelle of Angoulême, had married Hugh of Lusignan, count of La Marche, and even if they were not so black as they were painted by the contemporary chroniclers, there is still little to be said for them. But the Savoyards, who followed in the train of Henry's young queen, Eleanor of Provence, were exceptionally able men. Her uncle Pierre, later to become count of Savoy, showed this ability by keeping on the right side of the English, who do not seem to have begrudged him even his lucrative earldom of Richmond. The other members of his family and their followers were soon classed in the popular mind with the Poitevins as foreigners who, in Richard of Cornwall's paraphrase of the Psalmist, broke down the hedge of England so that every passerby could come in and pluck her grapes. As money flowed out of the country to aid the popes in their war against the Hohenstaufen, to swell the coffers of the already overbearing Lusignans, and to establish Savoyard power as far afield as Flanders, where another of Queen Eleanor's uncles was ruling as count, the English were swept by a wave of xenophobia that caused the smoldering resentment of the barons to burst into flame. The result was another civil war, the second of Henry's reign, which ended in a royalist victory when the baronial forces were defeated by Henry's son, Edward, and their leader, Earl Simon de Montfort, was left dead on the field of Evesham (1266). That Simon, who was to gain imperishable glory as one of the greatest of English heroes, happened to be a Frenchman, shows how far xenophobia and nationalism still had to go before attaining their full growth.

In spite of all these troubles and many others, both foreign and domestic, Henry, perhaps merely by hanging on "with the persistence of a querulous realist," to use Powicke's lovely phrase, left the monarchy so much stronger at the end of his reign than it had been at the beginning that Edward, who was overseas when his father died, did not come home to claim his crown until almost two years later.

Such, in brief summary, were the events that had set the stage on which Othon was to play his many parts, for to the north, Scandinavia scarcely came within the scope of western European history, while the kingdoms of the Iberian peninsula were just beginning to be involved again in the affairs of their Christian neighbors, now that the ambition of centuries was almost realized and the few remaining Moors were penned into the small emirate of Granada at the southernmost tip of Spain. Only one more region, the Holy Land, remains to be considered. It can scarcely be described as stage scenery, for little more was left of the Crusader kingdom than a few beleaguered towns along the coast; rather, it performed the function of the lighting that, as it changes the relationship of various parts of the backdrop to each other and to the actors in the play, can alter the whole atmosphere from one moment to another. Far too little attention has been paid to the persistence of the crusading ideal in the late Middle Ages, and although it is easy enough to see why, this neglect is none the less regrettable. The Age of Faith was nearing its end before it could even finish the great cathedrals and with Jerusalem once again in Moslem hands: the future belonged to the rising secular bourgeoisie with its utterly different philosophical and economic orientation. Even geographically interest was shifting; the Ottoman Turks, who were finally to close the eastern trade-routes, had gained their first victories against Christendom under the leadership of the Osman (1290–1326) from whom they took their name, and already in Othon's lifetime the men were living who were to make the first tentative voyages of western discovery. All these reasons for writing off the crusading plans of the early fourteenth century are valid if we are interested in history solely because it can be useful in explaining the institutions in which we still live, but this is too self-centered a viewpoint to be completely satisfactory. There is another one, most appropriately expressed by Winston Churchill: "History, with its flickering lamp, stumbles along the trail of the past, trying to reconstruct its scenes, to revive its echoes, and kindle with pale gleams the passion of former days." If we study Othon and his contemporaries with this end in view, we are led to the inescapable conclusion that for most of them their spiritual home was still Jerusalem.

The upper classes were well aware that the rulers of Europe, both lay and clerical, had prostituted the crusading ideal to their own political ends and had used the money raised for the recovery of the Holy Places to enlarge their own territories: when even a courtier of the old school like Joinville could advise Saint Louis to stay at home and govern his own realm instead of going out to seek death in the desert, it is not surprising that in secular literature the crusading knight-errant was already well on the way to becoming a Sir Thopas; and yet men of all conditions, from kings to the riff-raff of the Italian trading towns, still took the Cross, and whenever a pope, however weak or self-seeking he may have been otherwise, issued the call for a crusade, a real honesty of purpose sounds even through the involved periods and endless scriptural quotations with which the papal chancery was in the

9

habit of veiling its meanings. For a moment we seem to hear once more *"—Ah! que ce cor a longue haleine—The horn of Roland in the passages of Spain."*

It is to this music that Othon emerges once and for all from the wings; it is this lighting that singles him out from the crowd that made up the Household of the Lord Edward, eldest son of Henry III of England. Until then there had been nothing noteworthy about him, except perhaps the stage directions that announced his first brief appearance. Even they were not so unusual, for as the eldest son of Pierre, lord of Grandson, and of Agnès, his wife, he was from his birth a person of some importance, and it was natural that every precaution should be taken to safeguard his future.

> There was formerly in Savoy a certain lord of Grandson
> to whom a son was born. The astrologers summoned to
> examine, calculate, and cast his nativity, said that the
> new-born child, if he lived, would be great, powerful, and
> victorious. There was a man present, perhaps superstitious,
> perhaps gifted with second sight, who, taking a log
> from the fire, said that the boy would survive so long as
> the log lasted; he then closed that log up in the wall so that
> it should last longer. The boy lived, grew, reached old
> age, and then extreme old age, always increasing in honor,
> until when he was very old and wearied by the tedium
> of living, he had the aforesaid log brought out from the
> wall and thrown upon the fire; and soon after it was
> completely consumed, the knight swiftly died.[1]

It seems unjust to cast doubts on the veracity of those honest Savoyards who more than a century later repeated the story to the chronicler, Jean d'Ypres, but the closing sentence alone makes it seem improbable, for Othon, at the age of ninety, far from being *vivendi taedio pertaesus,* was still on his travels when he died a good fifty miles from home on the road that leads to Italy.

[1] Jean d'Ypres, *Chronica sive historia monasterii Sancti Bertini,* p. 751.

This auspicious birth probably took place in 1238,[2] and most of Othon's childhood must have been spent within the shelter of the gray castle walls where his ancestors had lived for two and a half centuries. The children—there were twelve altogether, six boys and six girls—were brought up on stories of them: of their grandfather, Barthélemy, who had ridden to the crusade and died in the Holy Land; of the wicked Adalbert, who had raided the lands of the neighboring abbey of Romain-môtier and had arrived there at the summons of Pope Leo IX to answer for his misdeed in no spirit of contrition but with a large body of armed retainers at his back; of Adalbert's son, Conon, called the Falcon, who had decided to marry Adelaide de Roucy, one of the great French heiresses. Her father, Count Hilduin, proudly aware of his relationship with the royal house of Aragon and with Robert Guiscard, met the proposal with the biting remark that he would never give his daughter to a Burgundian, but he underestimated his future son-in-law.

> It happened that Philip, king of France, sent this same
> Count Hilduin, with the lord Helinand, bishop of Laon, and
> several other princes, to the Lord Pope to treat of business
> touching the realm. When news of this was brought to the
> aforementioned Lord Falco, he laid ambushes in several
> places to catch them on their way home, and when they
> had been taken on their journey and robbed of everything
> that they had, he would not let them go until the count
> had promised on his oath to give him his daughter. After
> the engagement was accepted, he set them all free,
> loaded them with many gifts, and sent them home with
> great honor.[3]

Barthélemy, one of the sons of this marriage, became bishop of Laon, and it was from him that the chronicler got the story.

    [2] Letter from Kingsford to Burnand, published by the latter in "La date de la naissance d'Othon Iᵉʳ, sire de Grandson," *Revue historique vaudoise* (1911), pp. 129–32.

    [3] Hermann of Laon, *Gesta Bartholomaei Laudunensis*, pp. 267–68.

In addition to the past, the present was always pressing on them too, for Grandson, whence Conon had swooped falcon-like on his prey, commanded the roads leading over the Jura, so that the children early became accustomed to the bustle that heralded the arrival of travelers. Sometimes one of their episcopal uncles, Aymon or Ebal, would appear with his retinue, to be welcomed with the honors due to his rank but then to be treated as a member of the family at a banquet in the great hall, where Aymon brought the latest news from nearby Geneva, and Ebal, with tales of his far-off see of Lacedaemon, first awoke in Othon a desire to travel in foreign lands. Above all, the emissaries of their overlord, Pierre of Savoy, were always coming and going, for during his long absences in England, Pierre de Grandson and his brother Henri, lord of the castle of Champvent in the foothills of the Jura, were his lieutenants in the Pays de Vaud. Probably Pierre of Savoy himself would stop by on his way to his Vaudois capital at Moudon to stir the thoughts of the older boys with tales of the chances that awaited them at the English court, and it was undoubtedly under his auspices that Othon and his brother Guillaume, and Pierre de Champvent, Henri's son, were taken to England to be entered in the households of various members of the royal family.

We can even make a guess at the date of their arrival. Matthew Paris, sounding far more like the harassed father of many marriageable daughters than like a detached and celibate historian, had complained peevishly of the shipload of alien spinsters whom Pierre of Savoy had brought into England in 1247 with the charitable intention of finding them rich husbands, and it was probably at about the same time that he took the Grandsons and their cousin over. On June 17, 1252, Pierre de Grandson was granted an annual pension of twenty pounds by Henry III,[4] and it is tempting to believe that this was for his sons' services, for at that time he was

[4] *Close Rolls (1251–53)*, p. 109.

castellan of Moudon for Pierre of Savoy,[5] so that it seems improbable that he would have had an opportunity just then to leave the Pays de Vaud: Pierre de Champvent was already one of King Henry's squires in 1254;[6] and in 1263, when the widowed Agnès de Grandson leased the tolls of Grandson to Pierre of Savoy and sealed the deed for her two minor sons, Pierre and Guillaume, the three others, Girard, "Jacquet," and Henri sealed it for themselves and for their brother "Ottonin."[7] Years later, when Edward I granted the wardenship of the Channel Islands to Othon, he said that it was because "the said Othon is a member of our Household and because of his longstanding, laborious, and faithful service to us from his earliest youth and our own,"[8] which sounds as though Othon and the king, who was born in 1239, were much of an age and also gives us grounds for supposing that Othon was quite young when he was brought to England. Moreover, from the moment of Edward's coronation in 1274, Othon was employed as an expert in Gascon affairs, and he could have gained his knowledge of their intricacies only if he had been with the prince between 1254, when Edward was created Duke of Aquitaine, and the outbreak of the Barons' War in 1263.

Perhaps he found time to go home in 1258, when his father's death made him lord of Grandson,[9] but all that we know definitely is that once the fighting started, both he and his

[5] Bernard de Cérenville and Charles Gilliard, *Moudon sous la régime savoyarde*, p. 36 and n. 2.

[6] *R.G.*, I, No. 4091.

[7] *Minutes of Evidence*, p. 169.

[8] *C.P.R.* (1272–81), p. 188.

[9] Pierre de Grandson is last mentioned September 18, 1257, and he died July 15 (J. Grémaud, *Nécrologie de l'église cathédrale de Lausanne*, p. 155), probably in 1258, for on July 15, 1259, a letter from the papal chancery in favor of Girard calls the latter "natus quondam P. domini de Grançono" (J. Bernoulli, *Acta pontificum helvetica*, p. 678).

cousin, Pierre de Champvent, did good service in the king's cause. In October, 1265, Othon was granted the houses in Queenhithe that had belonged to one of the king's enemies,[10] and a month later he and Pierre were jointly given all the properties of William le Blund, who had fallen fighting for Earl Simon at Lewes.[11] But what these services were we have no way of knowing, for none of the records of the active career that had already taken Edward from the learned court of Burgos to the Welsh Marches mention his young and impecunious squire, who does not even seem to have been able to afford the expensive honor of knighthood until he had acquired some English lands. Up until then, even in official letters, he is still "Ottonin," and since by that time he was in his late twenties there must have been affection as well as habit in the continued use of the childhood name that he brought with him from Grandson. But in 1267,[12] when he first appears as *Sir* Othon, with his new gold spurs twinkling at his heels, he is definitely one of the prince's Household, that small group of Edward's relatives and intimate friends whom he was to learn to know so well over the long years during which he worked with them in the tortuous courts of Paris and Rome or among the tangled affairs of Gascony.

[10] *C.P.R.* *(1258–66)*, pp. 465, 467.

[11] *Ibid.*, p. 514; *Close Rolls* *(1264–68)*, p. 185.

[12] *C. Ch. R.* *(1272–1300)*, p. 177.

If I forget thee, O Jerusalem,
let my right hand forget her cunning.

Psalm 137

ii. The Crusade

For the moment, however, they had more straightforward business on hand. Once again the pope had called for a crusade, and once again the kings of Europe, their quarrels laid aside, were taking the Cross. The need was urgent, for every messenger from the Holy Land brought blacker news of the shrinking beachheads that were all that remained of the Crusader kingdom.

In 1244, when Jerusalem had fallen to the Saracens, Othon had been only six, but he was old enough to realize some of the sorrow that filled his family with their strong crusading tradition, and his young manhood had been punctuated with the news of one Christian defeat after another. The sultan of Egypt, Baibars, the Panther, once a Tartar slave going cheap in the market of Damascus because of a blemish, later his Mameluke master's most successful general, was now by the murder of that master ruler in his place. Since seizing the throne in 1260, he had devoted himself to the systematic and irresistible conquest of Syria.

The Barons' War, like all wars between Christians, was doubly reprehensible because it postponed the recovery of the Holy Places. In 1265, when Cardinal Ottobuono de' Fieschi was sent to England as papal legate to pacify the battle-torn country, he was also empowered to preach the crusade. In the beginning he seems to have left this to the professional preachers, the Franciscans and Dominicans. But in the summer of 1268 came news that stirred him to undertake the job himself. Baibars had stormed and taken Antioch, the great bastion of northern Syria. Nothing was left to the Christians but the isolated harbors of Tripoli, Sidon, and St.-Jean d'Acre, and even this last survived only by his forbearance and only so long as its citizens continued their policy of refusing an alliance with Abagha, the Nestorian Mongol khan of Persia and Baibars' greatest enemy. Spurred on by this disaster, the legate preached one sermon that persuaded his colleague, Tealdo Visconti, archdeacon of Liège, to take the Cross, but his greatest triumph came at Northampton in June, 1268, where Henry of Almain, King Henry's nephew, the earl of Gloucester, and a host of other notables followed the example of Edward and his brother, Edmund of Lancaster, and joined the ranks of the crusaders. Among such a glittering throng the chroniclers do not stoop to mention any of the lesser names, but since Othon was with Edward in July and September of the same year,[1] it is most probable that he took the Cross at Northampton with the prince's other followers.

Among any group of crusaders there were always a few whose purpose was just what they said it was—to deliver the Holy Places from the hands of the infidel. Everything that we know of Edward and Othon seems to show that they belonged in this category, and to them the ensuing delays must have seemed interminable. But most of them were necessary. It

[1] C. Ch. R. (1257–1300), pp. 177, 149.

was no small matter to collect and equip an army, to procure the ships and horses in good condition, and to arrange for the transportation of what Othon, when he later drew up crusading plans of his own, was to list as "the ladies and women and children of the host, as well as the other heavy things."[2] All that took time; it also took money, and Edward had to make the journey to France, where he pledged the revenues of his city of Bordeaux as security for the loan of 70,000 *livres tournois* made to him by King Louis. There were other and less excusable delays, the recalcitrance of the earl of Gloucester and the worse than recalcitrance of Gaston, vicomte de Béarn. This last was hardly surprising, for Gaston, the most powerful of the Gascon lords, had been making trouble for Edward ever since King Henry had sloughed off the responsibility of Gascony by giving the duchy to his son, but this time Gaston outdid himself, for he pocketed the 20,000 *livres* that was his share of the French loan and spent them on fomenting rebellion at home instead of going with his lord overseas. But finally all the preparations were completed, and by the summer of 1270 Edward and his immediate followers were at Portsmouth ready to sail.

The fleet moved off, a blaze of color under the August sun, with the lions of England and Leon and the castles of Castile flying above the brilliant line of shields hung from the quarterdeck, where the golden cockleshells of Grandson sparkled between the scarlet chevrons of Clare, the cross sable of Vesci, the checky gold and azure of Clifford, and the arms of half the noble families of England. Even if their heads stayed at home the younger sons were following Edward to the crusade. Edward sailed to Bordeaux and, after a roundabout journey through the Spanish Pyrenees, arrived at Aigues-Mortes towards the end of September. There he was met by the rest of his army, who had

---

[2] Charles Kohler (ed.), "Deux projets de croisade en Terre-Sainte composés à la fin du xiiie et au début du xive siècles," *Revue de l'Orient Latin*, X (1903–4), p. 427.

taken the easier way down the Rhône, and ten days later they embarked on their twelve ships for Tunis.

Why Tunis was chosen as the goal of a crusade was then and still is a vexed question. To the strategic mind it presented a constant danger, for its navy, based on a cape jutting into the Mediterranean, was in a strong position to attack Christian shipping bound on trade or conquest for the East. It also offered a religious challenge: the emir had written to Saint Louis hinting that he was willing to be converted, and the king's imagination caught fire at the idea of restoring Christianity to the very region where it had flourished so conspicuously in the days of Saint Augustine. But there may have been a third and more sinister motive. Across the narrow straits lay Sicily under its new ruler, Louis' brother, Charles of Anjou. Not content with being king of the Two Sicilies, vicar of Tuscany, and senator of Rome, he had adopted and improved upon the eastern policy of his Hohenstaufen predecessors and was aiming at nothing less than an Angevin empire that would include both Jerusalem and Constantinople. Since after 1268 both the Imperial throne and the Chair of Peter were empty, there had been no one to stop him from furthering his designs by preparing an attack on the Greek emperor, Michael Paleologus, until his brother's call to a crusade threatened to disrupt all his carefully laid plans. He could not well refuse, but the last thing that he wanted was to be forced into a position hostile to Baibars, whose friendship was necessary to protect the flanks of his future empire. But there lay Tunis. Although Charles was inordinately pious—he was in the habit of making his bored courtiers sit through the interminable sermons that were his delight—one doubts whether he was particularly interested in re-establishing Augustinian Christianity at its birthplace, and he certainly did not want to drive out the emir. Indeed, he wanted to keep him in power so that he would resume payment of the yearly tribute that had been granted to the Hohenstaufen kings of

Sicily but refused to their Angevin successor. By joining a crusade against Tunis he could please his brother, remain on good terms with Baibars, and if successful strengthen his own financial position.

He had many cogent arguments, not the least of which was the large army that he could contribute to swell the crusading host, for Pope Clement IV had declared that all those who had taken the Cross against the Hohenstaufen could commute their vows to a crusade in aid of the Holy Land, but whether this influenced Louis or not there is no way of knowing. Whatever had passed between the royal brothers, it was Charles whom the English found practically in command at Tunis when they arrived there in November, 1270. They had been shocked, on touching at Sardinia on their way from Aigues-Mortes, to learn that Louis had died at the end of August. They were even more shocked to discover on their arrival that a peace had already been concluded. It is true that there were saving clauses in it, dealing with the liberation of prisoners and giving permission to missionary friars to preach, baptize, and build monasteries within the emir's borders; but all the crusaders' expenses were to be paid, and Charles would continue to receive the annual tribute. Edward's Plantagenet temper flared out:

"What is all this, my dearest lords? Did we not come together here and take the sign of the Lord to go against the enemies of Christ, and not to make peace with them? This I will never do, for here is only the beginning, and the highway shall be made plain before us so that we may go on to the holy city of Jerusalem!"[3]

His indignation fell on deaf ears. Charles had, if not what he had planned for, at least what he wanted; the rest of the army, kings and commoners, were worn by sorrow and sickness and exhausted by an indecisive summer campaign against an enemy who never left the palm-shaded wells of the city to

[3] Walter de Hemingburgh, *Chronicon de gestis regum Anglie*, I, 331.

give battle but only to stir up by its trampling the sand that lay thick without the walls, so that the hot wind would blow it into the camp of the weary crusaders.

Only Charles was, quite naturally, feeling expansive. He invited everyone to stay with him at Palermo, and even persuaded Edward to winter there, sensibly pointing out that it was far too late in the year to start for Acre. Letters dated "in camp near Carthage" streamed into Sicily ordering lodging, provisions, and fodder to be ready for the English, and shortly afterwards the fleet set sail.

On landing at Trapani the four kings of France, Sicily, Aragon, and Navarre were immediately taken ashore in small boats, but that evening a terrible storm blew up in which over a hundred and twenty people were drowned, several ships sunk, and many more damaged. Men saw in it the hand of God, for the vessel bearing the first instalment of the Tunisian tribute went to the bottom, while of all Edward's twelve ships not one was missing or even harmed, "because he had not consented to the counsel of the wicked."[4] He did not consent either when the kings agreed to put off their crusade for another three years, but swore with a second outburst of temper:

"By God's blood! if all my companions and fellow-countrymen desert me, I shall go on to Acre, if only with Sowin, my groom, and keep my word to the death!"[5]

The roar of approval from the English was heartening to their leader, but it did nothing to lessen the tension at the Sicilian court, and Charles must have spent the few weeks between his arrival from Tunis and his departure for Viterbo, where the cardinals were sitting in conclave, in regretting the impulsive hospitality that had surrounded him with such uncongenial guests.

His first queen had been Beatrice of Provence, daughter of

[4] *Ibid.*, I, 332.

[5] William Rishanger, *Chronica*, p. 68.

that Raymond Bérenger who "quattro figlie ebbe e ciascuna regina," so that by marriage he was uncle to the two English princes, Edward and Edmund, and to Philip III, the new king of France, and stepuncle to Henry of Almain. Since both Queen Margaret of France and Queen Eleanor of England had openly accused their sister Beatrice of making off with more than her fair share of Provence, of which Charles was now count, his relations with his nephews were somewhat strained. In addition, he could never forget that the crown of Sicily had been offered first to Edmund of Lancaster, but no one could hold a grudge for long against that sweet-tempered prince, and there was a more dangerous rival among his guests. King James of Aragon's son, Peter, was married to Constance of Hohenstaufen, who had been left as sole inheritor of her family's claims to the island ever since Charles had defeated and slain her father, King Manfred, only four short years earlier, and two years after that had shocked all Europe by beheading her fifteen-year-old cousin, Conradin. Added to all these family complications there was a more immediate political one as well, since Edward's crusading ardor promised to interfere with his uncle's plans for the acquisition of an empire.

It is clear that Palermo, during the Christmas festivities of 1270, was no place for hasty actions or for ill-considered statements. It was, however, an excellent school for future diplomats, and Othon probably learned there many lessons that would stand him in good stead later in his career. He also had a chance to develop further the mastery of petty administrative detail that was to become one of his outstanding characteristics, for Charles had granted to Edward complete jurisdiction over his own men so long as they were on the island, and that involved a daily round of routine duties as unavoidable incidents arose between the idle men at arms and the Sicilians, who were seething with unrest under the hated Angevin government. There was also much to be learned about the mechanics of crusading, as the ships were refitted and the horses turned loose on the stony pastures of the south to be put in condition after one sea trip in preparation for the one to follow.

But there was more than diplomacy and business at the court of Palermo where, although the glory had departed with the Norman-Hohenstaufen kings, their works remained as monuments to their many-sided genius. Far to the north, as the dark afternoons drew to a close, Othon and his friends had gathered in the firelight to listen to the tale of Charlemagne's visit to the enchanted palace of Constantinople, and here where the intoxicating winter sunlight left no corner dark, they felt as though the stories were coming true. They heard mass in the Palatine chapel and watched the mosaics glimmer like autumn leaves through wood smoke as the incense billowed to the golden ceiling. They walked in the pleasure gardens of La Ziza and La Cuba, where the palms and cypress gave so little shade that only the murmur of the Moorish watercourses kept the heat at bay. A year ago Othon had followed the bones of Edward the Confessor to his shrine in the new-built Abbey of Westminster, whose sober glory of Caen stone and Purbeck marble was relieved only by the occasional light falling through the colored windows or reflected from the jeweled tomb; now he was at Monreale and Cefalù, and even the brilliant polychrome arcading of the exteriors was not enough to prepare his unaccustomed eyes for the blaze of porphyry and gold within.

Charles' predecessors had been not only builders; the slopes above the Conca d'Oro were full of game. Edward could indulge in his favorite pastime and hunt the descendants of those stags that William II had caused to be depicted in mosaic on the palace walls, but there was even better sport to be had, for here were the best falcons and falconers in the world, trained in the expert school of Frederick II. Some of the latter had even been trained by him, for he had laid it down in his book that the falconer must be diligent enough to pursue his calling even in old age, since the cultivation of an art is long and new methods are constantly being introduced. Besides, those tough and hand-picked men, fat enough to bear hard work and cold but not too fat to stand heat and exertion, light sleepers and neither gluttons nor drunkards, with well-controlled tempers and a passionate interest in their job, were the type that lives long, and Frederick had been dead only twenty years. Although praise of the great emperor may have been forbidden above the salt, Sowin and his fellow grooms doubtless listened to interminable stories of the good old days and invidious comparisons between the old and the new masters.

For the rainy weather that even in Sicily can make outdoor sports uninviting, there were the usual amusements of the castle, though here touched with something exotic and unfamiliar. Othon's fellow crusader, Rusticiano of Pisa, busy adapting tales of King Arthur from the book that Edward had lent him, had little new to offer—unless his expurgated version, which carefully omitted the story of Lancelot and Guinevere, can be considered a novelty—but in the mouths of the local minstrels the Matters of Brittany and Troy took on a strange glamor, blown across the sea from the couch of Shahriar or down from the inland vale of Enna, which had opened long ago to the pawing black horses of Minos. Their stories and the world-renowned agility of Palermo's Saracen dancers helped make time pass at the protracted banquets where the English, like their compatriot, John of Salisbury, a century earlier, felt sated rather than impressed by the endless procession of imported delicacies and longed for the far fresher fish and vegetables of the island, undisguised by fancy foreign sauces. It was easier to appreciate other things brought from the four corners of the earth, to admire King Roger's coronation robes with the Sassanian lions ramping over its silken folds, or to go out into the fascinating temptations of the market, where the overflowing booths gave them a foretaste of what the bazaars of the East would have to offer and whetted their impatience to reach their journey's end.

For since the days of Ulysses the charms of Mediterranean islands have ultimately palled on men whose hearts lay elsewhere, and Othon and the Lord Edward were glad when spring came at last and they could be on their way to the Holy Land. But the high hopes with which they left Trapani were to end in bitter disappointment. The great days were gone when whole armies had shaken to the sob, "Jerusalem! Jerusalem!" but even the hard-headed, who looked no further than Acre, were disillusioned when they reached that sordid trading-town. Othon's great-grandfather, Barthélemy, had faced physical danger and hardship, strengthened by the conviction that he shared with Roland and the paladins, "Paien unt tort e chrestien unt dreit," but in 1271, though life ran smoothly in the luxurious palaces, a blind warfare went on in which no man could tell who was friend and who was foe. The Christians fought, but against each other: Templar and Hospitaller were at odds, and the trade war between the Venetians and Genoese often broke out into armed conflict. The Saracens, on the other hand, fought very little; in fact, emirs of neighboring towns sent friendly messages professing their interest in Christianity, while the streets of Acre itself were thronged with a bright and mongrel breed of French-speaking Moslems who might be on good terms with everyone or no one. No experience gained in the royal courts of Europe had prepared Edward to follow this tangled web of intrigue whose threads disappeared behind the bales piled high in the spice-scented Italian warehouses, and after one attempt to punish the Venetians for their too flagrant trading with the enemy, he stepped back onto more familiar ground. It was easier for a prince whose motto was "Keep faith!" to turn his back on the town and march into the desert against his enemies, for once the Saracens were beaten the tortuous affairs of Acre would straighten out by themselves.

But it was impossible to attack them with the forces that Edward had on hand. When the armies of France and Sicily, Aragon and Navarre, had gathered before Tunis, the arrival of the English contingent encouraged men to hope that with this added strength not only the Holy Land but even the whole Saracen empire might be conquered. Now that the English were fighting alone their numbers were insufficient for anything more than the few disappointingly futile raids into infidel territory, which had shown that it was madness to think of attacking Baibars' main forces until help was assured. Edward turned to Persia and Cyprus. The response from the latter was prompt, satisfactory, and somewhat surprising: at least, the older men among the English must have listened in blank amazement as the Cypriot ambassador solemnly assured them that King Hugh would send help, on the grounds that he owed obedience to Edward since Edward's ancestors had once ruled over the Lusignan lands in France. For Hugh was a member of that pervasive family that, in the great days when the kings of England had been lords of more than half of France as well, had caused them as much trouble as all the rest of their French subjects put together. The lands to which he so touchingly referred lay in the debatable ground where the English possessions marched with the French, and their owners did homage first to one king and then to the other as their humor and convenience dictated. Since Hugh was titular king of Jerusalem as well as king of Cyprus, it was the most natural thing in the world for him to back up the one crusading army that had reached the Holy Land; this marked insistence on the sacredness of the feudal contract must have warned anyone who knew the Lusignan temper that Hugh was up to no good. But help was help, and Edward welcomed it gladly.

Persia, under its Christian khan, was another matter. Ever since the Mongols had won their first victories over the Saracens the crusading kings of Europe had looked upon them as allies, but when Abagha wrote promising reinforcements that never materialized in sufficient strength, it began to look to Edward as though Persia too were part and parcel of the disheartening intrigue to which there seemed to be no end. How could he find out what the Mongols really planned to do? It was impossible to rely for information on the natives of Acre, for their very existence depended on their alliance with the Moslem sultan against the Christian khan. As for the Italians, they would swear to anything so long as it did not interfere with their trade. Yet no one knew more about the Mongols than they did, for where business was concerned these scheming merchants became bold as tigers, and some of them had followed the silk roads deep into the heart of Asia. There were two of them in Acre at the moment, Niccolò and Maffeo Polo, outward bound from Venice on their second visit to the court of the Great Khan. Kublai, they reported, was anxious to know more of Christendom than they could tell him, and they had promised to ask the pope to send him a hundred learned theologians and scholars. But when they had reached Acre in 1269 they discovered that Clement IV was dead and his successor had not yet been chosen, and after spending two years in Venice, during which time the conclave had remained deadlocked at Viterbo, they had decided to start for China again, taking with them Niccolò's young son, Marco. They asked Archdeacon Tealdo Visconti to give them letters to Kublai, explaining why their mission had failed, and set off at once on the long journey that they knew lay ahead of them. But no sooner had they left than two friars arrived from Europe to announce to Visconti that the cardinals had finally reached a decision and that their choice had fallen on him.

The English were overjoyed; not only was it an honor to have a pope chosen from among Edward's train, but for the first time there were hopes that something might yet be achieved, for Gregory, as he now called himself, was a convinced and enthusiastic crusader. While Edward started preparing one of his ships to carry the new pope to Rome, messengers were sent posting after the Polos. They caught up with them in Cilician Armenia, and the brothers, their impatience to be off mastered by the good news that there was finally a pope whose answer they could take to Kublai, returned once again to Acre. Gregory could not give them the hundred able teachers that they had asked for, but he did order two Dominican friars to go with them and sent the khan some fine crystal vases as an earnest of things to come. So eager were they to be on their way that they do not seem even to have waited to hear the farewell sermon that Gregory preached in the church of the Holy Cross. At least, a quarter of a century later in the Genoese prison where Rusticiano of Pisa was taking down, at the dictation of a fellow captive, stories more marvelous than any that he had ever found in Edward's book of the Round Table, neither he nor Marco Polo thought the incident worthy of mention. Yet it lived on in the minds of those who heard it, and twenty years afterward, when Othon drew up his plans for a crusade that never came to pass, he described the scene. The church was crowded as the pope announced his text: "If I forget thee, O Jerusalem, let my right hand forget her cunning. If I do not remember thee, let my tongue cleave to the roof of my mouth, yea, if I prefer not Jerusalem above my chief joy." Out of consideration for his brave but unlettered congregation he went on: "My dearest sons, I shall now explain to you in French what I have just said in Latin. 'Nisi meminero tui, Jerusalem' shall apply to me." The rest of the sermon was drowned out by the weeping of the crusaders as they prayed through their tears that God would grant Gregory a happy life and the fulfilment of his desires.[6]

Even with a crusading pope and with the help that finally came from Persia and Cyprus, the English could do little more than continue their raids against the Saracen towns. But they

6 Kohler, *op. cit.*, p. 431.

were always driven back to Acre, for on the march the mail-clad crusaders died like flies under the Syrian sun, and when they reached their goal and attempted to quench the unbearable thirst of the journey with the grapes and figs that ripened to such sweetness wherever there was water, dysentery picked off the survivors. The nearest they ever came to the Holy Places was when on one of their forays they attacked and took Nazareth;[7] there, at least, they were rewarded for their labors as they knelt under the low roof that had once echoed to the words of the Annunciation. But Jerusalem still eluded them, an unapproachable mirage on the desert, and any hopes they had of taking it were cruelly dashed in the spring of 1272 when the citizens of Acre, Hugh of Cyprus, and Charles of Anjou made a ten-year treaty with Baibars. Whether Edward had known that it was coming or not he refused to have any part in it,[8] and Baibars decided to get rid of the one obstinate opponent who still stood out against him. With everything going in his favor he was anxious to wind up the whole affair; it would be too long to wait for heat and disease, defeat and treachery, to complete their work; assassination would be quicker and easier.

The Assassins had been suppressed sixteen years earlier, but it was simple enough to find one of their graduates and introduce him into the English quarters; the emir of Joppa sent messages to the prince with the old story, which never failed to carry conviction, that he was willing to turn Christian. Such

[7] Hemingburgh, *op. cit.*, I, 333. Other authorities say that they went to Nazareth not as conquerors but as pilgrims, taking advantage of the terms of the treaty between Charles and Baibars.

[8] All the English historians state that Edward refused to agree to the treaty, but Delaville LeRoulx (*Cartulaire général de l'ordre des Hospitaliers de St. Jean de Jérusalem en Terre Sainte*, III, 170) contradicts this, basing his contention on a passage from a letter dated September 30, 1275, from the Master of the Hospital to Edward: "Encore sache vostre hautesce que de cele trive, que vos plust que fust . . . [en]core se maintiengt." Considering the gap in the manuscript, this argument does not seem to be too convincing, especially as it would leave no good reason for the attempt on Edward's life.

negotiations were tedious, and by the time they were approaching completion the French-speaking ambassador was well known to the English guards. They still searched him before admitting him into Edward's presence, but it had become a perfunctory performance by the Thursday in June when he arrived with the cheering news that the emir had finally set the date of his baptism for the following Saturday. It was not far from the longest day in the year, and Edward, who had been forced to succumb to some local customs, was just waking from his siesta when the messenger was announced. Othon and the other members of the Household stood around the bed, which had been drawn near the window to catch the little breeze that sometimes blew off the snows of the Lebanon to temper the sweltering heat of the late afternoon, and listened to the emir's message, but when the man said that he had further news for Edward's ear alone they left the room. As the emissary fumbled in his belt for the second letter, Edward turned to the window for another breath of air and was taken completely off his guard when the Assassin attacked him. Unarmed and too drugged with sleep to reach for his dagger, Edward could do nothing but aim a formidable kick at his assailant; it knocked him to the floor, and after a short struggle Edward got hold of the knife and dispatched the man with his own weapon. It all happened so quickly that the Assassin was dead before the prince's followers could reach his side and discover with relief that he had received nothing worse than two slight wounds. Their optimism was not shared, however, by Brother Thomas Bérard, the Master of the Temple, who hastened to the scene to put at Edward's disposal his hard-won experience of the ways and wiles of Assassins. He gave him an antidote to keep any poison from spreading, but a few days later the wound in Edward's arm began to fester. The only remedy that the doctors could suggest was the heroic one of cutting away the mortified flesh. Edward took the news calmly when they assured him that the operation would save his life, but his wife, Eleanor of Castile, forgetting that she was a crusader and remembering only that she was a Spaniard passionately in love and far gone with child, burst into hysterical sobbing. By Edward's orders she was led from the room by her brother-in-law, Edmund, and John de Vescy, who tried to calm her with the rational, and masculine, remark that it was better that she should shed tears than that all the English land should weep, and the operation was successfully performed.

So far the early chroniclers, who are in substantial agreement. But it was too good a story not to grow with the telling. In the pages of Ptolemy of Lucca, writing after a lapse of forty years, the weeping Eleanor becomes the intrepid wife who put her lips to the wound and sucked away the poison, and there is a still later version. The worthy Savoyards who had told Jean d'Ypres the Meleager story of the baby Othon and the burning brand went on to say:

> That predestined lord of Grandson, gone with others beyond the seas, when he heard that the son of the king of England, that valiant man, had been thus poisoned, trusting perhaps in the fate foretold him by the log, sucked the wound and so Edward was healed. And because of this, that lord of Grandson and his family were raised to honors at the English court.[9]

One can only go on to say with the chronicler, "I do not affirm this; I have it only on hearsay." It is true that a few days after the attempt on his life, Edward made his will and named Othon as one of the executors,[10] but he was far too shrewd a judge of character to be swayed by a solitary act of calculated heroism, and if the other men were all chosen because they had already proved their loyalty by years of faithful service, this must have been particularly true of Othon, who alone of the eight owed almost nothing to his rank. The list was headed by the prince's brother-in-law, Jean, duke of Brittany, and by

[9] Jean d'Ypres, *loc. cit.*

[10] Rymer, I, 495.

his uncle, the earl of Pembroke, one of the greatest of the Lords Marcher; then came Roger de Clifford and Pain de Chaworth, also members of two of the Marcher families whose responsibilities along the Welsh border had gained them a particular and privileged status, and Chaworth's son-in-law, Robert Tybetot. Last of all the laymen came Othon, lord of Grandson in the Pays de Vaud but an almost landless man in England; he was followed by two clerics, Robert Burnell, who later became chancellor and bishop of Bath and Wells, and Antony Bek, the fiery hunting parson who was to die bishop of Durham and patriarch of Jerusalem. Othon's inclusion in this group clearly proves that Edward held him in particular esteem, but it is typical of him that we have no way of knowing what he had done to merit it, for he seems to have possessed his full share of the old-fashioned knightly virtues of modesty and humility. However, for this reason the story of his sucking the wound may be true, even though it was told of him only many years after his death, for it would have been in keeping with his character to say nothing about it. Only in his old age he may have grown garrulous, and it could well be that the first to hear the tale were the home-keeping Vaudois squires who gathered at Grandson to hear their famous countryman tell of long-dead popes and kings and adventure beyond the seas.

Even before the attempt on his life, it was clear to Edward that he could accomplish nothing more by staying in the Holy Land. His army, small to start with, was decimated by heat and disease; there was no prospect of getting help in the near future, for Abagha was unable to send enough troops to be of any real use and Hugh of Cyprus, for all his noble protestations, had proved himself a true Lusignan and untrustworthy ally. Nor was the distant prospect any brighter, for of the four kings who had postponed their crusade for three years in the autumn of 1270 one, Thibaut of Navarre, was dead, neither Philip of France nor James of Aragon showed any signs of starting the preparations that even then, in the early summer of 1272, should have been under way, and Charles of Sicily had made it quite plain that his crusading vows would never be allowed to interfere with his ambitions. Indeed, by the April treaty he had rendered Acre useless as a base for the English, for even if they had been strong enough they could not continue to raid Saracen territory from the city that, thanks to the treaty, could look forward to a ten years' respite from enemy attack.

Edward, with unconquerable optimism, made arrangements for leaving a small force behind under the command of Jean de Grailly, another of his faithful Savoyards, but it was a dispirited band that sailed for Trapani in the autumn of 1272. Their expedition had been ill-fated from the moment they arrived at Tunis, and all the pomp with which Charles welcomed them back to Sicily could not make them forget their resentment against the man who, more than anyone else, was responsible for the double failure of the crusade. Nor were their misfortunes at an end, and it was from the unsympathetic lips of his uncle of Sicily that Edward heard that his son, John, his other uncle, Richard of Cornwall, and finally his father had all died during his absence.

There was another ghost, too, who haunted the golden palace at Palermo, for it was there that Edward had last seen his cousin, Henry of Almain. Henry had taken the Cross with Edward at Northampton and come with him as far as Sicily, but there it appeared to them both that he could accomplish more by returning home than by continuing on the crusade. Edward intrusted to his cousin the management of his Gascon lands for so long as he should be away and also empowered him to receive back into the king's grace the banished sons of Simon de Montfort, who had come down into Italy with Charles and remained there, one of them, Guy, being his vicar for Tuscany. Henry was a most suitable person for both these undertakings; as the husband of Constance of Béarn he might conceivably exercise a restraining influence on his irrepressible father-in-law, the Vicomte Gaston, and as an early partisan of Earl Simon his words might carry weight with his sons. Accordingly, he started north with Philip of France and Charles of Sicily. At Viterbo, where the conclave was sitting, they broke their journey, for the outcome of the papal election was naturally a matter of the greatest interest to both of them. Henry also remained there, for he was hoping that a new pope would recognize his father, Richard of Cornwall, as king of the Romans, while Viterbo, lying near the borders of Tuscany, was an ideal spot from which to open negotiations with the Montforts. But the brothers were in no mood to make peace. Soon after Henry's arrival, Guy and his brother Simon, with Guy's father-in-law, Aldobrandino, the Red Count of Pitigliano, burst into the church where he was hearing mass and stabbed him to death at the foot of the altar to which he clung for sanctuary. This sacrilege and the brutality of the murder, for Guy had cut the fingers from Henry's clutching hand and actually gone back into the church to drag the corpse into the open the better to avenge his father, outraged the feelings of all Christendom. But although Charles had promised Edward that his new vicar of Tuscany would do all in his power to bring the criminals to justice, they were still safely hidden at Pitigliano in the inaccessible fastnesses of the central Apennines.

Edward evidently suspected that Charles had some part in the crime, and though he naturally absolved the pope of any responsibility he was shocked by Gregory's apparent laxness in proceeding against Henry's murderers. He was eager to reach the papal court at Orvieto as soon as possible, and leaving Palermo probably at the end of the year was already at Capua by the middle of January, 1273. Here he bade farewell to young Charles of Salerno, who had been sent by his ever meticulous father to escort the king of England to the frontiers of the Regno, and pressed on with such haste that he was in Rome by early February and shortly afterward arrived at Orvieto. Here his presence spurred Gregory to action and the papal chancery to torrents of vehement and indignant prose. Guy was cited to appear before the papal court, and when he refused on the grounds that it would endanger his life to do so as long as Edward remained at Orvieto he was excommunicated and the lands of any man who should help him were threatened with interdict.

Once this was done, the English delayed no longer. They climbed the interminable ridges of the Apennines, only to see from each summit a vista of yet more hills, paling one behind the other into violet infinity; they left winter behind them on the heights and came down on the far side to find summer blazing on the treeless plain, where they picked up the Via Emilia, a white chalk line drawn straight across Lombardy, until the air blew fresh from the glaciers and the pitiless sun was hidden behind the granite crags of the Mont Cenis. They crossed the pass when the snows had scarcely melted, and by the middle of June were in the green and pleasant valleys of Savoy.

After taking the homage of Count Philippe for St.-Maurice and the castles of Bard and Avigliana, which had come to the English crown in his father's reign, Edward went on into France, but it seems probable that Othon asked and received permission to go home. Apart from filial affection and his responsibilities as lord of Grandson, there was a more immediate reason why he should return to the Pays de Vaud, for while he was still with Edward in Savoy word had come that Jean de Cossonay, the old bishop of Lausanne, had died. Since the bishops were titular counts of Vaud, and the see of Lausanne the greatest landowner in the country, it was to the interest of the Vaudois nobles to make certain that the episcopal crosier was in safe hands. This time, after a delay of several weeks, the chapter had elected Othon's first cousin, Guillaume de Champvent, the brother of the Pierre who had settled in England and the son of that Henri who had acted with his brother, Pierre de Grandson, as Pierre of Savoy's lieutenant in the Pays de Vaud.

From the very beginning of his episcopate Guillaume ran into difficulties. Ever since the counts of Savoy had extended their holdings into the lands across the lake they had met with opposition, first from the bishops of Lausanne and, as they moved further east, from the German emperors. The bishops had naturally relied on the latter for support against the Savoyard encroachments, while both Pierre of Savoy and Count Philippe, his brother and successor, had found an ally in the always turbulent bourgeoisie of Lausanne. When Guillaume became bishop his ancient enemies, the Lausannois, were in an even more obstreperous state than usual and, since the Great Interregnum was just coming to an end, he could expect no immediate help from the Empire. Count Philippe looked on with ill-concealed delight, and as for the bishop, until the new emperor, Rudolf of Habsburg could come to his aid, he had no one to rely on except such of the Vaudois families as might prove friendly. The greatest of these was his own, with its Grandson–La-Sarraz ramifications, and of all its numerous members none could give him better advice and stronger support in his present straits than his cousin Othon, the friend of King Edward and fellow crusader of Pope Gregory, a man hardened on the field of battle and already experienced in the more complicated warfare of the council chamber.

For this reason, and since there is no mention of Othon's being with Edward that summer after the end of June,[11] it is most probable that when the king left Savoy for Paris and Gascony, Othon was riding northeast along the Jura. It was now full summer, even on the Col de la Faucille, and the distant snow of the Alps was almost invisible in the heat-haze, but as the small band of sunburnt men at arms came down to the Lac de Joux, the lesser mountains shifted until they took on the outlines familiar to Othon's childhood. Here after all

[11] Rymer, I, 504.

his wanderings he was back on his own lands and could claim hospitality at the Abbaye de Joux or from his cousins at Champvent, until his journey ended where the towers of Grandson rise beside the waters of Lake Neuchâtel. Here the weary crusader could rest among the sounds and sights and smells of his boyhood. This, and not that Canaan that he had barely seen, was the promised land flowing with milk and honey, where the cowbells rang in the upland pastures and the bees hummed through the long northern days in the linden outside the castle gate. Here, after the glare of the desert, were the cool gray shadows of the beech forests; after the acrid stench of the bazaars, new-cut hay drying in the sun and the aromatic gloom under the pines. To quench the easy thirst of that tempered climate there were the acid little wines of Corcelles and Yverdon instead of cloying Cypriot Malmsey or Sicilian Marsala, and over and under everything, a constant reminder that he was really at home, the nostalgic stale smell of the lake.

Another man might have been tempted to stay; the lord of Grandson would find plenty to do in that corner of the world where the conflicting claims of Church and Empire, of Genevois, Burgundian, and Savoyard, gave rise to never-ending quarrels and complications. But the energy that drove him over the face of Europe until death caught up with him on his travels would not let him rest, and soon he was off once more. He and his fellows had served their apprenticeship in the Household of the Lord Edward: now Edward was, by the grace of God, king of England and Ireland and duke of Aquitaine and stood in need of all their loyalty and experience to help him bear the heavy burden of sovereignty.

On ne saurait trop admirer l'activité du roi anglais:
il était à la fois sur la brèche du côté de la
vallée du Rhône et du pays de Galles; les fils de toutes
les intrigues européennes, en Castile, en Aragon,
en Italie, se raccordaient entre ses mains;
et il trouvait le loisir de veiller sur le continent à
ses intérêts comme duc d'Aquitaine.

LANGLOIS, *Le règne de Philippe III*

iii. The Business of the Realm

It is like an allegory labeled REX in a stained glass window, this picture of King Edward, sitting robed and crowned, one imagines, in his palace at Westminster with the threads of history gathered like reins into his capable hands. From the center the different colored lines radiate to the roundels and quatrefoils that border the design, each one of them showing a different scene: a battle on the purple slope of Snowdon, a Florentine banking house, a meeting of the Imperial Diet at Frankfurt, kings dancing with queens in a castle in Spain. In some of them the glint of a golden crown denotes that Edward was there in person, fighting in Wales, holding court in a Gascon town, or doing homage in France, but most of them show little groups of nameless men distinguished only by their costumes. There are mitered bishops among them, and knights in armor, and gowned and hooded doctors from Bologna, for the king could not go everywhere himself and someone had to follow the threads up the rivers and along the roads of Europe to their beginnings. To the casual observer whose eye is caught and held by the majestic figure at the center the little men on the edges remain anonymous, but after a time one of them begins to take on an identity if only because he appears so often: whether the roads lead to Wales or to Flanders, to Paris, Gascony, or Savoy, over the Pyrenees to Aragon or across the Alps to Rome, even once again to Acre and to far-off Armenia, the azure and argent surcoat with the bend gules bearing the Grandson cockleshells is more often than not found at the journey's end.

One does not know whether to be more amazed at the amount of territory that Othon covered or at the equally extensive variety of things with which he was called upon to deal. The thirteenth century was in many ways a gloriously unspecialized era. Geographically, there were, of course, boundaries, but the important entity was still Christendom, whole and entire. The kings of Europe, related to each other and to most of the greater nobles by a complicated network of marriages, were well aware that what touched one touched all, and Othon, dealing, for example, with the count of Savoy, could never for a moment lose sight of the unbroken chain of relationships that linked Savoy to the Empire, the Empire to Sicily, and ran from Palermo through Aragon and Gascony to England, until it came full circle in Savoy to the foot of the Grand St.-Bernard, where the counts held St.-Maurice, the very cradle of Savoyard power, as a fief of their cousin, the English king.

These geographical or matrimonial ramifications, for they amounted to the same thing at a time when it seemed that only lands married each other and the bride and groom became involved merely as a minor though unavoidable afterthought, did not form the whole pattern of Christendom; interwoven with the scarlet lines of blood relationship ran the golden web of finance. At its center was the pope, who, freed, *ex officio,* from the pleasant entanglements of marriage, relied on his agents, the Italian bankers, to perform for him very much the same services that their nubile daughters did for the laity. They were as pervasive in their influence as the latter and almost more necessary, for although a man could remain a bachelor if he wished, it was growing increasingly difficult to live without money. Not only did these sober businessmen have a seemingly inexhaustible supply of ready cash always on hand, but they also had evolved a system of transferring it from one country to another, not by the obvious method of packing it on muleback and sending it out to take its chances on the hazardous roads of Europe, but in a way puzzling to the uninitiated but undeniably convenient, by making out notes to the family banking house on a dark Florentine street or a sunny square in Siena or even to their partners in still more remote towns.

A man like Othon proved that he was as capable of dealing with a king whose poets traced his lineage back to the royal house of Troy as with an upstart Italian moneylender, but even more was expected of him. In the administrative field, too, specialization was still in an embryonic stage and no more so than among that closely knit but curiously unorganized body of men, the knights of the Royal Household. They still performed personal services as their predecessors had done in the days when there was no distinction made between the king's private and public capacities, for on the shoulders of many of them fell the burden of directing the motley crew who made up the ordinary medieval *familia.* They were also used in what we should consider government jobs, as administrators, diplomats, and auditors of accounts, and in addition were called upon to fight whenever the need arose. This arrangement owed its continued existence partly to the lack of specialization, but there was another, more obvious, reason: England was sparsely populated, educated men were rare, and since a surprising number of them were of humble birth, the lettered knight was even more of a rarity. Edward simply did not have a large class to choose from who combined both brains and breeding. That is why, over and over again, the same men turn up in every conceivable capacity and why it was taken for granted that any of them could turn his hand to anything that cropped up in the line of duty. For instance, in 1278 Othon was sent with Robert Burnell to Gascony with plenary powers to act in the king's name, which laid on them a heavy load of responsibility, for the issues of war and peace might be decided by their dealings with the Gascon and French magnates; but at the same time they had to take cognizance of such causes as that of the euphoniously named Desirata de Mente, who claimed for herself, her husband, and her heirs "in fee or emphyteusis the right of crying publicly whatever is used to being cried in Bayonne," and to decide whether the heirs of Oger de Murlens should pay on the Feast of St. Peter's Chains four pounds or one red hawk for the two mills that they rented on the outskirts of the same city.[1] This weighty choice was left up to the lessees, but that the chancellor of England should have been used by his king to settle matters such as these makes one draw an unavoidable comparison between Burnell and Tom Canty cracking nuts with the Great Seal, since the former, when he was at home, was guardian of that august bit of metal.

For over fifty years the dry entries in the Calendars bear witness to Othon's goings and comings and from their very bulk build up an image that takes on color and substance. He is continually moving across the face of Europe, reliable and versatile, diplomatic and responsible, a great noble, sure

[1] *R.G.*, II, Nos. 376, 386.

of himself and of his position, a fighter, and yet with an almost endless patience that no amount of detail could weary. An unattractive list of virtues in the main, and it is hard to see what were the characteristics that made him Edward's friend as well as his servant. It is not the business of government officials to draw character sketches, and whatever Othon's more human qualities may have been, they were not of the kind that appealed to other writers, for there is no description of him in the contemporary chronicles. But the argument *e silentio* is a poor one at best, and in two of the letters that Edward wrote to him and that have been preserved it is clear that the king felt for him a warmer affection than mere efficiency or even loyalty could have called forth. We must infer that along with his other unmistakably Vaudois qualities, he possessed some of their more sympathetic ones as well—perhaps the native wit, dry as their wines—just as we can draw the more obvious inference, though the records are naturally silent on this point, that he must have been a man of inexhaustible physical endurance.

To live to be ninety was in the thirteenth century something of a prodigy in itself, but to succeed in doing so when it seems as though half his life had been spent on the road argues a phenomenal toughness. Travel was still at the stage when a pilgrimage could be imposed as a penance, and it could hardly have been conducive to longevity when, even apart from the more obvious dangers, the mere business of getting from one place to another entailed so many and such varied hardships. The roads might be paved in the towns, but in the country they were so rough, so dusty in good weather, so mired, when not impassable, in bad, that to make the average day's journey of twenty miles or so and to do it day after day took physical energy and dogged perseverance. Everyone who could went on horseback, for jolting over the potholes in springless wagons was so desperately uncomfortable that even women big with child avoided it when they could: Queen

Isabelle of France, on her way back from Tunis and Sicily in 1271, died in Calabria as the result of a miscarriage brought on by a fall from her horse while she was fording a river. Rivers, indeed, were another hazard, for bridges when they did exist were not always properly kept up, and even the best could be swept away by floods or destroyed by fire—stone bridges were still so rare that they were usually attributed to the Devil—in which case there remained only the choice of finding a ford that offered safe enough footing or of intrusting oneself and one's horse to a ramshackle ferryboat. All these difficulties were increased because in most instances men had to ride armed. Chain mail offered no protection against the heat and after several hours of cold and gusty rain must have been sheer misery, but the forces of nature were not the only obstacles that lay between the traveler and his journey's end. The roads, especially where they ran through the dense forests that still covered a great part of Europe, were infested with bands of robbers or of outlaws more dangerous still, who stopped at no crime, since nothing could make their plight more hopeless than it was. In an attempt to remedy this, Edward had ordered that all highways between the principal market towns should be cleared of trees, brush, and ditches for two hundred feet on either side, but at best this can have afforded only a little more time to prepare for the attackers who might spring at any moment from the shadows. Even the towns were not safe; at least, Othon and his men became involved in some fracas in Canterbury of such a serious nature that the citizens were punished for it by a ten marks' fine and the temporary loss of their liberties.[2] Only at the day's end he may have found himself better off than some of his fellow travelers: the lord of Grandson, riding on the king's business, could be sure of a night's lodging in many of the castles that guarded the roads, and the monas-

[2] C.F.R. (1272–1307), p. 45.

teries would prepare their best guest-chamber for him when pilgrims and other benighted wayfarers had to be content with the common dormitory. But such a minor accident as a horse's falling lame might cut him off from even these amenities, and then he had to take shelter in any inn he could manage to reach and stand his chance of smoking chimneys and crawling blankets, until the slow creaking of the ox carts on their way to the fields roused him to the realization that yet more traveling lay ahead of him.

Whenever his road ended in some harbor town new perils awaited him. They are more familiar to us than those that he met by land, for he never seems to have encountered shipwreck or piracy, and in other respects the character of the Narrow Seas has not changed noticeably through the centuries. Once he had embarked on one of the noisome ships that sailed straight across the Channel or took the longer way by the Bay of Biscay to Bordeaux, he was facing only such dangers as every traveler over those notoriously rough waters has had to encounter. One need not take the famous poem on the Compostella pilgrims too literally; it was so obviously written by a good sailor who, like all good sailors before and since, though on land they may be the kindest of men, find seasickness in others a perennial source of amusement. The author's matter-of-fact assumption that everyone else finds it equally funny only serves to heighten his description of a painfully familiar scene: the stewards twitting the passengers on their sudden and inexplicable loss of appetite or congratulating the master on how much he can save on food *this* trip; the poor sufferers with basins beside them, turning away from the savory fumes of good roast meat and asking weakly for toast; or if they are made of sterner stuff, trying to keep their eyes from the tumbling horizon and reading until, blind and dizzy, they close their books with the desperate cry, "Alas! my head will burst in three!" The inexperienced or even the heartless could pass this off as a poetic exaggeration of stock jokes on a stock theme, were it not repeated by the stern voice of the law:

> Solomon Attefeld holds lands at Keperland and Atterton in the county of Kent on serjeanty, to wit that, whensoever the Lord King may wish to cross the sea, the said Solomon and his heirs are bound to cross with him, to hold his head on the sea, if need be.[3]

The amazing thing is that in spite of all hardships and dangers the roads and sea-lanes were crowded. It is true that Othon, riding through the short winter days, might go for miles and meet only a few straggling groups of men who, like himself, were forced to be abroad in all weathers, merchants on their way to the January fair of Lagny in Champagne or barefoot friars, two by two, hurrying one behind the other on the business of their Order. But on the March evening when the first blackbird whistled in the lengthening twilight all the doors of Europe flew open and the whole bright pageant of life spilled out along the roads.

There were men on seasonal business then, too, for it was the time of year when kings go out to war, and the highway glittered and clanged with armor, but others were there for no clear reason at all or even in the face of express prohibitions. St. Benedict in the sixth century had found it necessary to devote part of the Rule that laid the groundwork of Western monasticism to strictures against the *gyrovagi*, the wandering clerks, but in this he was no more successful than the Council of Nicaea two hundred years earlier, which, although strong enough to enunciate once and for all the articles of the Catholic faith, was yet too weak to impose the cloistered life on its incurably footloose scholars. In spite of repeated thunderings from popes and councils they still kept the roads musical with their songs, the inns turbulent with their drink-

---

[3] T. Blount, *Fragmenta Antiquitatis*, pp. 61, 56; quoted in G. C. Coulton, *Mediaeval Panorama*, p. 325.

4 4

ing bouts, and, it must be admitted, the universities alive with their ferocious eagerness for knowledge. Even so, they were only one part of the ever-moving crowds that filled Europe, and at nightfall, when a band of strolling players, forbidden by the city ordinances to pass through the gates, would set up their stage on the threshing floor of some outlying farm, they had few scenes to show more variegated than those that their audience had had before its eyes all during the day.

The road had other joys, too. The nonsense that the generation that wrote goliardic songs and carved Gothic doorways was blind to the beauties of nature may be passed over; even if it were true, Othon, though neither a poet nor an artist, was a huntsman and to such men a ride across the open country is always a delight. The tall deer in the woods and the hawks wheeling over the downs, the changes of wind and the shapes of the hurrying clouds, were not only of perpetual interest to him but also afforded valuable object lessons for the young squires who rode with him and whom it was his duty to instruct in that complicated jargon of woodcraft, proficiency in which was a mark of their rank. Rarely, indeed, could he point out to them a pride of lions, but they could learn that what to the peasant who drove them to the oakwoods was a herd of swine was to the gentleman who hunted their wild brethren a sounder, nor must they ever confuse this with a singular of boar; they must learn to speak of a skulk of foxes, to listen for an exultation of larks, and to distinguish a gaggle of geese from a wisp of snipe.

The towns promised travelers fascinations of another order when first the disproportionate bulk of a new cathedral loomed on the horizon, and though there might be a moment of disillusion as they rode up to the gate through the stench coming down from the blackened scarecrows that dangled from the gibbet and rising from the city ditch, which served the double purpose of a first line of defense and a convenient place to throw garbage, the promise was more than fulfilled once they had passed through into the swarming, painted streets. Each one of them hoped, when he had made his fortune in this world, to assure it in the next by building, if not a complete church, at least a chapel to the greater glory of God and of his patron saint. In the thirteenth century the "white mantle of churches" that had suddenly covered Raoul Glaber's Europe at the turn of the millennium still survived in many places, but wherever it was patched and shabby the master masons were cutting away the worn material and filling it in, not with the solid Romanesque fabric of the original but with a tissue of lace that grew more and more transparent as their skill and their pride increased. It is no wonder if Othon and his companions, whether they gave thanks for their safe arrival in a church whose evening shadows were barely pierced by the glow fading from the west window or heard mass next morning while the altar-candles paled in the first sunlight flooding the apse, found their attention wandering. The temptation was too great, for all around them rose the finished work, while the cheerful noise of hammer and chisel drowning out the priest's voice and the mingled smells of wet plaster and new wood overpowering the incense, lured their minds from the altar to the other eternally fascinating miracle of a building taking shape under the workmen's hands.

Othon's travels with the Lord Edward had already made him familiar with both the dangers and delights of the road; under the king he was now to learn more of its responsibilities. Heads of missions were chosen from among the members of the Household; during the first years of the reign, Othon was constantly leaving Westminster and returning to report on his success or failure, only to be briefed on a new appointment and sent off again. In the beginning, while Edward was organizing his administration and clearing up unfinished routine business, all that we usually know of these missions are the names of the men who carried them out and the affairs that they had to deal with. But after following Othon's career through the thirty-three years that he traveled as Edward's ambassador, we gain an insight not only into his own character and capabilities but also into the methods that the king used in choosing his envoys.

By reading backward and forward we can even hazard guesses that fill in the bare outlines of the earlier notices. For example, there is no record of Othon's appointment on a mission to Savoy in the late autumn of 1274. But he had been at St. Georges d'Espéranche in June, 1273, when Count Philippe did homage to Edward,[4] and with the king at Northampton in November, 1274, when the annual pension for that homage was renewed.[5] He was familiar with the legal and financial aspects of the transaction and, moreover, as lord of Grandson, was one of the count's greatest feudatories. It would therefore have been both politic and courteous to send him to announce to his overlord that the payments would be continued, so that when we find him back at St. Georges for the Christmas festivities of 1274[6] there can be little doubt that it was the business of the pension that had taken him across the stormy Channel and wintry roads of northern Europe to the foothills of the Alps.

From Savoy he went on to Paris, for in January, 1275, he and Antony Bek were sent to raise a loan from the Italian bankers there and to use the money in paying off some of the king's clamorous Gascon creditors.[7]

He was back in England, probably by April[8] and certainly by May, when he attended the first Parliament of the new reign[9] and heard discussions of yet another phase of the Gas-

[4] Rymer, I, 504.

[5] *Ibid.*, p. 519.

[6] A. J. Taylor, "The Castle of St.-Georges d'Espéranche," *Antiquaries' Journal*, XXXIII (1953), 38.

[7] *C.P.R.* (1272–81), pp. 77, 85, 98.

[8] *Ibid.*, p. 85.

[9] Francis Palgrave (ed.), *Parliamentary Writs*, p. 2; index, p. 642.

con question. All the difficulties in the situation stemmed from Edward's anomalous position as king in his own country and vassal in France, and in this secondary capacity he had been summoned to attend the Martinmas Parlement of Paris. Edward obviously could not leave his kingdom unattended, and someone would have to present his excuses in such a way that the well-trained French lawyers could pick no flaw in them. This also seemed like a suitable time to press once again for the return of the Agenais, one of the parts of the duchy whose ownership had been in dispute ever since Henry III and Louis IX had settled most of their difficulties by the Treaty of Paris in 1259. The well-thumbed rolls were brought out once again, the lawyers and clerks who had special competence in these two matters gave their opinions, the king discussed it with his most trusted counselors, and in October Othon was once again on his way to Paris, this time with Edward's cousin, Maurice de Craon, and the Marcher lord, Roger de Clifford.[10]

Another of the difficulties of Edward's position was the right of the Gascons to appeal over their duke's head to the court of the king of France. There were always Gascon cases pending before the Parlement, and when Othon reached Paris he found the seneschal of Gascony, Luc de Thanney, already there as Edward's proctor. Thanney had expected to go on to England to report on how matters stood in the duchy—"the situation is good in spite of French troublemaking," he wrote to Edward,[11] but Craon and Othon, acting on later instructions, ordered him back to Bordeaux. When he left, Othon went with him to accept the resignation of the seneschal of Limoges, Cahors, and Périgueux, pay him for his services, and appoint a new seneschal in his place.[12]

[10] Rymer, I, 530.

[11] *Chancery Miscellanea*, VII, 31, given in Ch. Langlois, *Le règne de Philippe III*, p. 221.

[12] *C.P.R.* (*1272–81*), p. 113.

Once again Othon returned to England, but by July, 1276, he and Stephen Penchester were off again to Gascony, this time to see about a subsidy of food and shipping required by the king of France from the duke of Aquitaine—another annoyance of Edward's dual position—and also to try to settle the quarrel with the archbishop of Bordeaux over the revenues of his see.[13]

The names of Othon's fellow emissaries are very revealing. Bek, his companion on the money-raising expedition, had been Keeper of the Wardrobe and was therefore well-versed in financial affairs; Craon and Clifford were great nobles, suitable ambassadors from one king to another; Thanney, the seneschal, was of course familiar with the administrative difficulties of Gascony; and Penchester, as Warden of the Cinque Ports, was able to haggle on equal terms with the French naval officials in Bordeaux. Each man was a specialist in his own line; that Othon was sent on four such diverse missions, which had nothing in common except that they all dealt with Gascon affairs, shows that he must already have been considered an expert on the question of the duchy as a whole. As such, he might have been kept shuttling indefinitely between England and France if new troubles had not arisen to call him back from the sunlit south to that country of which the chronicler, Piers Langtoft, wrote bitterly, "Quand [aillours] est l'esté, en Gales est yver."

Llewellyn ap Griffith, Prince of Wales, was Edward's vassal, but he had disobeyed one summons after another to come to England to do his homage to the new king and pay the long overdue arrears on his tribute. For two years Edward had kept his Plantagenet temper remarkably well in hand, until suddenly Llewellyn decided that the time had come for him to fulfil his engagement to marry Eleanor de Montfort, the daughter of Earl Simon. This move was too much for the

13 *Ibid.*, p. 155.

49

king's forbearance, for he was never to forgive her two brothers for the murder of Henry of Almain. Eleanor, sailing from France under the escort of a third brother, Amaury, was captured and sent up to London to be put in the gentle but safe custody of the queen, and in November, 1276, Edward sent one last summons to Llewellyn. When this too was disobeyed, he declared war on him and ordered the feudal levy to assemble at Worcester the following July.

But long before that, the spearheads of his armies were driving into Wales. Their ranks included the knights of the Household, and in the early months of 1277 Othon and John de Vescy, who had been his companion on the crusade, each led a force of four knights under the banner of the earl of Lincoln.[14] Othon not only saw his share of the fighting but used his administrative ability as well, for between March 24 and May 7 he received, either directly or indirectly, the sum of £1,079 from the fifteenth in the counties of Shropshire and Staffordshire "for the expedition of the king's affairs."[15] It seems like a large amount of money for one man to disburse, but Edward was laying his plans carefully, and his preparations were so successful that once the feudal levy moved from Worcester in the first week of July, it was a matter of barely two months before Llewellyn was brought to terms.

Edward himself made only a short campaign into Wales, and Othon went with him when he returned to Cheshire in August for the splendid ceremonies celebrating the foundation of the new Cistercian abbey of Vale Royal. If the sun was shining—in spite of Langtoft, it can sometimes be summer in Wales, at least on the border—the sight must have been dazzling, and even a gray sky would have failed to dim the brilliance of the crowds, for the retinues of some of the greatest names in England filled the quiet valley. Burnell was

14 J. E. Morris, *The Welsh Wars of Edward I*, p. 121.

15 *C.P.R.* (1272–81), p. 198; *C.C.R.* (1279–88), pp. 20–21.

there to say the mass of consecration, assisted by the bishop of St. Asaph, and Edward himself laid the cornerstone. Two other stones were laid by Queen Eleanor, one for herself and one for her eldest surviving son, Alfonso, and the foundations were further strengthened with stones laid by the earls of Gloucester, Cornwall, Surrey, and Warwick, and by Maurice de Craon, Jean de Grailly, Robert Tybetot, Robert de Vere, and Othon.[16]

Othon was still with the king on August 22[17] and probably the next day as well, when Edward and David ap Griffith came to a rather unsavory agreement as to just what lands the latter would get when his brother was overthrown, but although Llewellyn's downfall was near, he was still safe in his mountain stronghold of Snowdon. Edward had no intention of trying a frontal attack on those impregnable slopes behind which the Welsh princes had always managed to protect themselves against any attacking armies. It was easier to starve Llewellyn out. The English fleet drew a blockade around Anglesey, the granary of Wales, and before the corn was down, Othon and John de Vescy, with a force of some two thousand men, landed on the island.[18] There was nothing for Llewellyn to do but surrender. Othon, Antony Bek, and Robert Tybetot were appointed to draw up the peace terms,[19] and their combined efforts resulted in a treaty that Llewellyn agreed to on November 9 and that Edward ratified at Rhuddlan the next day.

Its provisions were harsh, but no sooner had the prince submitted to them than Edward relented. He remitted the war

[16] *Ledger-book of Vale Royal Abbey*, trans. J. Brownbill, p. 5.

[17] *C.P.R. (1278–81)*, p. 227.

[18] Morris, *op. cit.*, pp. 134–35.

[19] *Ibid.*, p. 142 and n. 2. "Grandison's name does not appear in the printed text, but his services are clearly shown by a document which contains entries of money for the expenses of the commissioners."

indemnity and also the annual rent for Anglesey, and on the very day that the treaty was ratified, ordered Othon, as keeper of the island, to hand it over to Llewellyn's men.[20] This inexplicable behavior could not fail to be galling, and it might have been more farsighted either to have spared Llewellyn the humiliation of yielding to such crippling terms or else to have given him the satisfaction of making a martyr of himself if he had tried to live up to them. Even more infuriating was Edward's generosity the following summer, when he paid all the expenses of the magnificent wedding that finally united the Prince of Wales with the heiress of the Montforts.

Othon was not present at that ceremony, for now that he was no longer needed in Wales he was sent off once more to Gascony. In January, 1278, he and Robert Burnell, now bishop of Bath and Wells and chancellor, were appointed, nominally as Edward's plenipotentiaries but in reality as joint seneschals, with Jean de Grailly, now seneschal of Gascony, put under their orders.

They did not sail straight to Bordeaux but landed in the north of France, for Burnell was to go to Paris where he probably treated once again for the return of the Agenais, while Othon went to Compiègne with Henry Lacy, earl of Lincoln, and John de Vescy to take the oath of the duke of Brabant to observe the provisions of the marriage contract between his eldest son, John, and Margaret of England, and, since Margaret was not quite two and a half at the time, to make sure that the contract should be equally valid between any other daughter of Edward and any other of the duke's sons.[21]

However, in this case Margaret did grow up to marry her youthful bridegroom, and all the other affairs that Othon and Burnell transacted abroad seem to have turned out equally well. At any rate, Edward wrote them a long letter thanking them for

[20] *C. Chanc. R., Var.*, p. 157.

[21] *D.K.R.*, VI, appendix II, No. 1119.

the efforts that they had already made in his behalf and giving them helpful advice on how to conduct the business that still lay ahead of them. The Gascons, he points out, have the reputation of being an unreliable lot who make a mockery of all their agreements, plans, promises, and doings, and the only safe way to deal with them is to have everything put firmly (*firmiter*) in writing; at the same time, Othon and Burnell are to show the faith of Blessèd Mary, the Mother of God, rather than that of St. Thomas, for Edward promises to back up any decisions they make; and finally, although he hopes that they will be in London by Michaelmas when the king of Scotland comes there to do homage, they are on no account to overlook anything in their eagerness to get home, "for we have no one about us who can understand these things better or be more useful to us in them then you, and even if we were there to attend to them ourselves, we do not believe that they could be better managed."[22]

They needed the faith of all the saints as well as the patience of Job over the long months during which they moved from one Gascon town to another, for their commission had given them sweeping powers to transact any business with any persons or communities on any subject.[23] It is true that they were not alone; they had the advice of the local officials, and once at least Edward sent one of his clerks, William Blyborough, from England to help them,[24] but they bore the chief responsibility for all the decisions that fill the Gascon Rolls during the period that they were there and that were to be used for years afterward as a basis for claims and as precedents for further action. They paid the king's debts; they made grants and appointments in his name; they restored rights and properties to people who claimed that they had been unlawfully deprived of them. Because of the bad harvest they advised Edward to remit the hearth tax for the space of a year, and perhaps for the same reason saw to it that the royal forest of Bordeaux should be

[22] Rymer, I, 554.   [23] *R.G.*, II, Nos. 187–88.   [24] *Ibid.*, p. 180.

turned over to agriculture. They took under the king's protection those Gascons who were in trouble with the Parlement of Paris and received back into his grace not only a couple of minor criminals but also Gaston de Béarn, thereby putting a temporary stop to that nobleman's troublesome vacillation between his allegiances to the French and the English kings. They soothed the affronted barons of Bazas, who complained that their rights had been infringed by the building on their properties of *bastides,* those free towns that were always a thorn in the side of everyone except their sponsors, and promised that the seneschal of Gascony would not only hear all their complaints but would also arrange to have their eldest legitimate sons recognized as their heirs if they so desired.[25] The conventional image of the medieval knight, ignorant of everything except war and the chase, and of his contemporary, the bishop, an unworldly saint or a far too worldly moneygrubber, pales before the reality of these two efficient and hard-working men.

That it was hard work there can be no doubt, and perhaps it was exhaustion brought on by four months of unremitting attention to Gascony and the Gascons that effected a temporary weakening in Othon's indomitable energy; at any rate, for the first and last time in his life he found himself tempted by the allurements of matrimony. The lady in question was a daughter of Count Othon IV of Burgundy and a valuable pawn in the game whose rules have been summed up as "Let me not to the marriage of true fiefs admit impediments." In contradistinction to the duchy of Burgundy, which was already a part of France, the county, the Franche-Comté, lay within the borders of the Empire, and Count Othon was under a cross fire of proposals from both French and Imperial matchmakers. On the latter side, Othon de Grandson's overlord, Count Philippe of Savoy, was undoubtedly in favor of the marriage, which would have strengthened the alliances along his frontier, and it would have

25 *Ibid., passim.*

been equally advantageous for Othon himself, for the Grandson lands marched with the Franche-Comté, and he even received an annual pension raised on the salterns belonging to his prospective father-in-law.[26] On the other hand, the French had already started the pressure against Count Othon that in the following century was to make Burgundy a Capetian appanage by the marriage of another of his daughters to the future Philip V, and in this earlier venture, French interest won out as well, for a year later Othon's intended bride or one of her sisters of marriageable age was betrothed to the duke of Burgundy.

The imperialist plans may have been defeated because French diplomacy was as usual more successful than that of other countries, but we cannot help holding Othon partly responsible for their failure since, to put it mildly, he does not seem to have been an impassioned lover, and he allowed his glowing prospects to be all too easily extinguished by the rather dampening letter that he received from Edward:

> The worshipful nobleman and our dearest friend, the
> count of Burgundy, has written us that there has lately been
> some talk and conversation between you both as to your
> marrying one of his daughters. But since we are as anxious
> for your well-being and honor as for our own, we hope
> with all our heart that you will marry neither there nor
> anywhere else, except in our presence, or at least, not until
> we have discussed this and other matters with you, so
> that the business may be carried out with the honor that we
> wish for you and that is fitting to your station, and be the
> more solemnly expedited in our presence. However,
> seeing that the wishes of the contracting parties usually win
> out in these matters, we agree that if you have this really at
> heart, and if our noble and belovèd Othon of Burgundy,
> your relatives, and any others zealous for your profit and
> renown, advise you to accomplish it, then may the
> foregoing arrangements which you have discussed with

[26] A.C.V. 1 B 349/1, No. 2/1.

the aforesaid count be brought to a fitting end, according to your desires and their advice, and that everything be done as you see fit. We are writing the same to the count.[27]

In spite of Edward's references to the self-willed wishes of those involved, the engagement never came off, and Othon settled down to a half-century of single blessedness.

However, the count continued to pay him his annual pension, which was some consolation, for he needed every penny that he could lay hands on. All his traveling was expensive, and when the loans raised in his behalf from the Italian bankers proved insufficient he had to make the rest up out of his own pocket. The king rewarded him for this not only with lands but also with other profitable gifts, whose very variety proves that the royal financiers were men of infinite resource and sagacity. In November, 1275, Edward had granted to him the lease of the Channel Islands in return for a rent of 500 marks a year,[28] but in January, 1277, this was changed to a free grant for life. It was at this time that Edward referred to his long and faithful service; he also expressly stated that the grant was made to pay for the debts that Othon had incurred while on the king's service and further added that his executors should hold the islands for the same purpose without rendering any account therefor for five years after his death.[29] His actual holdings in Irish lands were not yet as large as they were later to become when he was given wide tracts bearing unpronounceable Gaelic names, but he had already held in wardship the lands of an Irish heiress,[30] and in May, 1275, he had been granted a share in the forfeiture of all wools, fells, and hides exported from the island

[27] A.C., XIII, 51; transcribed in C. L. Kingsford, "Sir Otho de Grandison, 1238?–1328," *Transactions of the Royal Historical Society*, 3d series, III (1909), 188–89.

[28] *C.F.R.* (*1272–1307*), p. 65.

[29] *C.P.R.* (*1272–81*), p. 188.

[30] *C.C.R.* (*1272–79*), p. 142.

without a license.[31] This last is a good example of the intricacies of thirteenth-century finance. The king had induced the magnates of Ireland to let him have the customs on such exports, and he had appointed "Luke de Luk" and his fellow merchants from the same town to collect them for him; at the same time, almost as if to encourage smuggling and certainly to the despair of the businesslike Italians, he had allowed the claims of Othon and eleven others like him to their share of the illegally exported materials.

Other people besides the king and the count of Burgundy loaded Othon with presents. Some, like Robert Burnell, who, after they returned from Gascony, granted him in fee the manor of Sheen in Surrey,[32] may have done it out of friendship, for Burnell was notoriously avaricious where lands were concerned and stood as high with Edward as Othon himself, so that it was unnecessary for him to curry favor by such a gift. But when Jacques de Molay, Grand Preceptor of the Order of the Temple in England, granted him a yearly income of £2,000, there may have been other motives than those stated in the deed, that it was in recognition of Othon's services to the Order.[33] If the magnificent Templar found it helpful to have such a friend at court, Othon was indeed a man to be reckoned with.

There is no doubt that he was becoming increasingly valuable to Edward, who may have had an ulterior motive in quashing his friend's budding romance. Even the most patient of Griseldas, if she had not charmed Othon by her sweetness, would have wearied him by her reproaches had he been forever on the move; as it was, he could continue to come and go as the king saw fit. In fact, even as Edward was writing his letter of matrimonial advice in March, 1279, he was about to cross the Channel himself and was in need of Othon's services.

[31] C.F.R. (1272–1307), p. 60.
[32] C.C.R. (1272–79), p. 520.
[33] Reg. Clem. V, No. 2938.

The king was in France from May to July attending to Gascon affairs; a treaty was made at Amiens, settling among other things the twenty-year-old dispute over the Agenais, and as usual Gaston de Béarn was in the middle of a quarrel that had to be straightened out. Since Othon was familiar with both these problems, he must have been with Edward during that time, and since there is no mention of his being in England until the following November it is possible that Edward left him behind at the French court.

For Paris was a center of international intrigue, most of it stirred up by the two formidable dowagers, Eleanor of England and Margaret of France. Their two sisters, Beatrice, queen of Sicily, and Sanchia, queen of the Romans, were long since dead, but Margaret and Eleanor were kept alive by their hatred for their brother-in-law, Charles of Anjou, and spent their time laying endless plots and schemes in the hope that some day they might outwit him. In their maneuverings they could call on four generations for help, for old Count Philippe of Savoy was their uncle, the kings of France and England and the queen of Scotland were their children, and Eleanor's granddaughter was queen of Norway. They could also make sure of support from some quarter, for almost everyone disliked Charles for one reason or another. His two sisters-in-law hated him because on the death of his wife Beatrice he had annexed not only her share of Provence but all the rest of it besides, thereby depriving them of their inheritance; Eleanor further disliked him because he had supplanted her younger son Edmund as king of Sicily; and Edward distrusted him on both these grounds as well as for his betrayal of the crusade and for his continuing and questionable lenience to Guy de Montfort, the murderer of Henry of Almain. As for Margaret of France, she feared his influence over his nephew Philip III and to offset it was always trying to strengthen the pro-English party at the French court.

Their dearest scheme was to oust Charles from Provence. Together with the Franche-Comté, Dauphiné, and Savoy, the county had formed part of the old kingdom of Transjurane Burgundy, which had belonged to the Empire ever since the last of its kings, dying childless in 1032, had left it to his nephew by marriage, the Emperor Conrad II. The Arelate, as it was now called, is a proud and lovely region, stretching along the whole course of the Rhône, from the glacier that gives it birth to the olive orchards at its mouth, and it had never forgotten its royal past. With Italy and Germany it was always considered as one of the three kingdoms that made up the Empire, and the emperors had always received the crown of Arles at a separate ceremony. But after Barbarossa, the custom had fallen into disuse, and, although nominally still Imperial, it was coming more and more under French influence even before Charles, claiming Provence in right of his wife, appropriated the county for himself.

The situation bristled with complications, to the delight of the intriguing old ladies. There were innumerable grounds for enmity between the Emperor Rudolf and Charles, and Margaret of France used them one after the other to further her plans. She had the brilliant and legal idea of doing homage to the emperor for her share of Provence, which would have substantiated her claims, and her impatience knew no bounds when this had to be postponed because the Bohemian war kept him busy on the far side of Germany. Even that would still have left Charles with some uncontested rights over the county, while the sisters-in-law would never be satisfied until he could be driven out completely. To that end they planned a marriage between Edward's daughter, Joan, who had been born at Acre shortly after the attempt on her father's life, and Hartmann, Rudolf's son. If Hartmann could be proclaimed king of Arles, with an English queen to share his throne, Provence would once again be in safe hands and Eleanor and Margaret would have won their final victory.

By 1276 negotiations for the marriage had already gone so far that the council of the realm affirmed that it was too late for either side to back out. Four of the surviving Grandson brothers had taken part in them. Othon, in the autumn of 1277, had been one of the English commissioners who met the German embassy when it came to London to discuss the terms of the marriage contract;[34] Jacques had been sent by Edward to look over the lands that Rudolf was to grant to the bride and groom;[35] Girard, the bishop of Verdun, had taken part in the discussions almost from the beginning;[36] and after Girard died in 1278 it was the next bishop and fourth brother, Henri, who wrote Edward the news that his prospective son-in-law had been drowned when the boat that was carrying him down the Rhine hit a tree in the fog and capsized.[37]

This had checked the two old ladies, but another marriage that they arranged was more successful. A few years earlier Margaret had persuaded Philip III to agree to the marriage of Edmund of Lancaster and the recently widowed queen of Navarre, who was also countess of Brie and Champagne. This move delighted both dowagers, for it contained no less than three features distasteful to Charles. First, one of the great fiefs of France went to the loyal and loving brother of the king of England; second, Charles could never quite discount the possibility that Edmund might revive his claims to the Sicilian throne, and, moreover, by this marriage he became connected with yet another claimant, for his new stepdaughter, Jeanne, the baby heiress of Navarre, was betrothed to one of the sons of James of Aragon, whose heir, Peter, was married to Constance of Hohenstaufen. Finally, the new count of Champagne was not only earl of Lancaster but earl of Leicester as well, a title that had come to him after the Barons' War, when he had been given all those lands of Earl Simon that the Montfort brothers, with the support of their friend, Charles of Anjou, were still

[34] C. M. Fraser, *A History of Antony Bek, Bishop of Durham, 1283–1311*, p. 16.

[35] Rymer, I, 563.   [36] *Idem.*

[37] J. Böhmer (ed.), *Die Regesten des Kaiserreichs*, No. 1427a.

clamoring to have returned to them. All in all, the old ladies could congratulate themselves on having achieved a perfect masterpiece of vexation.

It was business connected with Edmund of Lancaster that in 1280 took Othon on his first embassy to the Curia,[38] and although the nature of this business is never explicitly stated it is safe to assume that it had to do with the possible substitution of Edmund for Edward as leader of the hoped for crusade. As far back as 1276 Edward had realized that he would probably be unable to keep his crusading vow himself, and he had written to Pope John XXI, promising that if he could not go he would send his brother in his place. Nothing had come of this suggestion and now, four years later, when the troubles in Wales made it more than ever impossible for Edward to leave England, he decided that it was time to send a messenger to Rome who would bring the matter to a satisfactory conclusion. Othon, the fellow crusader and trusted counselor of both brothers, seemed particularly fitted for this mission, and if Gregory X had still been alive, he might have been more successful. But Gregory had died in 1276 and although the popes who followed him succeeded one another so rapidly that it was impossible to tell what their policies might have been, it was easy to see that they all were too weak to take the place of their great predecessor. They left to one side the business of Christendom while they took part in the Angevin-Italian squabbles that tore the peninsula, and the political position of each one was determined by his gratitude to the party that had engineered his election. When Othon left England in July, 1280,[39] the reigning pope was Nicholas III, of the great Roman house of Orsini. As the Italians look down on the transalpine barbarians and as the Romans look down on the other Italians, so do the Orsini look down on everyone else except the Colonna. Nicholas was the bitter enemy of Charles of Anjou, the interloping Frenchman who could glory in the title of "senator of Rome" and who

[38] Rymer, I, 584.   [39] *C.P.R.* (*1272–81*), p. 389.

thought his niece too good to marry the pope's nephew. Because of this enmity, had Nicholas lived, Othon's embassy might have turned out differently, but by the end of August Nicholas had gone to wait for Boniface VIII in that *bolgia* of the Inferno reserved for simoniacal popes, and Othon reached Italy in time to witness what proved to be an unusually long and stormy conclave.

The six months that he spent waiting to see whether he would have a friendly or an unfriendly pope to deal with gave him an opportunity to learn just how things were done in the capital of Christendom, and what he saw must have been very difficult for a man of his type to understand. Rome even at the best of times was an unruly and tumultuous city; during a papal election, and especially such a particularly troubled one as this was to be, all semblance of law and order vanished, and by comparison London and even Bordeaux must have appeared miracles of well-policed tranquillity. It is true that the conclave was not sitting in Rome, for long ago the popes had fled from the pestilent nobles and pestilential vapors of the Campagna to the safer and more salubrious hill towns of Viterbo and Orvieto. It is comparatively rare to find a papal letter dated from Rome, for the city was left to the great families, who built their castles among the ruins and tried to erect on crumbling and half-forgotten traditions their own half-understood form of feudalism. A strange thing they made of it. In urban Italy, even among the smaller towns of the north where the open country could still be seen at the end of the street, feudalism had never flourished, and here where the influence of *the* City extended in wave after concentric wave until it broke on the foothills of the Apennines it was more out of place than ever. It is hard to make sense of this mixture of barons who had for their castle the Colosseum and of senators who were at the same time French counts and Sicilian kings, for Rome, true to the fate predicted for it by Vergil, produced neither artists who could portray them nor poets who could describe them. By now it had lost even those arts that had been promised to it, and the Romans, whose destiny it was to rule the world with peace and justice, were carried helplessly along by the torrent of Angevins and imperialists, foreign nobles and Tuscan bankers, who poured through the city on their way to Viterbo, where the cardinals had been sitting month after month behind the locked doors of the episcopal palace.

It had been Gregory X who, at the Council of Lyons, drew up new and stricter rules to govern the procedure of future conclaves so that there might never again be an interregnum as long as the one that preceded his own election, but it must have seemed to Othon that his old friend had not been foresighted enough. As the vintage passed, and the olive harvest, and the first pink almond twigs blossomed, still no pope had been chosen. There was always plenty to do, for half the saints in the Calendar had met martyrdom in Rome and the city was full of their relics, while no amount of death and disturbance could lessen the passion of the Romans for dramatic ceremonial, although with no pope to say the Christmas masses at Santa Maria Maggiore and at Sant'Anastasia or to bless Sant'Agnese's little white lambs, even these solemnities lost some of their splendor. Luckily for the faithful, Martin IV was elected just before Ash Wednesday, 1281, and crowned on *Laetare* Sunday, so that Othon's long wait was rewarded: he heard the Lenten and Easter liturgies carried out with all the pomp that a new pope could bring to them and witnessed as well the interesting and sometimes peculiar rites of a papal coronation.

Pope Martin was a Frenchman, Simon de Brie, and he turned out to be the docile friend and creature of the Sicilian king. After this, all Othon's diplomacy was in vain. It is too much to say that the pope remained obdurate, for that was not his nature; rather, he vacillated for two years and only then did he write Edward that, although he regretted the king's inability to lead the crusade himself, he refused to accept Edmund in his place.

Although Othon may have had his instructions in regard

to the papal election, no hint of such a thing has survived. There can be little doubt that messengers crossed the snow-clad Alps or sailed into the port of Ostia, but whatever they had to say was relayed by word of mouth. All we know of any other business that kept Othon in Rome all that winter is con-tained in a perfectly open and aboveboard letter from Edward to Charles of Salerno written the previous July. Young Charles had been urging his cousin to send someone to treat with Guy de Montfort, so that the latter might be reinstated in Edward's favor and be given back the Leicester lands, but the king had always refused, on the grounds that it would not be to his honor to do so:

> ... nevertheless, since we have seen the goodwill that you
> have put into this business, we should be very glad if the
> aforesaid Guy or his friends would remit the guarantee
> and the conditions that he is willing to make with us to our
> faithful and loyal Otes de Gruntson (who is in those
> parts on our brother's business), so that the said Otes can
> advise us of them and we can take more certain counsel with
> those whom the matter touches most nearly, for without
> that counsel we are unwilling to undertake any
> important business.[40]

This grudging reply held out little promise of success; Guy was not the man to make humiliating concessions nor was Ed-ward in the mood to accept any other kind, for the events of the last few years had done nothing to diminish the anger that he felt against the whole house of Montfort. For political rea-sons he had set Eleanor free so that she might marry Llewellyn, but her brother, Amaury, who had been captured with her, was still held prisoner in England, and neither her tearful appeals nor papal demands for his release, backed by requests from Archbishop Peckham, had so far brought his liberation any nearer. If Edward was so unrelenting against Amaury, whose only sin lay in his being a Montfort and who had no connection

---

[40] Rymer, I, 584.

6 4

with the murder of Henry of Almain—he had been studying at Padua when it was committed, and the whole University, masters and scholars alike, as well as all the friars in the town, had sworn with startling unanimity that he was at death's door with a fever on the day of the crime—there was little chance that he would forgive the actual culprit. Moreover, Guy's vicissitudes during the last few years prejudiced his chances, for it was clear that he was being protected not only by the Sicilian Angevins and by his powerful relatives in both Italy and France but even by the popes, and Edward would not willingly listen to those who were helping the murderer of his cousin to escape justice.

Othon must have listened to countless arguments, from Charles of Salerno, from Guy's cousin and greatest friend, Jean de Montfort, perhaps even from Guy himself, for the Angevins were at Viterbo in force to make sure that this time they would get a French pope. But he could only repeat his master's orders: Edward remained inflexible and Guy was to go to the Holy Land and remain there, or at least stay south of the Alps, and never without Edward's permission go back to France, let alone to England. The permission never came; and Guy, the son of a French father and of an English mother—insofar as any of the Plantagenets can be called English—was to spend the rest of his life fighting in Italy and to die in a Sicilian prison without ever revisiting either of the lands from which he sprang.

Othon was back in England by June 1, 1281,[41] and seems to have spent the summer in attendance on the king, as his name appears repeatedly in the bewildering variety of documents that make Calendars of Rolls such diverting reading. He never had to witness one of those frequently recurring entries by which the king, to avert suspicion, categorically states that the recipient lost his ear by the bite of a sow, but he was there to put his seal to the letter by which an injured husband forgave the two men who had kidnapped his wife and, to make it worse,

[41] *C.C.R.* (1279–88), p. 124.

had taken all her goods and chattels as well,[42] and to those granting to the lady Dionisia de Monte Canisio, who judging from the context was probably as pretty as her name, the right to hold her lands directly of the king by the service of a rose.[43] Othon's testimony by itself was sufficient for this latter grant, but a weightier and less sweet-smelling matter required a whole cloud of witnesses. It took the bishops of Worcester and of Norwich, Edmund, earl of Lancaster, the king's brother, William of Valence, earl of Pembroke, the king's uncle, Henry de Lacy, earl of Lincoln, and a host of others, including John de Vescy, Robert Tybetot, Othon de Grandson, and the seneschal of the Household, to confirm the license granted by King Henry to the men of Biarritz to fish for various kinds of whales, "balenam, balenatum, et cavalatum, sint masculi vel femini," on the payment of fifteen *livres Morlaix* a head and on the understanding that if the king or his heirs were in Gascony one of these whales should go to him at a price to be agreed on by four worthy citizens of Bayonne.[44] As usual, Othon also had to look after the affairs of his friends and relatives,[45] and it is pleasant to know that when he left the court at the end of a tiring day he had his own house in Westminster to go home to. Although Edmund of Lancaster's cook lived just around the corner,[46] Othon's house must have been in a desirable situation and of a convenient size, since Parliament once met there; the lord of Grandson could live there in a state befitting his rank.

But the comparative peace of this interval was broken in the autumn when news came from Savoy that the long-standing quarrel between Edward's great-uncle, Count Philippe, and Rudolf of Habsburg had at last flared into open warfare. The origin of the conflict is obscure; it seems to have dated from the days of Richard of Cornwall, who when he was king of the

[42] *Idem.*

[43] *C. Ch. R.* (*1257–1300*), p. 254.   [45] *C.P.R.* (*1272–81*), p. 442.

[44] *R.G.*, II, No. 479.   [46] *Ibid.*, p. 435.

Romans had given the homage of certain towns near Bern and Fribourg to Pierre of Savoy and to his male heirs after him. Since Pierre's only surviving child was his daughter, Béatrice, these rights should have gone back to the Empire, but his brother and successor, Philippe, still kept a tenacious hold on Morat, Payerne, and Gümmenen, and during the last years of the Great Interregnum there had been no one to dispute his claims. Even when there was an emperor again Rudolf was at first too busy with more important affairs elsewhere to force the issue, and during the early years of his reign a temporary truce had sufficed to keep the peace between them.

The saintly Gregory X had done his best to put a stop to this quarrel when he came to Lausanne in 1275 to consecrate the newly rebuilt cathedral of Notre-Dame, but in spite of his efforts relations between Rudolf and Philippe grew steadily worse. The emperor still hoped to regain the three towns by peaceful means, the more so as war on his eastern frontier required all his attention, and in May, 1278, just before he took the field against King Ottokar of Bohemia, he had empowered Edward to act as arbitrator in his quarrel with Savoy and to draw up the articles of a permanent treaty. Edward's efforts were no more successful than those of the pope had been, but he continued them even after the fighting started and in February, 1282, appointed Othon, with John Derby, dean of Lichfield, and Philippe's brother, Thomas of Savoy, to try to bring about a peace.[47] Rudolf refused even to grant them an audience,[48] and the best that Othon could do was to meet with the Savoyard and Imperial plenipotentiaries. His advice must have carried some weight, for later in the summer when a truce was drawn up, Edward was expressly mentioned, together with Margaret of France, who of course had her finger in the pie, as one of those by whose request the agreement was reached. However, neither that truce nor the others that succeeded it led to a permanent

[47] Rymer, I, 589 (incorrectly dated 1281. Cf. *R.G.*, II, Nos. 557–64).
[48] Fritz Kern (ed.), *Acta Imperii Angliae et Franciae*, No. 22.

treaty, and the war came to an end only with the fall of Payerne to the Imperial forces in December, 1283.

The war within a war that Othon's cousin, the bishop of Lausanne, was waging against his insubordinate flock dragged on even longer. The Lausannois had seized on the outbreak of hostilities as a chance to rise against Bishop Guillaume, and the latter had been driven from his see and was in exile at Belfaux near Fribourg when Othon reached the Pays de Vaud. The peacemakers in the larger quarrel tried to end this one as well, but even after the Savoyard-Imperial treaty was sealed the dogged Lausannois kept on fighting, and it was not until the spring of 1284 that the emperor was able to bring them to terms.

Othon found time during the winter of 1282 to look after his own affairs, and he made arrangements to buy from his nephew, Girard d'Oron, the homage of "Perrin," lord of Vaumarcus, for the village of Concise and the forest of Seyte, both lying north of Grandson. The sale, which cost him 200 *livres lausannois*, did not go through until the summer,[49] by which time Othon was once again fighting in Wales. He must have left the transaction in his mother's capable hands, for in the following year she approved Perrin's donation of these properties to his daughter.[50]

Agnès, ruling from the castle in the stead of "my illustrious lord Othon, knight, lord of Grandson and my son," as she called him in her more official moments, was in effect the head of the greatest of the Vaudois fiefs and exercised all the responsibilities that that position entailed. Her visits to her overlord, the count of Savoy, when he came to the Pays de Vaud and held his court at Romont, were occasions of some ceremony, on one of which she dined with Philippe and ranked just below the dauphine of Vienne.[51] Of her six married daughters at least

[49] G. A. Matile (ed.), *Monuments de l'histoire de Neuchâtel,* Vol. II, No. 79.

[50] *Ibid.,* No. 84.

[51] Wednesday, August 15, 1272, Romont: "presentibus Octolino [de Burgo] et episcopus gebennensis et comitessa de Vienna et domina de Grandson et pluribus aliis," given by Mario Chiaudano (ed.), *La finanza sabauda nel secolo XIII,* II, 272.

five lived nearby, and although her sons were scattered to the four winds, they were always on the move, and Grandson lay where all their paths crossed, so that letters frequently arrived from Jacques and Henri in Viterbo, while Othon himself or Bishop Girard, passing by on business for the pope or the emperor or the king of England, would take time to spend a few days at home with their mother.

Girard, the first of her sons to become bishop of Verdun, died in 1278, and his brother Henri, who succeeded him,[52] found the affairs of his bishopric in great disorder. He and Jacques wrote to Edward from Viterbo asking for his support. One infers that they got one of the clerks in the papal chancery to help them with the composition of their letter, for very few other people were capable of writing in such a flowery style. The gist of it—shorn of moving references to the shipwrecks of life and other extraneous matter—is that the chapter of Verdun had come to the late bishop's funeral not to bury him but to rob him and had laid hands even on his personal property; would Edward permit Edmund of Lancaster, as count of Champagne, to give them refuge in his castle of Passavant and to protect their rights, and would the king let them know his will in the matter through their brother Othon, by whom they were sending him this news?[53] When Henri finally went north to his bishopric, Jacques must have come with him as far as the Pays de Vaud, for he was later captured by the Imperial forces during the siege of Payerne.[54]

Probably Agnès died before this family misfortune, for we hear no more of her after April, 1283. She died on December

[52] M. Dessemontet has pointed out that the recent discovery that Agnès de Grandson was born a De Chiny helps to explain this succession. Chiny was in Luxemburg, and its powerful counts seem to have had almost as much influence in the nearby diocese of Verdun as the Grandsons had in that of Lausanne.

[53] J. Champollion-Figéac, *Lettres*, I, 161–62.

[54] Böhmer, *op. cit.*, I, 1804.

20[55]—the year is not known—and as she lay on her deathbed she watched the reflections from the fireplace as she had watched them on the day when her first son was born. The fate foretold for him by the burning brand was well on the way to fulfilment; she had seen two of her sons become bishops; she had married her daughters well; she had held the property together. In short, she had conscientiously done her duty as *domina Grandisoni*, and it is a pity not to know more about her, for as she lay dying, full of years and honor, she was a far more sympathetic character than either of the fighting dowagers of England and France.

Had she lived a little longer, she would have seen her first-born son raised to even greater dignities. In March, 1282, while Othon was still in Savoy, David ap Griffith had been reconciled with his brother Llewellyn—a proceeding that the English likened to the sudden friendship between Herod and Pilate—and on Palm Sunday he made a sudden attack on Hawarden Castle in Flintshire, overcoming the garrison and mortally wounding the justiciar of Wales, Roger de Clifford. The whole country flared into open rebellion, but the resultant war was short-lived. Llewellyn was killed at the battle of Orewin's Bridge in December, and David was betrayed and taken in the following June.

Although it was such a short campaign, the accounts of it are full of contradictions, for it was in the main a guerilla war, and the news of sudden sorties and aimless retreats, of captured castles and unfinished negotiations, became badly garbled before it reached the remote safety of the scriptoria where the monks were writing their histories. It makes it no clearer if we try to follow it through the eyes of one man, especially when that man is Othon. He was in Wales from May through July,

55 B.M. Roy. MS, 2, A, xviii. This is the Grandison breviary, which belonged to her grandson, John Grandison, bishop of Exeter.

1282, as castellan of Montgomery,[56] where he led a force of seventeen lances;[57] he sent men to his Channel Islands to buy food for the army;[58] he was in attendance on the king when Edward took the field himself[59] and later at Rhuddlan.[60] During all the winter and most of the spring of 1283 he and John de Vescy were once more commanding at Anglesey,[61] and during the following summer he was once more with Edward.[62]

By September, 1283, David's head had gone to join his brother's on the Tower and his four quarters were each hanging in a different city. Wales, with the last of her princes dead, had no one left to keep up the legend that she could remain free, and "The king through the land, to nourish love, Causes his peace to be cried in the manner of a conqueror; Establishes his laws, makes the state better; He appoints in his name wardens and rulers."[63] Chief among these was Othon, who held the post first of justiciar of Snowdon and later of all Wales from before March, 1284, to September, 1295. Needless to say, since he was rarely to spend eleven months, let alone eleven years, in one country, it was in the nature of an honorary position, and during most of his tenure of office he was represented by deputies.[64] However, Edward did keep him in Wales until the end of 1285, for during the crucial period that saw the inauguration of English rule in the former principality, the duties of justiciar of Snowdon were too onerous to be intrusted to any-

56 P.R.O., Exch. Accts., 4/1, m. 1, in A. J. Taylor, "A Letter from Lewis of Savoy to Edward I," *E.H.R.*, LXVIII (1953), 60, n. 4.

57 Morris, *op. cit.*, p. 156.

58 *C. Chanc. R., Var.*, p. 222.

59 *Ibid.*, pp. 223, 233–34, 237.

60 *Ibid.*, pp. 240, 241, 243.

61 Morris, *op. cit.*, pp. 189, 193.

62 *C. Chanc. R., Var.*, p. 271; Morris, *op. cit.*, p. 199.

63 Piers Langtoft, *Chronicle*, II, 183.

64 T. F. Tout, *Chapters*, VI, appendix I, 58–59.

one but a man of proven ability. These duties, as laid down in the Statute of Rhuddlan, were that he "shall have guard and governance of our royal peace in Snowdon and in our lands of Wales adjoining and shall administer justice to all, according to our royal writs and to the laws and customs that follow."[65] He thus occupied very much the same position in Wales as he had done while in Gascony with Burnell, but in the newly conquered territory there were other and unfamiliar difficulties to contend with. Apart from the natural reluctance of the North Welsh to come under English law, there was the added complication that although the region comprising Anglesey, Carnarvon, and Merioneth was now shire ground, it was still separately administered and had its own separate legislation, for the Statute of Rhuddlan stipulated that the courts of Westminster should have no jurisdiction there. The eighteen months during which Othon kept his state at Carnarvon must have been a time of endless experimentation and revision—or as a native of another Celtic country put it, of "muddling through"—and it is surprising that even a man of his boundless energy should have found time for anything more than the judicial duties of his office. But he was called upon to display yet another facet of his many-sided character.

One step that Edward was taking to "nourish love—in the manner of a conqueror" was to build anew or to rebuild a number of castles, and the supervision of this work was added to Othon's other responsibilities. All in all there were to be eight of them; four had been started after the first Welsh war and were well on the way to completion by the time that the second broke out, but one of these, Aberystwyth, having been largely destroyed in the rising of 1282, now had to be rebuilt, and three new ones, Harlech, Carnarvon, and Conway, began going up soon after peace was made. Baumaris, the last, was started only in 1295.

It has been estimated that the whole operation, between

65 *Statutes of the Realm*, I, 55.

1272 and 1301, when Edward turned the principality over to his son, cost as much as £80,000 and that as many as 4,000 men were sometimes employed at one time. The amount of detail involved was staggering. That Conway castle, the greatest of them all, could have been finished within ten years— or rather, in ten summers, for no work could be done in winter —speaks volumes for the efficiency of Edward's government. Even before construction could be started, Othon had to see to the hiring of the men who felled the trees and mined the coal and then find more men, carters and boatmen, to bring them to Wales, for almost all the workers came from England; he had to see that once there they were sheltered and that land was bought on which their living quarters could be built; and, above all, he had to pay them. Their wages, together with all other expenses, imposed a heavy strain on Edward's already shaky finances, and the king must have been secretly thankful when the archbishop of York died in 1285, for while the see was vacant its revenues came into his hands; he could find no better use for them than to turn them over to Othon and to his deputy, Malcolm Harley, to go toward the cost of the Welsh castles.[66]

In addition to all this time-consuming work, Othon had his own affairs to consider. As a man of influence he had many friends and hangers-on, and he seems to have been most assiduous in looking after their interests.[67] He also had his own financial worries, although these were probably connected with his official life, since, as also happened on his embassies, when funds were not forthcoming from the king he made good out of his own pocket, hoping to be reimbursed later. The joint debt that he and John de Vescy contracted[68] was almost certainly

66 *C.P.R.* (*1281–92*), p. 193; *C.F.R.* (*1272–1307*), p. 220. They came to £1,812 12s. 4d.

67 *C. Chanc. Warrants*, p. 16; *C.P.R.* (*1272–81*), p. 442; *C.C.R.* (*1279–88*), p. 259; *C. Chanc. R., Var.*, p. 288.

68 *Calendar of Letter-books of the City of London*, A, p. 87.

for expenses in Wales, and financial pressure was probably also responsible for an otherwise inexplicable occurrence, when a strangely assorted group of seventy people, headed by the prior and cellarer of Ixeworth, fell upon one of his servants, Ralph de "Bonevill," and carried off some of the goods belonging to his master and to his master's cousin, Pierre de Champvent.[69] Ixeworth was one of the properties of William le Blund that had come to Othon and Pierre after the Barons' War; it had been in the family for several generations, and the villagers and monks probably resented their new owners, so that when the latter, in financial straits, bore down upon them too heavily, they met force with force.

Othon was also called away to perform such odd jobs as swearing that the king would observe the terms of the marriage contract between Earl Gilbert of Gloucester and Edward's daughter Joan.[70] Joan, who had been only five at the time of her betrothal to Hartmann of Habsburg, had now reached the ripe age of twelve, and Othon had known her since she was born, but there is no sign that either he or her parents felt any qualms about marrying her off to one of the brilliantly unstable Clares, a man old enough to be her father, who had already had one unfortunate matrimonial experience and, indeed, was still in the process of divorcing his first wife and getting a papal dispensation to marry her next of kin.

As though that were not enough, other people as well were clamoring for Othon's services. In 1283 Edmund of Lancaster was in Paris, acting for Edward in discussions about the disputed episcopal election of Bordeaux and also dealing with his own unruly city of Provins, which he owned in right of his wife, the countess of Champagne. It was quite typical of the gentle

---

[69] *C.P.R. (1281–92)*, pp. 89–90. "Bonevill" is probably a more than usually accurate English approximation of a continental name; Bonvillars is a small village near Grandson.

[70] Rymer, I, 628–29. See P. Chaplais, "The Making of the Treaty of Paris (1259) and the Royal Style," *E.H.R.*, LXVII (1952), 237 and n. 1.

Edmund that in the midst of such pressing matters of state he found time to adopt for his emblem the sweet-scented rose of Provins—*R. gallica,* var. *officinalis,* in the cold language of the horticulturists, the Red Rose of Lancaster to the historians—which had been brought from Syria by Blanche's father-in-law, Thibaut of Champagne. He did not mention this in the letter that he wrote to Edward to tell him how things were going, since he obviously tried to make his report as brief as possible. By his own efforts he had reached an agreement on the question of Provins, which "I would have sent you in writing, only it is very long, so I am writing it to mother, who will show it to you if you want to see it." But Gascon affairs proved to be beyond the competence even of the king's brother. He needed expert help to straighten out the tangles of the Bordelais election and, after that last charmingly domestic remark, went on to say: "You must remember, Sire, that I have asked you by letter and by word of mouth, if you would lend me my lord Otes de Granzon to help me in my business, for which I need his counsel; and I am asking you again, please to lend him to me for a short time. He can come back whenever you want."[71] It is possible that Edward heeded this urgent appeal, for from May to September of that year Othon is not mentioned in the English records. With another man we might simply think that he was resting from his arduous labors, enjoying some stag-hunting on his new Irish lands of Clonmel and Tipperary[72] or even nearer home at his manors of Sheen in Surrey or Seal in Kent.[73] But such delights were not for him so long as the king and the king's brother had need of him, and events in Europe were soon to make him more valuable as a diplomat on the Continent than as an administrator in Wales.

[71] Rymer, I, 631.

[72] *C. Ch. R. (1257–1300)*, p. 254.

[73] *Ibid.,* p. 284.

*Dominus rex Sicilie pro cuius liberacione tantum
laboravit dominus rex noster modicam graciam
vel potenciam habet ad regendum regnum suum.
Unde timeo quod in vanum multum
laboravimus circa ipsum.*

WILLIAM HOTHAM, *to the prior of Holy Trinity, Cambridge*

iv. The Sicilian Vespers

When Othon had last seen Charles of Anjou in 1281 at Viterbo, it looked as though all the latter's ambitions for the formation of a Mediterranean empire under Angevin rule were on the point of being realized. Already his influence was paramount at the French court, in spite of the frantic opposition of his sister-in-law, the queen dowager Margaret; and the election of Simon de Brie as Pope Martin IV assured him an equal supremacy at the court of Rome. By the agreements made at Lausanne in 1275, Rudolf had given him a free hand in Italy, and the bonds between them had been further strengthened by the betrothal of his grandson, Charles Martel, to the emperor's daughter, Clementia. Peter of Aragon, the husband of Constance of Hohenstaufen, could apparently be discounted as a possible rival for Sicily, for he was in trouble with the papacy, having refused at his accession to hold his kingdom

7 6

as a fief of the Church and moreover had his hands full at home putting down a rebellion of his Catalan nobles.

Othon had left Rome and was far away with Edward on the Welsh March when they received their first inkling that even Charles's luck might change. Ferrante of Aragon, writing from France toward the end of May, 1282, ended a routine letter of recommendation with a startling piece of news told in a most casual way:

> Also, my lord, know that I have learnt from certain merchants who lately came to Court that it is decided that the pope will soon arrive at Marseilles; they also told me as sure that five Sicilian cities have risen against King Charles and killed all the French living in them. There is no other news in Paris worth repeating.[1]

That last sentence was not so ingenuous as it sounded, or else Ferrante was very badly informed; there was other news in Paris, for King Peter's extensive naval preparations had raised grave suspicions at the French court, which the carefully non-committal answers that he gave to Philip's questions concerning them did nothing to allay. Henri de Grandson, writing to Edward from Orvieto three weeks later, had no reason to hide what everyone suspected:

> The news at the Curia is that all Sicily is in open rebellion against the king, and it is feared that the king of Aragon, who had a great fleet at sea, will land in that kingdom. The king of Sicily is gathering a great army at Naples, intending to make for Sicily; and unless something new turns up, the pope plans to go at Whitsun to Bologna and from there, around Michaelmas, to go into France.[2]

By the time that Edward had received a letter from Peter himself, informing him that he had been offered the crown of Sicily and was planning to accept it, the Aragonese fleet was

[1] Rymer, I, 609.

[2] C.-V. Langlois (ed.), "Notes et documents relatifs à l'histoire du xiiie siècle," *Revue historique*, LXXXVII (1900), 67.

already riding at anchor in Trapani harbor and the new king was in Palermo.

The whole contradictory story of the Sicilian Vespers is so fantastic, from Giovanni da Procida's seemingly autobiographical account of his cloak-and-dagger doings between Constantinople, Rome, and Saragossa to the actual events of that Easter Monday afternoon, when the exasperated Sicilians crying "Mora! mora!" finally rose against their French conquerors, that it is hardly surprising to find it turning into melodrama. Suddenly, at the very end of December, 1282, the air, which was growing heavier day by day with bulls of excommunication against Peter of Aragon, with defiant letters passing between the rival kings, and with the dusty wrangling of the lawyers, was cleared as though by a clap of thunder: Charles and Peter had decided to fight it out, with a hundred knights on a side, in a duel to be held at Bordeaux the following June, with the king of England guarding the lists.

Edward was at Conway when this astounding suggestion reached him, and he seems to have hesitated for a moment out of sheer surprise. But long before Pope Martin's frenzied appeals to him to stop the duel had arrived in Wales, he had made up his mind to have no part in it. He wrote to his uncle:

> We cannot find it in our heart, nor in any manner possible,
> that such great cruelty should be done in our presence,
> nor within our power, nor in any other place where we could
> put a stop to it. And, dear cousin, it would be a very
> strange and grievous thing to us that we should receive you
> on our lands in such a manner when you did us such honor
> and received us so handsomely in yours when we
> returned from beyond the seas. . . . For know truly, that not
> even to gain two such kingdoms as Sicily and Aragon would
> we guard the lists where such a battle should take place.[3]

The courteous reference to his reception at the court of Palermo may have concealed a hidden barb, but when he ended his

[3] Rymer, I, 626–27.

OTHON DE GRANDSON

THE BERN ALTAR-FRONTAL

The altar-frontal, now in the Bern Historical Museum, is a most lovely thing. It measures 3.28 m. by 88 cm. and consists of a large central panel and two endpieces. The latter are of scarlet silk embroidered with golden vases out of which grow very boldly designed and executed golden grapevines. The work on the central panel is very different and far more delicate in character. It shows the Virgin and Child enthroned between the two archangels, Sts. Gabriel and Michael, represented without their attributes and bearing censers. The figures are all embroidered in gold, except the faces, hands, and feet, which are of white silk, the blue in the Virgin's veil and in the cushions of the throne, and the red and silver cross on the Christ-child's halo. Above the left-hand figure is written SAINT GABIEL *(sic), above that to the right,* SAINT MICHIEL, *and above the central figures, their monograms,* MAT DNI IC IC .

Between the archangels and the throne are gold vases from which spring golden vines with green silk leaves and white silk fruit. To the left of the throne kneels a small figure in chain mail wearing a blue and silver surcoat, with a red band running diagonally from the left shoulder to the right hem and a red armlet from shoulder to elbow; both of these bear three golden shells. At the far ends of the central panel, just under the outer wingtips of the arch-angels, are two identical shields with the Grandson arms, "paly argent and azure on a bend gules 3 escallops or."

Unfortunately, although all signs point to Othon de Grandson as the donor and to the cathedral of Lausanne as the recipient of this frontal, nothing is definitely known as to its provenance. It is mentioned neither in the cathedral inventory of 1529 nor in that made in 1536 after the Bernese conquest of the Pays de Vaud, although the latter lists a blue damask cope, a set of black silk vestments, and two cloth of gold frontals, all bearing the Grandson arms and therefore gifts of the family. However, since this too bears their arms, and since the work is of the late thirteenth or early fourteenth century, it is safe to assume that Othon was connected with it; while from its size and magnificence, and also because the central figure is of the Virgin, it probably did belong to the cathedral of Lausanne. It is also worth

noting that the statue of Notre-Dame de Lausanne, which made the cathedral a place of pilgrimage, showed Our Lady seated with the Baby on her lap.
Earlier authorities also differed as to its style. J. Stammler (La trésor de la cathédrale de Lausanne [*Lausanne, 1902*]) *thought that the central panel came from a French-speaking country, basing his argument on the French names of the two archangels, since the Greek monogram for the Christ-child was common everywhere, and that the two endpieces were Palermitan work of the end of the Hohenstaufen period. On the other hand, Lethaby, the architect in charge of the fabric of Westminster Abbey, as quoted in Burnand's two articles on Othon, said that the center was Palermitan and the two endpieces were* opus Anglicanum *and must have been made in London. Because of this, I was at first inclined to believe that Othon must have picked it up in Sicily.*
I began to change my mind after seeing the fragments of the fresco on Queen Eleanor's tomb in the Abbey and the water colors of them in Kerrich's sketchbook (B.M. Add. MS, 6728, fols. 87–88). Lethaby had already noticed the similarity between the embroidered and the painted knights; F. Rose-Troop had suggested that the fresco represented Othon praying before the Holy Sepulchre but thought it impossible that he could have gone to Jerusalem after the queen's death and therefore suggested that he had been sent there after the attempt on Edward's life. But there seems little reason for having portrayed that on the tomb, and if I could find a connection between the frontal and the events of 1291–93, it would bolster my half-formed theory that Othon had made his pilgrimage after the fall of Acre. Accordingly, I was delighted when Dr. Stettler, the director of the Bern Historical Museum, asked me if Othon had ever spent any time in Cyprus, as on purely artistic grounds he had decided that the frontal was of Cypriot origin.
As a proof that Othon did go to Jerusalem after 1291, this is a very tenuous line of reasoning, more fitted for a detective story than for a serious historical study, but it does justify my placing his purchase of the frontal during the years between the fall of Acre and his return to Europe.

CHÂTEAU DE GRANDSON

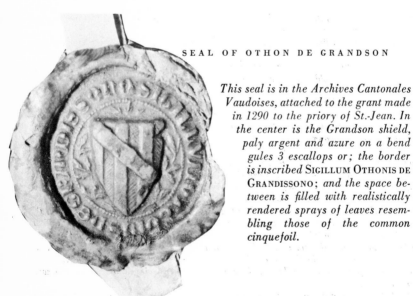

SEAL OF OTHON DE GRANDSON

This seal is in the Archives Cantonales Vaudoises, attached to the grant made in 1290 to the priory of St.-Jean. In the center is the Grandson shield, paly argent and azure on a bend gules 3 escallops or; the border is inscribed SIGILLUM OTHONIS DE GRANDISSONO; and the space between is filled with realistically rendered sprays of leaves resembling those of the common cinquefoil.

letter with an earnest offer to act as peacemaker Edward was completely sincere. Any war in Europe made a crusade impossible, and this particular war threatened as well to put him in a very precarious position, both as king of England and as duke of Aquitaine. Sooner or later Philip III must intervene on the side of his uncle, and if he summoned Edward to do his military service, the latter would not only be forced to leave his own kingdom, perhaps even before the Welsh were conquered, but would also find himself dragged into a war against King Peter. This would undo the work of eight patient years of diplomacy. Aragon, with its claims to various parts of southern France, had always been an uncomfortable neighbor to Gascony, and from the very beginning of his reign Edward had been striving to safeguard his southern frontier by arranging marriages between the royal children. It looked as though his pertinacity had finally been rewarded when Peter, in need of allies, agreed to the betrothal of the Infante Alfonso to Eleanor of England just before he left on the expedition that was to end in Palermo. Although his subsequent excommunication had put a stop to these plans, as Martin IV was not slow to point out, they could still be realized if Edward's offer were accepted and his efforts successful.

For the moment, however, his services in the cause of peace were not needed, for all Europe seemed to be standing still as it watched the preparations for the duel at Bordeaux. Edward appointed Jean de Grailly to guard the lists, but with a truly English genius for compromise he made sure that the duel would never take place by handing the field over to Charles, who entered the city on the appointed day, June 1, 1283, not only with his hundred knights but also with an army of 12,000 more, led by his nephew, the king of France. There was still no sign of Peter; only, as they waited, the arrival of yet another Aragonese messenger was announced. These had been coming almost every day, and Grailly knew just what to do; taking with him a lawyer, " . . . one of the best and most experienced in the English court," he went out to the field to meet the envoy. The latter asked the same question as all the others had done and received the same answer, for Jean repeated that he refused to take the responsibility of guarding the lists while there were so many French troops in Bordeaux; but there any resemblance to the previous interviews ended, for the stranger disclosed that he was none other than King Peter himself. Jean would have dismounted to make his obeisance, but the king refused to let him do so and bade him return to tell Charles, "king of Jerusalem and count of Anjou," that Peter, "king of Aragon and Sicily," was not forsworn. The experienced lawyer— who must also have been, or have had, an experienced secretary, for during most of the interview Peter was galloping up and down and round and round the lists—was taking it all down. He went back with Jean to tell Charles that the king of Aragon had indeed kept his day. But by the time the Angevin knights had thundered onto the field, Peter was well on his way to the border, going as he had come, disguised as the servant of a rich merchant familiar with the unguarded paths across the Pyrenees.

This anticlimax woke Europe from the trance into which the announcement of the duel had thrown it and, just as in the castle of the Sleeping Beauty, everyone took up his work where he had left off. The rival kings of Sicily went on fighting, and Peter won a great victory when his fleet, under Queen Constance's Neapolitan foster brother, Ruggiero da Loria, defeated the Angevins and took Charles of Salerno prisoner. Edward continued his unavailing efforts to make peace, "because of my love toward the kings, and for their state, and for that of the Holy Land and of all Christendom,"[4] but his representatives in Gascony were snubbed by the papal legate there, and in spite of the pensions paid to two of the cardinals and to the pope's notary, he was no more successful at the Curia itself, for Martin

[4] Rymer, I, 637.

was determined on war. In August, 1283, he declared Aragon forfeit and assured French support for his cause by offering the kingdom to Philip's younger son, Charles of Valois, and a month later he proclaimed a crusade against Peter and authorized the French clergy to grant a tenth for three years to their king.

This last papal move was particularly galling to Edward; it assured the French intervention that he had dreaded, it made the chances of peace more remote than ever, and it further complicated the already involved question of what would happen to the large sums on deposit with the Italian bankers from the money collected in the British Isles on the crusading tenth authorized by Pope Gregory at Lyons in 1275. These sums were the center of a vicious circle. Edward, alone of all the kings of Europe, must lead his crusade in person in order to touch the money and, as we have seen, his request to be allowed to send Edmund of Lancaster in his stead, even though it was backed by Archbishop Peckham, had been refused by the pope. On the other hand, it was obviously impossible for him to leave for the Holy Land so long as the Welsh were raging on the border; he needed money to bring his campaign to a victorious conclusion, and that money could come only from the tenth. His attempt to seize it in 1278 had raised such a storm that he was forced to give in, and he was no more successful during the second Welsh war. Undoubtedly, his suggestion that Llewellyn be excommunicated for starting hostilities in Holy Week had owed something to financial as well as to religious motives, for a crusade could be proclaimed against those under the ban of the Church, but this too came to nothing, and in May, 1282, he ordered that no money was to be exported from the kingdom. Perhaps he had already heard rumors of the Sicilian Vespers, for he remembered only too clearly from his father's reign how quick the popes were to call a crusade when their interests in Sicily were at stake and how much English money could be poured into Italian wars; and in March, 1283, to make sure that this could not happen a second time, he ordered his officials to raid all the monasteries where the tenth was held for safekeeping. Again the embattled clergy, led by Peckham, forced him to give it back, but by that time the Welsh were finally defeated and Edward could once more write to the pope of his unswerving determination to go to the Holy Land. But although Martin was urbanity itself on all other matters, congratulating him on his pious resolution and absolving him of all sins committed as far back as the Barons' War, he would not budge from his original position on the main issue, and the only concession that the English envoys could wring from him was that the tenth would be granted if Edward took the Cross before Christmas, 1284, and promised to set out within the next five years. But by that Christmas even his chances of fulfilling the first condition laid down by Martin looked hopeless, for Philip, as he had foreseen, had summoned him as duke of Aquitaine to follow him to the war on which he was embarking to win Aragon for his son.

Edward was already at Dover early in the winter of 1285 when news came that brought him at least a temporary respite: Charles of Anjou had died at Foggia in January. That same year was to see the deaths of the other three principal actors in the Aragonese-Angevin struggle. In March, Martin IV, whose years in Italy seem only to have heightened his native French appreciation of good cooking, died of a surfeit of his favorite dish and went to "purge himself by fasting of the Bolsena eels and of the *vernaccia*,"[5] the wine in which the unfortunate, milk-fed creatures were drowned to make them succulent enough to grace the papal table. The dynastic war waged by Philip III under the guise of a crusade brought death to him and disaster to the French, and by November his victorious enemy lay dead as well. But there was a bright side to this corpse-strewn picture and, for the first time since the quarrel started, it looked as though there might be a chance for the

[5] *Purgatorio*, XXIV, 23-24.

peacemakers. Even under the strong leadership of Charles of Anjou and with French and papal support, the Angevins had been roundly defeated, not only in Sicily, which they had been forced to abandon, but in Lombardy and Tuscany as well, and even in Rome itself, where the people had risen and imprisoned Charles's vicar. Now their future looked blacker than ever, for the lands that remained to them were ruled by a regent, the count of Artois, since Charles of Salerno was still a prisoner and his son a minor. Philip IV, like his father before him mourning the death of another king of France who had lost his life in defense of Angevin claims, was more anxious to settle his own affairs than to continue the war. The new pope, Honorius IV, could hope to reconcile the French and Roman factions in the Sacred College, for his family, the Savelli, was one of the greatest in the city, but at the same time it had always supported the Angevin cause. And, finally, the king of Aragon was no longer ruler of Sicily, for Peter had left the Italian kingdom to his younger son, James, while he was succeeded at home by Alfonso, whose kingdom was not necessarily forfeit just because his brother maintained his own claims to Sicily.

Edward redoubled his efforts. His first letter to Honorius after his accession, asking him to stop the quarrel, had received a discouraging answer, but the changed circumstances after the deaths of the two kings in the autumn made the pope more amenable, and when Edward next wrote, accompanying his letter with a present of jewels, his suggestions met with at least tacit approval. He decided to take immediate advantage of this by sending an impressive embassy to Rome, and the bankers of Lucca were soon in receipt of a mandate to pay to Othon de Grandson as much money as he might require of them for the king's affairs.[6]

The order was dated December 8, 1285, as were the letters of protection for Henry Cobham going to Rome on the same

[6] *C.P.R.* (*1281–92*), p. 213.

errand,[7] and the envoys probably set out soon afterwards, for Othon was at the Curia by February, 1286, and as usual Edward had found another job for him to do on the way. The king was going to France later in the year to pay homage for Aquitaine to his new overlord, Philip IV, and Othon, Antony Bek, and John de Vescy were sent ahead as his proctors to the French court.[8] The business there probably took some time, for the question of homage was still complicated by the problems left unsettled by the Treaties of Paris and Amiens, and, in addition, Othon undoubtedly took this opportunity of finding out all that he could about the French point of view on the Aragonese situation before starting out to discuss it with the pope.

It cannot have been before the end of January at the earliest that he found himself back in the bright, uncertain weather of a Roman winter, and once again he was to watch the spring come to Italy as his negotiations dragged on over seemingly endless months. But in every other respect this embassy was very different from the one of four years ago. Rome itself had changed for the better under its new senator, Pandolfo Savelli, who, although as crippled with gout as his brother the pope, was a man of equally strong character and knew how to rule his fellow Romans so that they were enjoying one of the few periods of law and order that fell to their lot during the Middle Ages. Honorius was a far easier person to deal with than the spineless Martin IV, in spite of his own uncompromising attitude toward the Aragonese usurpers in Sicily, and he seems to have developed a friendly respect for Othon's capacity for hard work and for his unremitting attention to the difficult business in hand which, as he wrote to Edward, "has weighed on us both equally."[9]

[7] *Idem.*

[8] *R.G.*, III, p. xxv and n. 3. If Bémont is correct in saying that they were sent in this connection, it must have been early in the year, for Edward did his homage July 5, 1286, and Othon did not leave Rome until after June 17.

[9] Rymer, I, 666.

The business was difficult, but the pope was on familiar ground in dealing with it, for it is clear from the questions that the king sent to Honorius about the crusade and from the answers that Othon brought back to him that it was all a matter of bargaining, an art in which the Romans have always been proficient. Othon had obviously been instructed to ask for far more than he hoped to gain, and there is no doubt that the pope countered his first demands by offering far less than he was prepared to grant; the final agreement, arrived at only after four months' negotiation, was a monument to Italian ingenuity and Vaudois patience. The two most important provisions of the bull that Honorius issued on June 17, 1286, were that Edward must take the Cross before Whitsunday, 1287, and leave within three years instead of within five, as he had asked to be allowed to do, and that he could not have the tenth for another seven years, but only for another three. The remaining answers followed the same pattern; in each one the pope conceded something less than Edward had asked for and at the same time made his concessions depend on the king's fulfilling certain conditions laid down in the bull.

But this was only the usual give-and-take of diplomacy and comparatively simple; the French-Aragonese war raised many more difficult problems, and nothing happened all that winter to make their solution any easier. Although other messengers came from England, Othon had to act on his own initiative, for things were happening too rapidly to allow the instructions that they brought with them to be of much practical use. The pope, on his side, was hampered by his own eagerness to see the affair settled and by the secrecy that this entailed, for he did not dare discuss it with the whole Sacred College and had to rely for advice only on those cardinals whom he knew to be in Edward's confidence. Besides, there were always the Sicilians to consider, and the princes of the Church and the crowned heads of Europe were powerless in the face of their obstinate determination never to go back under Angevin rule. They refused to abide by any of the treaties into which Edward and his ambassadors had put so much hard work and good will—although it is only fair to the Sicilians to say that these were usually broken more quickly by the popes than by anyone else; they paid no attention to the excommunication of their king and to the interdict laid on the island; and they cheered the news of the victories that the invincible Ruggiero da Loria gained in one great sea battle after another. In February, 1286, the Sicilians filled the cathedral of Palermo with impenitent rejoicing as the crown of his Norman and Hohenstaufen ancestors was placed on the head of James of Aragon, and although the new king immediately sent an embassy to Rome with a humble request that the pope accept his obedience and the devotion of the Sicilians, the way in which the story is told by the chronicler, Bartolomeo di Neocastro, who was one of the ambassadors, reflects the spirit of his countrymen far better than does the meekness of the petititon that he brought from their king. Honorius, who must have had a pleasant wit if Bartolomeo can be believed, told the envoys in a parody of their own pompous oratorical style that although he admired the way they marshaled their words and composed their discourse he could not say as much of their deeds: ". . . you Sicilians can talk well, but you do evil and you do not live soberly."[10] The ambassadors, seemingly far more puffed up by the implied compliment than cast down by the pope's flat refusal to grant their request, went home in the best of humors, which does not seem to have been overshadowed even when Honorius laid the interdict on Sicily, excommunicated King James and his brother, ordering them to leave the country by Ascension Day, May 26, and for good measure repeated all his anathemas against Alfonso of Aragon as well.

The arrival of the brilliant and talkative Sicilian embassy and its subsequent rebuff furnished an exhilarating topic of conversation for the Roman scandalmongers, but there were

[10] Bartolomeo di Neocastro, *Historia Sicula*, p. 1119.

other pieces of gossip to which Othon listened with even greater interest, for they concerned his brother, the bishop of Verdun. Henri de Grandson seems to have been something of a stormy petrel. No doubt he had devoted a certain amount of time to study during the two years that he spent at the University of Bologna, where he is known to have bought a copy of the *Decretals* enlivened by the gloss of Bernard of Compostella,[11] but that can hardly have accounted for all the debts that he ran up. In 1276 even a loan from the Bolognese bankers of 600 pounds—just double the annual salary that the university paid its professors[12]—had been insufficient to meet all his bills, and he had turned to his hard-working older brother, who had come to his rescue with the small but useful sum of a further 50 pounds.[13] In spite of that, Henri was probably a far better educated man than Othon, but he was completely lacking in the latter's native gift for diplomacy. He was still in the middle of his dispute with the chapter of Verdun when Edward sent him on a mission to Rome, where he promptly became embroiled in another fight, this time with Archbishop Peckham, a far more formidable antagonist. Henri had accused the bishop of Winchester, John Pontissara, of having imprudently divulged to members of the Curia certain things derogatory to the king's honor, and the bishop had thrown the blame on Peckham, saying that all that he had done was to bring a letter from the archbishop to the papal court but that he had had no suspicion of its contents. All this happened in 1282—Henri wrote about it in the same letter in which he reported on the Sicilian Vespers—but two years later Peckham was still furious. His relations with Edward were never very good at the best of times; he had received his archbishopric in spite of the king's effort to have the post given to his friend Burnell;

11 S. and S. Stelling-Michaud, "Étudiants vaudois à l'université de Bologne," in *Mélanges d'histoire et de littérature offerts à M. Charles Gilliard*, p. 190.

12 *Idem.*

13 Archivio di Stato Bologna, Memorialia Communis, 29, fol. 39. I am indebted for this notice to M. Ollivier Dessemontet.

and the uproar after the seizure of the crusading tenth during the Welsh campaign had not improved matters. Now someone was spreading rumors at the Curia that Burnell had failed to get the bishopric of Winchester because Peckham had said that he had too many benefices already, and the stories continued to circulate that Peckham was talking against the king. He wrote an indignant letter to the bishop of Tusculum which started rather calmly, mentioning no names, but ended with a burst of anger: "Know that it is Master Henri de Grandson who is reported to have said such things about me."[14]

Peckham was a Franciscan at a time when the Order still retained some of its original austerity, and he was by nature a strict and upright churchman, which may have been why he worried over his clergy's holding more posts than they could possibly look after. Not many others were troubled by such scruples, even though the Church was always inveighing against the practice; only a few years before, Edward, writing to Pope Martin in favor of his cousin, Aymer de Valence, had ingenuously pointed out that since in England the oldest son inherited all his father's property, which was not the case elsewhere, "it has been usual heretofore to provide the younger sons of magnates with maintenance by a plurality of benefices."[15] Primogeniture was not the rule in the Pays de Vaud, but even there the sons of good family had to be provided for, and it was probably at Othon's request that Honorius allowed Girard d'Oron to hold the deanery of Vevey and several benefices in the cathedral of Lausanne as well as the deanery of Sion in the Valais, which he already possessed.[16]

Girard was probably the brother of Rodolphe d'Oron who had married Othon's sister, Antonie, and was thus not a very close relative. Othon's nephews and cousins were the ones who really benefited by his frequent visits to Rome and by the in-

[14] John Peckham, *Registrum epistolarum*, No. 544.

[15] *C.C.R.* (*1279–88*), p. 188.

[16] *Reg. Hon. IV*, No. 288.

fluence that he wielded at the Curia; we can trace their careers over three generations through the dispensations for them "obtained by the lord Othon de Grandson." We see them first holding a few small livings in remote parishes in England or the Empire or minor stalls in some cathedral chapter; he asks that they may continue to enjoy their plural benefices and also be granted the next vacant living or prebend in a specified diocese. They were still too young or too busy to be ordained; in spite of that he sees to it that they shall be allowed to retain their livings. They still had not finished their studies; he gets them dispensations for non-residence.[17] With their way thus smoothed for them, it is not surprising that seven of his younger relatives became bishops,[18] not counting his cousin, Guillaume de Champvent, who had been elected to the see of Lausanne in 1273 and without his help.

It is hard to describe such unabashed trafficking in ecclesiastical positions without sounding slightly cynical, nor is the cynicism only a twentieth-century misunderstanding of the thirteenth, for the pages of a writer like Hemingburgh, the Benedictine chronicler, are full of it. But nothing could be farther from the truth than to imagine that it was universal and that Othon kept his tongue in his cheek while he used his influence at the Curia to gain favors for his friends and relatives. The whole tenor of his life proves the contrary, and if further proof is needed it can be found in the charming story told about him by the grateful chronicler of Vale Royal Abbey, where he had laid one of the stones.

> Now there was at that time with the King, a good and
> holy man and a most strenuous knight in arms, named
> Othon de Grandson, whose memory be blessed forever.
> Once he was sent as ambassador to the Apostolic See

17 *C. Pap. R.* (*1190–1304*), *passim*. These deal only with the English benefices. References to the others are scattered through the incomplete and generally unindexed volumes of papal registers published by the Écoles françaises d'Athènes et de Rome.

18 See genealogical table, end papers.

touching the business of the kingdom. And when he arrived
there, led, I believe, by the inspiration of the Holy Ghost,
he obtained from Pope Honorius IV the appropriation
of the church of Kirkham to the monastery of Vale Royal
forever. And when he returned to England after having
favorably accomplished all the King's business, he most
devoutly gave to the abbot of Vale Royal the bull of the said
church of Kirkham. And the abbot, on his side, mindful
of such great benefits, and considering that he held no
knights in his own pay, offered a not inconsiderable
quantity of gold and silver to the aforementioned knight.
But he, preferring to be rewarded by God rather than by man,
utterly refused to accept these things as vanities. Wherefore
the abbot, with the unanimous consent of his convent,
determined and decreed that the memory of the said knight
should be specifically preserved and cared for in the said
monastery forever. And for that reason, the deed of the
knight are recorded here, that thereby those who shall
come to the monastery may be induced to pray without
ceasing that he may receive an eternal reward in Heaven
for all his labor here on earth.[19]

This estimate of Othon's character is borne out by his
modesty so far as his own needs were concerned; he was given
permission, as was John de Vescy, no doubt at his request, to
have a portable altar on which mass could be celebrated for
himself and his household by his own chaplain, and he was
further allowed the liberty of choosing any discreet priest as
his confessor.[20] The confessor's lips were sealed then, and are
doubly sealed now by six hundred years of dust drifting over
a nameless grave, but one wonders about the sins. One also
wonders about the portable altar: on his way home, did
Othon stop in Siena, where Duccio was painting the earliest
of the small triptychs that would have been just what he
needed, or did he wait until he got back to France so that the
troublesome Limousins, whose affairs he had gone to settle

19 *Ledger-book of Vale Royal Abbey*, p. 11.

20 *Reg. Hon. IV*, Nos. 534–35.

ten years ago, could provide some of their famous enamels to give the altar a magnificence more suited to the northern tastes of its owner?

At any rate, he would not have been in Italy long enough to keep a careful eye on its manufacture, for a few days after this privilege was granted to him he had his last interview with the pope. It was a very private one, for Honorius did not want to put into writing his ideas on the Sicilian question, and the instructions that he gave to Othon were for his ears alone, unless, indeed, the cardinals friendly to Edward were allowed to be present. When Othon had kissed the ring on the twisted old hand and was headed north again, all that he carried with him to show for his five months in Rome were the pope's answers about the crusade and the crusading tenth and a short letter allowing the king to marry his children to any of their cousins within the fourth degree, excepting, of course, those of the excommunicated House of Aragon. Since that was precisely the marriage that Edward had in mind, the pope's reply on that score was not very satisfactory, but everything else that Othon had to report was gone over in the greatest detail, for the kings of France and Aragon had at last given Edward powers to arrange for a truce between them, and the palace of St.-Germain, where the English had been lodged ever since Edward had arrived in Paris early in June to do his homage, was in a fever of activity.

Now that the first step had been taken, Edward was impatient to get the discussions for a definite treaty under way, and two days after the truce had been drawn up he sent Sir Hamo de Solens and Raoul d'Allaman posting down to Rome with a copy, to get the papal approval without which Philip IV refused to consider it binding. He apologized for the insignificance of the two men—Raoul was another Vaudois connected with the Grandsons, for he had been Bishop Henri's clerk when the latter was a student at Bologna[21]—but he

21 Stelling-Michaud, *op. cit.*, p. 194.

explained that there had been no time to choose more solemn envoys. As well as requesting Honorius to ratify the agreement, he asked him to send plenipotentiaries to Bordeaux to meet with the representatives of all the other powers involved.

The truce was to take effect within a month of its proclamation and to run until the end of September, 1287, which gave them all just a little over a year to settle the peace terms, but considering the manifold difficulties that confronted them even that was scarcely time enough. Honorius delayed matters by refusing to grant plenary powers to his legates, the archbishops of Ravenna and Monreale; Alfonso's attention was diverted by the threat of civil war in Aragon and by difficulties with his pro-French uncle, King James of Majorca, and with King Sancho of Castile; and Charles of Salerno, fretting in his cell, had opened negotiations on his own account with James of Sicily, although the only result was that they reached an agreement so disastrous to Angevin power in the Mediterranean and to papal prestige that Honorius repudiated it at once. However, it was clear that Charles's liberation was the necessary preliminary to any treaty of peace, for neither France nor the papacy would come to terms with Alfonso so long as their champion lay in an Aragonese prison. Edward had been working to this end almost from the beginning, urged on by letters from all Charles's supporters and relatives and also by the real friendship that he felt for his cousin who, while he had not inherited his father's strength of character, was a far pleasanter person than the latter had been. Even Ramon Muntaner, the adoring chronicler of the House of Aragon, speaks highly of him, although he seems less impressed by Charles's more usual virtues than by the miraculous vision that had enabled him to rediscover the body of the Magdalen, buried more than twenty lance-lengths deep in the limestone soil of his county of Provence; ". . . you can well imagine and believe that if he [Charles] had not been good and just, God would never have revealed such a thing to him."[22]

[22] Ramon Muntaner, *Chronica catalana*, p. 318.

The year of negotiation that followed the truce of July, 1286, was a hard one for Edward, placed between the intransigent pope and the equally intransigent Sicilians, neither of whom were really prepared to make any concessions suggested by a northern king, but in 1287 two things happened to weight the scales in favor of Aragon: Honorius died in April and almost a year was to pass before a new pope was elected, and in June Loria won another naval victory, in which Guy de Montfort, who by then was commander in chief of the Angevin forces, was taken prisoner. With this delicate balance broken, the discussions proceeded at a faster rate, and arrangements were made for a meeting between Alfonso and Edward, to be held in July at Oloron in Béarn.

Whether it was the relief caused by something definite having been accomplished at last, or the effect of the mountain air after the heat of Bordeaux, all the participants threw off the strain of the last few months and indulged in a week of festivities before getting down to business. On alternate days Alfonso and Edward dined with each other, and there were tournaments, and dances in which the kings danced with the queens while the rich men of both nations joined in the fun. The ladies did not lack partners, for although neither Burnell nor the bishop of Norfolk were dancing-men, there were plenty of others to choose from—Jean de Grailly, who had come up from Aragon where he had been negotiating for the long-delayed marriage between Alfonso and the Princess Eleanor, William de Valence, Henry Lacy, John de Vescy, and of course Othon. Once again we have to admire his versatility, and we can only hope that after his long years in "the wild land of Wales," as Peckham called it, and among the aging ecclesiastics of the Curia, he was still able to keep his place in the *estampie* and the *danse du jaloux* as he led his partners out under the summer sky.

However, when the time came to discuss the matters that brought them there, he had to leave the dancing to men less experienced in diplomacy, for as Edward's principal envoy to Rome his advice was invaluable in drawing up a treaty that must satisfy the whole College of Cardinals, who in the absence of a pope were still guided by the pro-French policy that the Church had been following for the last twenty years. It was finally settled that Charles should be freed for a ransom of 30,000 marks; that he should use his influence on Philip to get the latter to agree to a three years' armistice, the time to be spent in arranging for a definite peace; and that he was to leave his three eldest sons and the sons of sixteen Provençal nobles as hostages in Aragon; they were to be forfeit and he was to return to captivity if, within the stipulated term, his efforts should prove unsuccessful. At the same time, the marriage contract between Eleanor and Alfonso, which had been under discussion for fourteen years, was at last drawn up. There had been a few trifling mishaps—Edward's lion had killed a horse belonging to one of the natives, who had to be reimbursed to the tune of 18s. 9d.—but in general the English and Aragonese could feel that some progress had been made, and with lighter hearts than ever they returned to their merry-making, which went on even more gaily than before.

Although Alfonso invaded the territories of his uncle, the king of Majorca, which caused Philip to accuse him of breaking the truce, there still might have been a chance to conclude matters favorably if the election of a new pope in February, 1288, had not undone all that had been accomplished so far. Nicholas IV, like his uncle, Nicholas III, from whom he took his name, was an Orsini and therefore unfriendly to the Angevins, but that did not make him look any more kindly on the Aragonese claims to Sicily. In March he abrogated the treaty of Oloron, and since Alfonso refused to free Charles under any other conditions, Edward, who still held the blessèd but thankless position of peacemaker, had to start all over again from the beginning.

Many of those who had turned their backs on the Pyrenees the year before with the dance music still ringing in their ears, took the road south again at the end of the following summer when yet another meeting had been arranged, this time at Canfranc in Aragon. Edward still had Othon, John de Vescy, and Burnell with him, and the archbishop of York had come to join the English party, and there were also the pope's representatives, the archbishops of Ravenna and Monreale as well as Charles of Salerno himself, who had brought with him two of the sons he was to leave as hostages. On October 27, another treaty was agreed to, but it was so like the first, except for some minor changes, that its abrogation by Pope Nicholas was a foregone conclusion even though it was drawn up and attested by the papal notary and in the presence of the papal legates. The two kings swore to observe the truce, Pierre de Champvent, Othon's cousin, pledging himself for Edward, and Charles was a free man once more. But Edward's responsibilities were not yet over, for Charles had brought with him only 23,000 marks of his 30,000 marks' ransom, and only two of the promised nineteen hostages, his oldest son and the sixteen other boys having been left behind in Provence, and now Alfonso demanded another 50,000 marks as guarantee that he would secure the three years' armistice within ten months of his release. It was for Edward to make up the difference, which so far as the financial provisions went he seems to have done with the greatest difficulty. Things were in desperate straits indeed when Gaston de Béarn had to be prevailed upon to pledge some of his lands for the rest of the ransom, and the receipt from Alfonso for the 23,000 marks that was all that Edward could advance on the 50,000 marks' guarantee sounds as though it had been collected from all possible sources, for it was paid partly in English money, partly in French, and partly in gold florins. It was easier to make up the tale of hostages, although even here Alfonso increased his demands, and Edward was forced to leave behind him thirty-six nobles and forty citizens as security for the missing Provençals and for the rest of the ransom. The citizens were mostly Gascons, but among the nobles were two of his closest friends, John de Vescy and Othon.[23] Their plight must have weighed on him, for being a hostage at the mercy of Angevin whims could be a long-drawn-out as well as a perilous business, but he did his best for them when he passed through Saintes on his return to Gascony, by asking the prior of St.-Eutrope to offer on their behalf the prayers and psalms appointed to be said for captives,[24] and that being done, he renewed his efforts to see that Charles carried out his obligations so that they might the sooner be set free.

If John de Vescy had stayed in Aragon, Othon would have had a companion on whom he could rely whatever happened, for they had been in worse places together before, and their friendship had survived the sultry heat that made a furnace of the streets of Acre and the cold monotony of day after day under the rainy skies of a Welsh winter. But Vescy, perhaps because of ill health, was given leave of absence to go north with Edward, and Othon was left to amuse himself as best he could while he waited impatiently for news from beyond the mountains. Some of the hostages were kept at Jaca, a frontier town whose protecting ring of walls with their twenty-eight towers and seven gates was guarded in turn by the surrounding white circle of the Pyrenees, but it is probable that Othon, because of his importance, was one of those who was sent down to the capital, Saragossa. There, captivity was irksome but not unbearable; to a man accustomed to having his retinue always about him, the presence of two extra guards made very little difference, and although the hostages had to return to their lodgings once a day, they could spend the rest of the time as they pleased, walking and riding through the half-Moorish town or hunting outside the walls.[25] A day's sport along the banks of the Ebro, on a horse whose neatly pricked ears and small proud head proclaimed his Arab blood, and with some of the famous Spanish falcons to bring down the herons that flapped lazily

[23] Rymer, I, 690.   [24] *Ibid.*, p. 697.   [25] *Ibid.*, p. 694.

from the river's edge, could make a man forget his worries, although they closed in again when the hunters passed through the gates at evening to discover that there was still no news of Charles. However, by March 9, 1289, he had carried out at least some of his promises, and it was probably soon after that that Othon was released, for by Easter Sunday (April 6) he was back in Gascony.[26]

His cousin, Pierre de Champvent, was there too, and other friends of his, Burnell and the earls of Pembroke and Lincoln, but one voice was missing among those raised to welcome him, for John de Vescy, whom he had last seen when he parted from him at Canfranc, had died. His death removed one of Edward's most trusted counselors at a time when such men were badly needed, for the Sicilian business was as far from settlement as ever, and the question of a crusade, which to Edward's mind was inseparably linked with it, became more urgent with the arrival of every messenger from Tartary and the Holy Land, for the Saracens were once again on the march. Another embassy must go to Rome, and now that Othon was back he was the obvious man to send; on May 10 he and William Hotham, the provincial of the English Dominicans, left for Italy.

They bore letters not only to the pope, the papal legates and various officials of the Curia, and to Charles of Salerno and his wife, Maria of Hungary, but also to the Ghibelline leader, Guglielmo Spadalunga, marquis of Monferrat,[27] which meant that they had to lengthen their already long journey by first crossing France to Lausanne before taking the Grand-St.-Bernard over the Alps to Piedmont.[28] By the time that they reached Rieti, where Pope Nicholas was spending the summer, they

[26] P.R.O., E 36/201, p. 79, in J.-P. Trabut-Cussac, "Itinéraire d'Édouard Ier en France, 1286-89," *Bulletin of the Institute of Historical Research*, XXV (1952), p. 180, n. 63.

[27] Rymer, I, 708-9.

[28] Othon was paid for his embassy in the currencies of Lausanne, Turin, Parma, Bologna, and Florence, which is a good indication that he probably followed what is still the most usual route from the north to Rome.

had covered more than a thousand miles of difficult country; except for the flat, hot ride down the Via Emilia from Parma to Bologna, most of their way led through mountains, and the endlessly twisting Apennine roads could be as time-consuming and wearisome as the more difficult but shorter Alpine passes. Since by the beginning of August Othon had already left Rieti for Gaeta on the second stage of his mission, he must have arrived at the Curia by mid-July at the latest, which means that he spent only a little more than two months on the road. Even for a solitary traveler this would have been excellent time, but Othon's retinue was so numerous that it took anywhere from forty to sixty horses to carry them and their supplies, and the very size of the embassy caused them continual delays. The horses themselves were a perpetual nuisance; they had to be stabled and fed; they fell ill and had to be doctored, and even so, eight of them died; their shoes and harness wore out and had to be replaced; and in addition to all this, they were useless when it came to crossing the Alps and had to be led over the pass, while their masters mounted the tough and sure-footed mules belonging to the Valaisan guides, who, if the charges made by their descendants are any criterion, took their full share of the £6,000 that the embassy finally cost the king of England. The human beings caused almost as much trouble; they too fell ill and four of them, including Aymon de Bonvillars, one of Othon's Vaudois followers, died, which meant further delays and expenses; they, too, had to be fed and, unlike the horses, wished to stay awake after sundown, so that large sums had to be spent on wax and candles for their use; and at least one of them, Raoul d'Allaman, came so completely unprepared that he had to buy not only a light cape for the sweltering Italian summer but later a complete winter wardrobe including such costly items as furs. But perhaps he was not too much to blame; even with all their experience at the Curia, Othon and Hotham may have underestimated the time that it would take him to remain in Rome after the rest of the embassy had left and see to the copying of the papal bulls in duplicate, triplicate, and quadruplicate, nor could they know that Raoul would twice be incapacitated, once when he came down with a "low flux" and once when he fell and broke his arm.[29]

However, even before Othon reached Rieti, he was aware of some of the complications that awaited him, for Hotham had already been in Rome earlier in the year and was able to report on how matters had stood up to the time when he had returned to Gascony. So far as the crusade went, things were progressing more favorably, for the desperate plight of the Holy Land had forced Nicholas to meet some of the terms laid down by Edward as his conditions for leading the expedition, but there was no such encouraging news as to the pope's attitude on the Sicilian question. He had rendered all Edward's work useless by abrogating the treaty of Canfranc as he had abrogated the treaty of Oloron; he had renewed the excommunication against Alfonso; and once again he had granted the tenth to Philip IV to be used in winning Aragon for Charles of Valois. As though this were not bad enough, while the embassy was still on the road, news reached it that seemed irrevocably to bar the way to any further negotiations. On June 19, Nicholas had crowned Charles of Salerno as king of Sicily and taken his homage for the island, and on the following day he granted him the tenth in his kingdom to pay for the war against Aragon.

The pope had made it perfectly clear that he had been using Edward as a cat's-paw in everything connected with Aragon and the crusade; the tenth that was so grudgingly withheld from a king desiring to use it for its original purpose could be granted to anyone, even to a perjured weakling at war with another Christian ruler; and all the painstaking and honest effort that went into the preparation of a treaty counted for nothing in the face of the pope's right to annul it at will and to release his favorites from any of the vows that they had taken

[29] Joseph Stevenson, *Documents illustrative of the history of Scotland, 1286–1306*, I, 134–38.

in connection with carrying out its provisions. Othon, in an
angry speech, laid Edward's case before the pope:

"My lord the king of England, censures the kings who,
wrangling over the realm of Sicily, are waging war,
although which of them has taken up arms with greater
justice, he cannot rightly determine. But in all friendliness,
he is amazed that Your Paternity, by which the whole
circle of the world is governed, should have suffered these
kings to become embroiled in such a wicked struggle. For since
the Sicilians, whether Italian or French or a mixture of
the two, are all Christians, is not the Roman See to blame?
Or would you consider it wrong to put an end to as many
of these disasters to your sons as possible? On the contrary,
it would be acceptable to God and seem good to men if,
turning the eyes of Your Holiness on the quarrelling
kings, you would interpose the grace of your clemency
between them, so that those whom you suffer to rage you
might persuade to peace or at least admit them to a
semblance of peace. For if you command, they will not
disobey. And therefore, considering what perils the whole
world undergoes from the dissensions of these kings and with
what good reason men hold you to blame, my lord humbly
prays that, so much as in you lies, you should put an end
to their raging and establish a truce for two years between
them and their allies, during which time my said lord,
together with you and the kings of France and of Castile,
should come to a final decision as to making a firm
peace between them.

"For otherwise, it will not be pleasing to you, Holy
Father, if the other princes of the earth and indeed all
Christian men, hearing of your wanton provocation of those
whom, however unwillingly, you allow to fight when you
might benignly make peace between them, treat you as an
enemy of our universal Mother and of the Christian faith, even
though they still pay all due regard to the honor of
Mother Church. And you can be sure that when all the
others are fighting you, my lord will not be the last to take
up arms against such perfidy, lest he too should be undone."

When the pope had heard this, he raised his eyes to
Heaven, a bitter sigh broke from the bottom of his heart, and
turning to the envoy, he said to him,

"What you have said, my son, is human, yet to accomplish it would be divine, nor should you reproach the innocent father unless you are also willing to chide the guilty son. I shall therefore give you a legate, with whom you shall go to those kings to treat with them of what you ask; and if they consent to it, I shall not gainsay it."[30]

The sprightly Bartolomeo di Neocastro, who gives the interview in full, makes the mistake of calling Othon "Hugo," and, moreover, since he was a Sicilian and a Sicilian orator at that, his account is open to question, for he would naturally emphasize the pope's responsibility for the conflict and would also put into Othon's mouth the involved and rhythmic periods on which his fellow countrymen had prided themselves ever since the days of Piero della Vigna. It is true that it was becoming more and more the fashion for ambassadors to paraphrase the instructions that they received—at least, those that were for the public ear—in long speeches loaded with facts and details, but judging by the homely and direct Latin of Hotham's letter to the prior of Holy Trinity, even he, with the advantage of two years' study at Paris, would have found it difficult to keep up for long a flow of such phrases as "nec minus est innocuum patrem corripere, quam culpabilem filium non mordere," and if Othon really did deliver Edward's ultimatum himself he probably made his point with fewer circumlocutions than Bartolomeo would have thought fitting for such an exalted business. But whatever the defects of his style, his speech carried such conviction that a few days later he was on his way to Gaeta in the surprising new rôle of papal envoy.

James of Aragon was besieging the town—Charles, of course, had accused his rival of breaking the truce, which was slightly comical, all things considered—and since Loria was in command, it was highly probable that the outcome might be another Aragonese victory. This may have been one reason why Nicholas had agreed so readily to Othon's proposals, but he still did not

[30] Neocastro, *op. cit.*, p. 1155.

want to involve himself too deeply and, in spite of the presence of the papal legate, it was Othon who was mainly responsible for concluding the new truce, at least if we can believe Charles, whose rather biased letter to Alfonso of Aragon gives by far the fullest account of the proceedings.[31] He is a little too eager to point out that he agreed to it against the advice of some of his friends, who were scandalized by the haste with which it was concluded, and that it was no more to the liking of the enemy, especially of Loria, who, with victory snatched from his grasp, seems to have found the whole business tedious and plodding and swore that he would not be forced out of Sicily even if Catalonia and Aragon took the Cross against him. But in spite of Charles's disclaimers, obviously made in preparation for the day when he would find it convenient to break the truce, the siege was raised, James set sail for Sicily, and another breathing spell had been reached.

Othon was not back in Rome until November 2,[32] so that he must have gone south with the Angevins when they left Gaeta for Naples. Certainly, it was wise to see whether his presence there might not help to circumvent some of the bargaining and trickery that seemed the inevitable aftermath of any Angevin agreement, and it was also politic to have an English representative at the magnificent ceremonies held in September to celebrate the knighting of Charles Martel by his father and his coronation with his mother's crown of Hungary. It is true that Edward might have found someone more suitable for this particular mission, for if the elder Charles had kept his promises he would have been working for peace at Saragossa and Paris instead of ruling in Naples, the younger Charles would have been a hostage in Aragon, and Othon would not have spent seven months of semicaptivity beyond the Pyrenees.

Although it was easy to forget such worries when Naples, always at its best in the brilliant October weather, was looking

[31] Rymer, I, 717–18.

[32] Stevenson, *op. cit.*, I, 136.

more fantastic than ever as the new French churches and castles rose in that incorrigibly Greek atmosphere, they must always have been at the back of his thoughts, like the wisp of smoke above Vesuvius that never leaves the Neapolitan sky completely cloudless; and they returned to trouble him as he tossed with the recurrent fever that kept him ill during most of the autumn.[33] The great medical school of Salerno had already seen its best days, and although he still got better care at Naples than he would have had anywhere else, it was probably owing more to his strong constitution than to the ministrations of the Salernitan doctors that by early November he was well enough to be back in Rome.

He arrived there just in time to see Hotham, who left for England four days later, and to hear how the business of the embassy had been progressing at the Curia during the three months that he had been away. Various minor matters had been settled: the pope, although refusing to grant a dispensation for the marriage of Eleanor of England to Alfonso of Aragon, had given his permission for the five-year-old Edward of Carnarvon to marry the queen of Scotland, one year his senior; gifts totaling £466 14s. 4d. had been made to two cardinals and to two papal notaries; and above all there was now the possibility of a new crusade. In August a Templar, a Hospitaller, and two Dominicans had reached the papal court with alarming news from the Holy Land, and a few days after they had left for England, bearing a letter for the pope to Edward, Tripoli fell to the Saracens, who were reported to have slaughtered forty thousand Christians and to have outraged the faithful by tying the statues of the saints to their horses' tails. Nicholas, blind as he was to everything but his own interests in Sicily, was roused to action by this disaster. He even went so far as to grant money from the crusading tenth to the patriarch of Jerusalem for the strengthening of the fortifications of Acre, the only town now remaining to the Christians, and he also promised to send him

[33] Letter of Hotham, *Hist. MSS Comm., Var. Coll.,* I, 256.

twenty galleys under the leadership of Jean de Grailly, who, after having been dismissed as Edward's seneschal of Gascony, had taken service with Philip IV as commander of the French forces in the Holy Land and had come to Rome to ask for reinforcements. More important, from the English point of view, Nicholas also confirmed the grant of the sexennial tenth that Honorius had made to Edward three years earlier.

It now only remained to pay the 6,000 marks in arrears on the tribute due from England as a papal fief, which Othon and Hotham did jointly on November 4,[34] after which the latter left for home, while Othon stayed on at the Curia. He was still on the king's business, for his embassy was not officially ended until he arrived at the English court on March 8, 1290,[35] but a great part of the time was spent in his efforts on behalf of his family and friends. Among those who benefited from his sojourn at the Curia were his nephew, Girard de Vuippens, who was later to succeed Guillaume de Champvent as bishop of Lausanne, and Guillaume's brother, Othon, who was to succeed Girard when the latter was transferred to Basel. Othon de Champvent was in turn succeeded by another of Othon de Grandson's nephews, Pierre d'Oron, which meant that for fifty years, from the election of Guillaume de Champvent in 1272 until Pierre's death in 1323, the see of Lausanne was in the hands of members of the Grandson family. This may explain Othon's assiduity where the preferment of his relatives was concerned; always to have a supply of bishops related to him and grateful for the favors that he had procured for them was the best way to make sure that the Pays de Vaud would not get out of hand while his errands for the king of England kept him so far from home. However, on this occasion he remembered his contemporaries as well; for his cousin, Guillaume of Lausanne, "the fruits of whose see have

[34] Rymer, I, 719.

[35] Stevenson, op. cit., I, 134.

been so reduced by war that his table cannot properly be maintained," he secured the grant of the annates in his diocese for the next three years,[36] and the same concession was made to Robert Burnell,[37] no doubt at his request.

Most of the indulgences for a plurality of benefices and for non-residence ended with the pious proviso, "so that the cure of souls be not neglected," but one doubts whether the dalesmen of Yorkshire or the parishioners of the other churches ever saw much of their Vaudois rectors, who rarely neglected their studies to see that suitable curates were taking their places. But at Grandson there was to be no lack of spiritual comfort. The year before, Othon had made a gift of 100 *livres* annually to the prior and monastery of St.-Jean de Grandson,[38] the sum to be raised on the revenues of the salterns of Salins, which he held from the count of Burgundy, and now that he was in Rome he took the opportunity of asking the pope to give to St.-Jean the revenues of two priories in the diocese of Besançon and the priory of St.-Laurent near Mâcon, so that with the churches of Giez and Concise, which it already possessed, it would be rich enough to support thirteen monks and a prior *in perpetuum* so that the divine office might be more worthily celebrated.[39] Not content with that, he was also given the pope's permission to build at his own expense a church for the Friars Minor on the banks of the Arnon near Grandson.[40]

Most of these dispensations were granted on December 13, which means that Othon probably left Rome soon afterward, for papal favors seem always to have been bestowed at the last moment. As he rode home through the winter fogs, he could

36 *Reg. Nic. IV*, Nos. 1864–65.

37 *Ibid.*, No. 2025.

38 A.C.V. 1 B 349/1, No. 2/1.

39 *Reg. Nic. IV*, No. 1771.

40 J. H. Sbaralea, *Bullarum Franciscanum*, Vol. IV, Nos. 95–96.

congratulate himself on having concluded his own business successfully, but he must have felt less sanguine about that of the king, for his sojourn at Rome and Naples had not increased his respect either for the pope or for Charles of Salerno. As Hotham had put it—and Othon undoubtedly agreed with him—

> The lord king of Sicily, for whose liberation our lord king has worked so long, has scant ability or power to rule his kingdom. And therefore I am afraid that all our work for him has been in vain.[41]

41 Hotham's letter.

*Non tamen jacte me rei facto interfuisse, licet
historiam dixeris transumtive; sed sicut a diversis
diversorum in cordis amaritudine resolutus gestorum
relationem aura avida suscepi, eorundem seriem juxta
meum arbitrium factam, muliebri narratione
duplici corda pie pungente, facti tamen continente
veritatem, adorior pandere fideli cuilibet legere cupienti.*

De excidio urbis Acconis

v. The Fall of Acre

Othon arrived home in England for the first time in four
years to find that at least some of his efforts had borne fruit and
that plans for a new crusade were already under way. In January, 1289, Parliament had met at Westminster and had listened
to the two Mongol ambassadors who had been sent by Arghan,
the son and successor of Abagha, to promise that his troops
would fight in the van of a crusading army as soon as the king

In my description of the siege of Acre, I have not attempted to quote
references to all my authorities, for there is scarcely a statement I make that
could not be challenged: not only do the contemporary chroniclers disagree

107

of England should come to lead it in person. The Mongols had already heard the encouraging news that Edward had been appointed commander of the expedition, for Rabban Sauma, the envoy of the Nestorian patriarch, had been with him in Gascony in the summer of 1287, shortly after he had fulfilled the terms of the agreement made in his name by Othon and had received the Cross from the hands of the papal legate. The Nestorian monk was heartened by what he had seen. When he had been in Rome, the cardinals had seemed to be more interested in the articles of his creed than in the Mongol alliance, but as he wandered through Bordeaux and along the tree-shaded banks of the Garonne, thinking, no doubt, of his native Peking, through which another river ran to another sea, the sight of the polyglot crowds who thronged the town and who had all come to ask the help and advice of the English king must have convinced him that here at last was a great ruler, one who would be able to turn the tide of battle in Syria. The other two envoys, on their return to Persia, were able to add that Edward would leave for the Holy Land by St. John's Day, 1293, and, moreover, that he had decided to send a messenger to prepare the way before him, as the scripturally minded English chronicler put it.

Edward was the last man to apply Malachi's prophecy to himself, but he realized very clearly that one reason for the

---

with each other, but modern writers contradict each other flatly as to the trustworthiness of the various sources. In general, I have followed the *Gestes des Ciprois*, adding anything that seemed illuminating or interesting from the other chronicles so long as they somehow fitted in with what I found there. My other sources were the anonymous *De excidio urbis Acconensis*, the *Historia de desolacione et conculcacione civitatis Acconensis* of Thaddeus of Naples, Marino Sanudo's *Secreta fidelium crucis*, and the short accounts given by some of the English writers.

It was not in order to spare Othon's rather tarnished reputation that I omitted Cotton's story that he and Beaujeu had 15,000 prisoners of war killed in cold blood, but only because none of the other chroniclers mentions it, and it could not possibly have happened just before the last attack on the Temple, as Cotton seems to think it did, for by that time Beaujeu was dying, if not already dead, and Othon was on his way to the ships.

failure of the last crusade had been that, although all the plans had been very well laid so far as they went, they had been agreed on by the kings of western Europe only and had failed to take into account the conditions prevailing at the far end of the Mediterranean. It was useless to repeat the mistake of going to Acre and spending long months in wrangling with his allies while heat and disease sapped the strength of his army; some-one must go ahead to make all the preparations on the spot, so that as soon as Edward arrived he could move at once against the enemy. It would not be an easy job. The man who undertook it must be a devout crusader and a tried soldier, possessing physical strength and courage; a pertinacious but resilient diplomat, experienced in Syrian intrigue; of high enough rank so that his words would carry weight with the masters of the great military orders, yet loyal enough so that he would never act for his own advantage but only in the interest of the king, whose thoughts he must know as well as he knew his own. It was a formidable list of requirements, but Edward had no difficulty in finding an envoy who embodied them all. Now that Othon was back from Rome and Gaeta, from Saragossa, Gascony, and Paris, he was clearly the man to be sent to St.-Jean-d'Acre.

If Jean de Grailly had still been serving the king of England instead of the king of France, Othon might well have had more than the few months that were allowed to him in which to enjoy the rare delight of being at home again, either in his house at Westminster or in one of his many manors scattered over the English countryside, for Jean would have been equally well qualified for the job. He knew the difficulties that awaited them even better than Othon did, for when Edward had sailed from Acre in 1272 he had left Jean behind with the resounding if empty title of "seneschal of the kingdom of Jerusalem"; ever since his return to the west he had been a loyal and vehement champion of English interests against the pretensions of the French kings and of their officials, both as seneschal of Gascony and in his numerous appearances as Edward's proctor before the Parlement of Paris; and his having been employed in the delicate negotiations for the Aragonese marriage and on the embassy to Mâcon in 1278, where the dowager queen of France, who had assembled all her friends to plan the conquest of Provence, found his presence so helpful that she begged Edward to let him stay longer, "for he is much beloved and trusted in the country,"[1] show that he was a reliable and experienced diplomat who enjoyed the king's full confidence.

This only makes his sudden fall harder to understand. The three years that Edward spent in Gascony from 1286 to 1289 had been mainly taken up with the Sicilian business, in spite of the patriotic conviction of most of the English chroniclers that he had gone primarily to settle the affairs of his duchy overseas, but one case in which he did "proclaim the right and redress wrongs" and see to it that "whoever misbehaved was sentenced as the law demanded" was that of Jean de Grailly. The seneschal was accused of having appropriated to himself the rights of high and low justice outside the town of St.-Émilion and in three other places, and in July, 1287, a commission headed by the bishop of Norwich sentenced him to make full restitution and to lose all his lands in Gascony. It is still a mystery why such a severe judgment should have been passed on a man who up to then had stood high in the king's favor, but there can be no doubt that he had a fair trial. Several of his friends were on the commission that found him guilty, Jean de Vescy, who had been with him on his embassies to Aragon, and Othon and Burnell, and their detailed report shows how carefully they went into the charges before reaching what must have been a painful decision to many of them. Rarely does legal Latin evoke a whole countryside as clearly as do the pages in which Jean's misdeeds are set forth, for the areas in which he usurped authority are described minutely and their boundaries fixed by local landmarks; we hear the clattering mills along the rivers and the nightingales in the trees that shade

[1] Champollion-Figéac (ed.), *Lettres*, I, 209.

their banks, and we feel the dark coolness as we turn from a sunbaked market square to enter the church known by the incredibly romantic name of "Cantemerle."

These details also afford some clue to the mystery. Among all the dry-as-dust legal and feudal and administrative squabbles that made up the "Gascon question" we are apt to forget the one aspect of it that was not dry at all, that was in fact unexcelled for quenching the thirst brought on by too many gritty arguments. But it was constantly in the minds of the landholders in such regions as St.-Émilion, and when in one year Jean received the tolls on over 40,000 casks of wine passing through only one of his towns, it is understandable that he wanted to assure his revenues by assuring his rights.

Jean had gone back from Rome to the Holy Land early in 1290, but Othon did not leave England until the middle of the summer. He spent the interval in putting his affairs in order with the same painstaking attention to detail that had always characterized the work that he had done for others. In England, he appointed his brother Guillaume and the prior of Wenlock, another Savoyard, as his attorneys[2] and left the livings of which he was patron to his friend, Burnell, to distribute as they fell vacant.[3] In Ireland the disposal of his properties was more complicated. His towns of Clonmel and Kilfeakle and the manor of Kilsheelan he also granted to Guillaume;[4] to his nephew, Pierre de Vuippens, went his lands in Estremoy and "Oheny," which were already rented to the earl of Ulster;[5] and another nephew, Pierre d'Estavayer, got the vill of Tipperary and Acconagh.[6] Since the two Pierres were going with him to Acre, he also provided that if they should die without heirs, the lands of the

[2] C.P.R. (1281–92), p. 362: C.C.R. (1288–96), p. 460.

[3] C.P.R. (1281–92), p. 462.

[4] C. Ch. R. (1257–1300), p. 366.

[5] C.P.R. (1281–92), p. 372: C.D.I. (1285–1300), p. 335.

[6] C.P.R. (1281–92), pp. 372–73.

former should go to yet another nephew, Girard d'Oron, and those of the latter to Jean d'Estavayer, known to his family as "Red" (Rousselet). He appointed William Drayton as his attorney in Ireland, with the proviso that he might be removed from his post and another official substituted if it seemed necessary,[7] and he also got an order from the king to the treasurer and barons of the Exchequer in Dublin, pointing out that all these Irish fiefs were held for the service of two knights' fees and not for the seventeen that they had been asking.[8] Guillaume and Burnell were made his attorneys for the Channel Islands, with one of his clerks, Denis of Tilbury, under them as bailiff,[9] and he took the precaution of securing a confirmation of Edward's previous grant of the islands to him for life and to his heirs and assigns for five years after his death in order to pay his debts.[10] Once this was all settled, there remained only the question of procuring money for his journey. Edward pardoned him the various debts that he had incurred as Justiciar of Wales, where his brother was now his deputy,[11] and raised a loan for him of 3,000 marks from the bankers of Pistoia.[12] He was also granted the first fruits of the archdeaconry of Richmond.[13] Even this did not prove sufficient, and in the following year the king squeezed every penny that he could from the long-suffering Channel Islanders for the same purpose.[14]

Othon had already made all the arrangements for the fighters and clerks who were going with him, and when the time came to celebrate the weddings of the two princesses whose marriage contracts he had helped to draw up when they were both children he was able to join in the festivities with the carefree assurance that everything was set for his departure. Both Joan's

[7] *Ibid.*, p. 337.

[8] *C.C.R.* (*1288–96*), p. 88.

[9] *C.P.R.* (*1281–92*), pp. 339, 367.

[10] *C.C.R.* (*1288–96*), pp. 85–86.

[11] *Ibid.*, pp. 78, 80; *C.P.R.* (*1282–91*), p. 397.

[12] *C.P.R.* (*1282–91*), p. 373.

[13] W. H. Dixon, *Fasti Eboracenses*, I, 337.

[14] *R.G.*, III, No. 1924.

marriage to Gilbert de Clare and Margaret's to Jean de Brabant were as much matters of business as that of the widowed Isabella de Vescy to Gilbert's enemy, the earl of Hereford, which took place at the same time and which Othon probably attended, since he had been one of her late husband's executors.[15] However, in the two former cases the brides were both young as well as royal, and their weddings were celebrated with great magnificence. Edward could still play as hard as he could work, and for all his position as the greatest king in Europe, he was not above enjoying a joke; earlier in the year he had made a sporting bet with the queen's laundress that she could not follow the royal hunt and be in at the death of the stag, and when she won, mounted on the horse that he had wagered, he redeemed the animal for forty shillings, realizing with kingly tact that in her daily vocation the money would be of more good to her than the best of thoroughbred hunters. As for Othon, there was never any doubt of his vitality, and he certainly joined in the merrymaking as heartily as the king during those long June evenings that turn Westminster into a city made for dancing.

He pursued his crusading plans with equal vigor. As soon as Princess Margaret was married he took the Cross from Peckham,[16] and by July 18 he was already in Paris on the first stage of the long journey that lay before him. There he continued his methodical arrangements for both this world and the next. He surrendered some of the lands that he held from the count of Burgundy in exchange for others of equal value,[17] and a few days later he made a second grant from the revenues of the salterns of Salins to the prior and monks of St.-Jean de Grandson,

---

[15] *C.P.R.* (*1281–92*), p. 356.

[16] Bartholomew Cotton, *Historia Angelicana*, p. 177.

[17] *Complete Peerage*, art. Grandson.

for I hope, and I trust to God, that through their prayers
and suffrages, Blessèd Mary and St. John will see to it
that my soul, after it has left my body, is presented to God
and received into Abraham's bosom. For I trust that through
these prayers and because of what I hope to achieve, I
shall, God willing, once I have put off this garment of flesh,
deserve to gain a heavenly prize.[18]

From Paris he probably went on to the Pays de Vaud, for he
did not reach Orvieto until the middle of September, and there
was nothing to keep him in France. The court was buzzing
with the latest news of the rival kings of Sicily, but the War
of the Vespers already seemed to belong to the past, for at its
worst it had been only a barrier blocking the way to the Holy
Land, and now the road lay open before him.

There were things of more importance waiting for him at
home. His new Franciscan church had been building for almost
a year and had already progressed so far that the pope could
grant indulgences to all who should visit it,[19] but the work
must be pushed on even faster, for the crusaders had no better
patron than the saint who had dared enter the palace of the
sultan and like another Moses had confounded the sorcerers
of Egypt. Also, someone must be found to whom the Grandson
lands could be intrusted now that Agnès was dead, and there
were farewells to be said, to Count Amadée of Savoy, his
overlord, who perhaps at this time made arrangements for the
two hundred pounds that were paid to Othon the following
April,[20] to his cousin the bishop, and above all to his two
sisters whose sons were riding with him to the wars. The young
men were too dazzled by the prospect of fighting under the
banner of their distinguished uncle to think of Syria as anything except a battlefield on which they might gain honor

[18] A.C.V. 1 B 349/1, No. 2/2.

[19] Sbaralea, *op. cit.*, IV, 165.

[20] Max Bruchet, *Inventaire . . . du trésor des Chartes de Chambéry . . . ,*
No. 338.

and advancement, and if they pictured it otherwise, it was in terms of the pleasant countrysides in which they had grown up. But Othon knew what lay before them, and as he followed the white roads that run along Lake Neuchâtel from Grandson to Estavayer and then twist over the hills to Lausanne and Oron, he must have felt a premonitory pang of homesickness, for the Pays de Vaud is at its loveliest in August, when the early green has brightened into the gold of the shorn wheatfields and the first faint bronze on the vines, and the snow peaks dream against the sky as though summer would never end.

Once they had left Chillon behind them and were riding up the valley of the Rhône, the country took on a more savage beauty. As the road between the mountains narrowed to the pass, the sun beat more and more fiercely to ripen the grapes on the hard-won terraces and the apples on the bending trees, and Othon and his men were grateful for the long shadows of the poplars and for the cool crypts where they stopped to pray to the soldier saint, St. Maurice, the commander of the martyred Theban legion whose bones had provided relics enough to fill all the churches of the Valais, from the great abbey itself to the smallest mountain chapel. Only when they reached Italy did they get a hint of what less favored lands might hold for them, for there the leaves, tattered and wilted at the end of the summer's heat, hung lifeless on the vines, and the riders moved in a white and choking cloud of dust. They stayed there scarcely long enough to watch October waken the country into brilliance once again, for when Othon had obtained an indulgence for William Burnell, the chancellor's nephew, to hold a few more benefices,[21] his business at the Curia was finished, and by the middle of the month he and his company were on their way to Acre.[22]

As they sailed into the bay a few weeks later, the city looked

[21] *C. Pap. R.* (*1198–1304*), pp. 517–18.
[22] *Reg. Nic. IV*, Nos. 3279, 4385–87, 4391–94.

very much the same as when he had last seen it twenty years before. The double line of walls that ran across the neck of the promontory on which it was built still stood with all its towers, and Italian cargo ships still rode at anchor in its harbor. But on land Othon found that the old atmosphere of apathy was gone; instead, a feverish expectancy filled the painted palaces and spread to the streets, where idlers gathered in the shade of the silken awnings to exchange the rumors that ran like wildfire through the crowds. In an effort to forget the doom hanging over them, "the fools and lustful, drunkards, players, and actors," to say nothing of the more than "thirteen thousand women who are everywhere described as leading a wicked and execrable life,"[23] gave themselves over to their various amusements, and vice and corruption flourished. The chroniclers, who could explain the subsequent disaster only as the just judgment of God, doubtless exaggerated the number of sinners. They would have done better to lay the blame where it really belonged, on the Cypriot and Angevin claimants to the throne, on the Italian traders, and on the commanders of the military orders, who had let the Holy Land slip through their fingers while they fought among themselves, and who were now faced with such a state of anarchy that they could no longer control their own underlings, let alone hope to put up a successful resistance to the approaching enemy.

The selfish incompetence that was the underlying reason for their downfall was also the immediate cause of the siege of Acre, which was to be the penultimate act of the tragedy. The year before, when Pope Nicholas had at last been stirred to action by Othon's eloquence and by the news coming from the Holy Land, he had not only given Jean de Grailly the twenty galleys, but in order to man them he had had the crusade preached in Northern Italy. The friars were authorized to promise loot as well as more spiritual rewards, but there

---

[23] Hemingburgh, *op. cit.*, II, 23, 25.

seems to be little doubt that the last flare-up of crusading fervor occurred in the unaccountable cities of the Veneto and Emilia, and when the galleys sailed from Venice they carried 16,000 crusaders, under the command of Giacomo Tiepolo. Almost all of them came from the lower classes—the merchant aristocracy was far too busy trading with the enemy to find time to fight them—and they presented the same problem as their predecessors had done in the days of Peter the Hermit. They could not understand the wisdom of their superiors in making a truce with the enemies of the Cross, and they wanted to fight, with Saracens if possible, and otherwise with anyone who looked like a foreigner. But this required weapons, and they had none, and soon they began to run out of food as well, for there was no one supreme commander in the city, and the half-dozen men who shared the authority did nothing for the undisciplined rabble that had suddenly been thrown on their hands. The Italians decided to rely on what arms they had, and one day, cutting down all those who tried to stop them, they robbed and killed some of the poor Saracen peasants who had come in as usual to sell the produce of the outlying farms in the city market.

Sooner or later the sultan would have found a pretext for breaking the truce, for he was resolved to drive the Christians out of Syria, and this was too good an opportunity to be missed. But the citizens of Acre had no sooner heard that the Mameluke army was on the march than they received the welcome news that the old sultan had died before he could even cross the Egyptian frontier, and since those with any experience of the Saracens knew that the death of a sultan was usually followed by a prolonged struggle between his would-be successors, they hoped that a breathing spell had been granted to them. But Malik el-Aschraf, the son of the dead ruler, immediately put an end to all controversy by inviting his rivals to a banquet and murdering them as they lay around the table. Once he was firmly settled on his throne, he lost no time in sending a demand to Acre that the truce-breakers be handed over to him. A council was held to decide what should be done, and Guillaume de Beaujeu, the Master of the Temple, and a thoroughgoing realist if ever there was one, made the suggestion that they empty the jails of all criminals lying under sentence of death and give them up to the sultan as the culprits. This was too much even for his hardened fellow soldiers, and instead they sent Malik the rather feeble answer that the criminals, who had come from overseas were not under their jurisdiction, "for the Christians were confident that they could win by themselves, and they put their trust in the man who had arrived shortly before with many followers and with treasure from the king of England, Sir Othon de Grandson."[24]

In March, 1291, Malik wrote again to the Master of the Temple, threatening to lay siege to Acre in revenge for the slaughter of the Saracens, and once more a council was held, this time a council of war. The leading men of the city were there, Jean de Grailly and Othon, the commander of the Cypriots, and the masters of the five military orders, the Temple, the Hospital, St. Mary of the Germans, St. Thomas, and the Holy Ghost. "These were the eight men by whose prudent counsel and skillful vigilance the city of Acre was then ruled, and if they could have agreed, as God is my witness, it would still be standing."[25] Certainly, the area of disagreement was limited, for there was nothing left to plan for but the defense of the town. It was to be based on the Tour Maudite, the great round tower at the salient where the line of walls running up from the bay met the other line that ran from the open sea on the opposite side of the point. The various chroniclers differ as to just how the troops were to be disposed, but it seems that the Tour Maudite was to be intrusted to the Cypriots under Amaury of Lusignan, King Henry's brother, while the Templars

24 *Ibid.*, p. 24.

25 J. Quetif and J. Echard, *Scriptores ordinis praedicatorum*, I, 423.

and Hospitallers, fighting side by side at last, were to have the main responsibility for guarding the wall to the south, and Othon and Jean were to protect the eastern line between the tower and the harbor.

When it comes to giving an account of the siege, the chroniclers differ even more; almost each one is bitterly prejudiced in favor of the order or nation to which he belongs and accuses all the others of treachery and cowardice, and in the nightmare days that followed the first appearance of the enemy troops no one could see more of the battle than his own hotly contested corner. Only two things are clear: the defenders were so heavily outnumbered that they were doomed from the start, and at the end the Templars atoned for all their years of lethargy and put up a magnificent stand in which they were killed almost to the last man.

No one even agrees as to just when the siege began, for the sultan was in no hurry to gain the certain victory and made his preparations with deliberate thoroughness. He pitched his vermilion tent among the vineyards and gardens belonging to the Templars, and from the entrance, which according to custom faced the direction of march, he supervised the installation of his four great siege engines, Ireful (Yrious), Victorious, and two others. It took a full week to get them in place, for they were brought up gradually under cover of darkness, and even then the engineers were protected by movable wicker breastworks. On the eighth morning the defenders saw that the engines were in position on the edge of the moat opposite the four principal towers, ". . . and if anyone should ask why they let them come so close, it was because they could not help it."[26]

Twice they attempted to halt the enemy advance. The first time, Othon and the Master of the Temple had ordered the commander of one of the gates to set fire to the engine being drawn up opposite it, but the man whom they sent out was too terrified to do the job properly, and the torch that he aimed

[26] *Gestes des Ciprois*, p. 808.

at the wooden scaffolding fell short and burst into flames on the ground. It was a bright moonlight night, and the defenders carried out the second part of their plan and made a raid on the Saracen camp. But that, too, was a failure, for their horses got entangled in the tent ropes, and although they killed some of the enemy, they lost eighteen of their own men.[27] Warned by experience, they waited for a moonless night before they attempted another sortie, but although they kept it so secret that no one knew anything about it until the order came to mount, the Saracens somehow got wind of it, and the raiding party emerged from the darkened city into the light of innumerable torches.

The siege now began in earnest. The air was filled with stones from the enemy mangonels, and the small darts, nicknamed "locusts," flew thicker than snowflakes, as Othon later told the chronicler of Lanercost.[28] On the walls the exhausted defenders fought day and night, for the enemy was always able to throw in fresh troops to replace the dead and relieve the survivors, and hand-to-hand battles went on even underground, where Christian met Saracen in the dark tunnels that the Saracens were digging in order to bring down the towers. By Holy Week the situation was already desperate:

> When they saw that the enemy was conquering the walls
> and that it would be impossible to defend the city any
> longer, they decided by common consent to win God's help
> with the arms of penance, and having confessed and
> communicated, to form ranks with the prisoners of war
> in front of them and to burst out of the city on the day of our
> common salvation and give their lives as the Author of
> life had imperilled His own.[29]

27 *Idem.* The text calls Othon "Jean," but as he was the only Grandson there, that is obviously a mistake.

28 *Chronicle of Lanercost,* p. 139. The writer says that his information came from someone who had been there, and since Othon was with Edward at Lanercost during the Scottish war, he probably gave him the details that he used for his description of the siege.

29 *Idem.*

The idea of the Good Friday sortie may have originated with Othon, for the chronicler of Lanercost is the only writer who mentions it, but it was never carried out, for the patriarch, "broken in soul and wearied by the counsel of the wicked," not only refused to give the enterprise his blessing but even forbade it under pain of excommunication.

Twelve days later, on May 4, when the sickly young king of Cyprus arrived with reinforcements, the city was still standing, and the garrison welcomed him with fireworks, but their joy was short lived. He sent an embassy to the sultan, and although the latter at first only demanded whether they had brought the keys of the city with them, he later relented and out of pity for the king, "who is a child, even as I was," offered to let the defenders march out with the honors of war, taking everything with them, except the actual stones of the city. Whether the envoys would have accepted the terms or not, at that moment an ill-timed bolt from one of the Christian mangonels fell through the roof of the tent, barely missing the sultan. He leaped to his feet with hand on hilt, and although the lives of the Templars were saved by one of the sultan's attendants, who begged him not to sully his steel with the blood of swine, the unfortunate stone had put an end to all possibility of negotiation.

The Saracens now concentrated their attack on the great corner tower, the Tour Maudite; on Tuesday, May 8, they set fire to the barbican that protected it, and once that was gone, they proceeded to bring down the tower itself. It took a whole week, for the defenders fought valiantly, although at times they could scarcely man the walls, the darts and quarrels were flying so thickly; but by Wednesday, May 16, so much masonry had fallen into the moat that the Saracens were able to use the rubble as a bridge, and in the afternoon they raised their flag over the ruins of the tower. From this new vantage point they commanded the whole outer line of walls, and although some of the defenders still held out in the smaller towers, the bulk of the garrison had to fall back behind the more lightly fortified inner ring. There was no room or place of safety in the shrunken city for all the civilians. That night the women and children were sent on board the galleys, but the weather had changed and such a storm was blowing that they preferred to die on land rather than drown at sea, and like frightened horses they ran back to their burning houses.

The storm continued all the next day, and Friday dawned gray and overcast. It was the date set by the Saracens for the last great assault, and any of the defenders who had managed to snatch some sleep were awakened before daybreak by the kettledrums whose horrible booming rolled from one end to the other of the ruined walls. Behind the camels that carried drums and drummers came the entire Saracen army, for this was no attack against one isolated tower but an onslaught against the whole line of fortifications from sea to sea. The defenders fought as best they could under the rain of missiles that darkened the sky and in the smoke of the Greek fire that was often so thick that it was impossible to tell friend from foe. The end came when the Master of the Temple, raising his arm in command was fatally wounded by a dart that struck him in the unprotected armpit. When those around him saw him carried off the field, they fell back; although the English and French fought every step of the way, it was impossible to stem the hordes that were sweeping into the city. Jean was wounded, but Othon managed to get him and as many of their followers as he could save on board one of the galleys in the harbor. Pierre d'Estavayer escaped with his uncle, but Pierre de Vuippens had been killed in the fighting; perhaps he was the poor English squire whom the chronicler saw burning in his armor, "like a tar-barrel," although it is to be hoped that he met a quicker and more merciful death.

By this time the whole city was overrun; the storm was still raging, but the light of the burning buildings illuminated the pitiful crowds who rushed to the water's edge in a vain attempt to get to the boats. Babies were snatched from their mothers' arms, to be thrown aside and trampled by the oncoming horses, and many of the women were torn in pieces between two of their captors, neither of whom would yield his prey to the other. In the words of Sanudo, "where you find a multitude terribly shaken by the fear of death, there you find confusion." Order reigned only in one corner of the city, where the Templars gathered around their dying Master. The sultan offered them a truce, but whether they refused it or whether they accepted it and then broke it when they saw the Saracens raping their captives, a last assault was made on the Temple, and Christian and Moslem perished together in the ruins of the tower that fell under the weight of the attackers.

It was a glorious end for those who resisted to the death, but those who saved their own lives did so at the expense of their reputations. It was too easy to make scapegoats of the survivors, and everyone who managed to reach Cyprus alive, from King Henry down, came in for his share of the blame. No one suffered at the hands of his contemporaries more than Othon. Although the *Gestes des Ciprois* especially mentions him and Jean de Grailly as having fought until resistance was no longer possible,[30] the author of the *Excidio* accuses them and some of their highborn followers of having abandoned both their posts and their men at the very first onslaught; worse still, once they were back in Europe, they protested that they would have preferred death to flight, though "truly, they did not flee from the battle, for into battle they had never gone."[31] Even an English chronicler could not resist a jibe; after telling how Othon came to Acre with the English funds, Hemingburgh goes on to say, ". . . since it took too long to pay off the enemy, he fled with the treasure to Cyprus, and there he changed his surname and was no longer the big noise in military circles" (*mutato cognomine, in congressu militari parvum sonum*

30 *Gestes*, p. 814.
31 *De excidio*, p. 701.

fecit).[32] The pun on the canting motto of his family, *à petite cloche, grand son,* was tempting, but the accusation was unfounded. Even if Othon did succeed in saving the money intrusted to him, he lost almost everything of his own, for early in January, 1292, his friends in England had to send one of his yeomen, Peter Weston, out to Cyprus with a horse, some clothes, and other necessities.[33] The situation of all the refugees was deplorable, for although King Henry did his best to provide for as many of them as possible, none of the other Cypriots raised a hand to help them and indeed were hard put to it themselves to cope with the inflation that followed the arrival of so many penniless fugitives as rents increased ten times in value and food prices soared.

Yet for all their hardships, they were still alive, and Othon had no doubts but that their preservation was due to the intercessions of Notre-Dame de Lausanne, who kept a watchful eye on her children however far from home their duties took them. He resolved to take a thank offering back to her cathedral church, and soon after he reached Cyprus he was deep in discussions with the Cypriot craftsmen as to just what form it would take. Once he had decided on a frontal for the high altar, there were other questions to be settled; which color to choose from among their rainbow bales of silk, just how to place the design so that it would also include St. Michael, the warrior-angel, to whom he had a special devotion,[34] and just how much gold thread was to go into its making. Once all that was arranged, he turned to other things, for the king of England's emissary could not spend his time in the cloister supervising the nuns who were to do the actual embroidery, and he probably left one of his clerks to oversee the work. Although the clerk may have had some artistic ability, he lacked

[32] Hemingburgh, *op. cit.,* II, 24.

[33] *C.P.R.* (1281–92), p. 465.

[34] *Cartulaire des Îles Normandes,* No. 104.

his master's passion for detail, for some mistakes crept in—"Gabriel" is spelt "Gabiel," and the small figure that represents Othon wears its sword on the wrong side—but once it was finished, it was a beautiful thing: a length of crimson silk on which golden archangels swing their censers before the enthroned Virgin and Child and delicate white and green vines grow from golden vases, while two shields bearing the Grandson arms and a knight wearing the Grandson colors leave the court of Heaven in no doubt as to the identity of the donor, kneeling through the ages at the foot of the throne.[35]

The gratitude of the living had found tangible expression; it now remained for Othon to do what he could for the dead. In theory, a mass said at the humblest chapel in Christendom would do as much for the souls in purgatory as one sung by the pope himself over the tomb of St. Peter, but in spite of the theologians, men could not help believing that there were some places from which prayers rose to Heaven more surely than from others. Chief among these was Jerusalem, and Othon, although he must postpone the day when he should approach the Holy City at the head of a victorious army, could still go as a pilgrim, his battered armor exchanged for a cowl and his tall charger for a humble ass. Neither Christian nor Saracen had yet reached the stage of evolution where total war was taken for granted, and on the roads through the sultan's dominions lines of captives from the fallen Christian towns crossed groups of pilgrims passing unmolested on their ways.

Perhaps Othon went on his own account, to pray for the souls of Guillaume de Beaujeu and Pierre de Vuippens and all the others who had fallen beside him; perhaps even in this he was acting as an emissary, for news had reached him while he was still at Acre that in the autumn of 1290, soon after he had left for the Holy Land, Eleanor, Edward's *chère reine*, had died. Edward was inconsolable, and Othon not only sympathized with his friend's sorrow but mourned the queen on his

[35] See illustration.

own account, for everyone seems to have loved her. She in turn had a particular regard for him, perhaps as the bachelor friend of the family who, when he returned from drawing up the marriage contracts for her daughters, could give her such details about her future sons-in-law as were beneath the notice of those financial and territorial documents but of the greatest interest to a happy wife and loving mother. One of her last acts had been to grant to him some of the houses in London that had come to her after the expulsion of the Jews in 1290,[36] and in her will she left to him two of her manors, Ditton in Cambridgeshire and Turweston in Buckinghamshire.[37]

Othon needed little urging to make the pilgrimage to Jerusalem both on his own account and because of the affection that he had felt for the queen, but he probably did go there as Edward's emissary, for the trip was commemorated on Eleanor's tomb in Westminster Abbey, where the few remaining flecks of paint still bear shadowy witness that he once knelt, wearing the familiar striped surcoat with the bend gules, before the enthroned Virgin and Child in the church of the Holy Sepulchre. Perhaps the clerk with artistic leanings accompanied him and drew the sketch from which the painting was made—he may even be one of the group of four pilgrims who survey the scene —for the frescoed knight on the tomb and the embroidered knight on the frontal are almost identical, the only difference being that the English painter, who probably knew more about military matters than did the Cypriot nuns, has this time placed the sword correctly on the left side.[37]

There were other shrines to be visited all along the road through what had once been Samaria and Galilee and in the neighborhood of Jerusalem itself, for if Rome had an abundance of relics, the Holy Land had more, and there was no lack of guides and guidebooks to point out the sites where the miracles

---

[36] *C. Ch. R.* (*1257–1300*), p. 465.

[37] *C.P.R.* (*1281–92*), p. 417.

of the Gospels had taken place or such interesting buildings as that in which the Virgin had gone to school. What she could have been taught there is a mystery, since the philosophers had established beyond a doubt that she was gifted with a perfect understanding of both the *trivium* and *quadrivium,* but sightseers are rarely skeptical, and to a noncritical and loving age it made little difference anyway. And if anyone had been inclined to scoff, Othon had the evidence of his own eyes that a miracle of major proportions had taken place within the last twenty years; the Holy House, which he had visited when he was on his first crusade, was no longer at Nazareth, for when the Saracen menace came too close solicitous angels had picked it up and carried it through the air, over mountains and seas, to the comparative safety of Loreto.

If Othon, like all tourists, was hypnotized by the insistent voices of the guides into believing everything that they told him about the past, it was far different when he looked at the countryside with an eye to the future, in preparation for the day when the next crusading army should come to the Holy Land. In this he took nobody's word for anything; he relied on his own experience, noticing every detail of the road and of the terrain through which it ran, the castles that guarded it, and the provisions that it afforded for both men and horses. It is very possible that instead of sailing back to Cyprus from Jaffa—the usual route—he took the road to Cilician Armenia instead, for that road played an important part in his plans for the next crusade. Besides, Armenia itself was now in jeopardy from the Saracens, for Malik, who had driven the last Christians out of Syria in July, was turning to threaten the northern kingdom. His letters to King Hayton after the fall of Acre were intended to strike terror into the heart of that unwilling monarch: the earth, he wrote, is empty of wild animals and the sky of birds, for they have all gathered to feast on the bodies of the slain Franks, from whose armor he is making shackles for the feet of the survivors, and even after the slaughter there are still so many prisoners that women are selling for a drachma apiece.[38] He followed up his threats by raiding Armenia in the two following years and was building an armada for the conquest of Cyprus, when his assassination at the hands of his emirs, who feared that his ambitious plans were endangering his country, brought a respite to the two Christian kingdoms.

It came just in time to save the Armenians, for while the Saracens were attacking them from without, they were suffering from dissensions within their borders. At a time when they had no allies left on the mainland except the remote and unpredictable Mongols and only their own unity could save them, the country was split in two by a bitter controversy over the date of Easter. At this critical moment King Hayton decided to abdicate and turn the throne over to his brother Thoros. The latter reigned for two years and then abdicated in his turn and restored the crown to his brother, but what with Saracen attacks, religious quarrels, and recurring abdications, the administration of the kingdom needed a thorough overhauling. Even before Hayton returned to the throne, he decided to ask for outside advice in the job of reorganizing his realm. Othon, Jacques de Molay, who had succeeded Guillaume de Beaujeu as Master of the Temple, and the Master of the Hospital were present at the coronation ceremony[39]—the first of Hayton's career, for when he succeeded his father he had been too humble to allow himself to be crowned—and they stayed on in Armenia to help him put the country back on its feet.

The moving spirit in the reorganizations was, according to his own account, Hayton, lord of Gorigos, the king's cousin, who called the three Europeans to witness that he spared neither labor nor expense in his efforts and worked and sweated

[38] Cotton, *op. cit.*, pp. 219, 217.

[39] Hayton of Gorigos, *La Flor des Estoires de la terre d'Orient*, p. 327.

1 2 8

day and night until he achieved his aim.[40] Othon was already on good terms with the Templar, for Molay had been Grand Preceptor of the Order in England, and now he struck up a friendship with Hayton of Gorigos that was destined to last long after their task in Armenia was accomplished. The administrative experience that Othon had gained in Gascony and Wales had made him an invaluable colleague, but an even greater bond between the two men was the passionate desire that they shared to see Jerusalem once again in Christian hands and their agreement on the methods to be used to bring this about.

Othon had already worked out a detailed plan during the years when he had discussed a crusade with the popes, with Edward, and with any of the fighting rulers of Europe who would listen to him, but the loss of Syria and his subsequent visit to Armenia caused him to modify it in the light of changed circumstances and of his greater knowledge of the questions involved. Even when it had still been possible to use the Syrian ports he had decided against them as a base of operations in favor of Lajazzo in Armenia, for it had a far better harbor than either Tripoli or Acre, and besides, the country behind them was in enemy hands, which would put insuperable difficulties in the way of procuring supplies for the troops. Now that he had seen Armenia he was more than ever convinced that he was right, for the harbor of Lajazzo fully lived up to his expectations, and the well-watered country could provide an abundance of good cheap forage for the horses and of fish, meat, and game for the men. There was the added advantage that the crusaders would not have to bring so many horses with them, for there were plenty to be had in Armenia and even more among the neighboring Turks, who could also sell them all the tents they needed. As a further inducement he mentions that the country was surrounded by a ring of high

40 *Ibid.*, p. 330.

mountains and fortified castles, so that there was always two or three days' warning of an attack. From the political point of view as well, Armenia was by far the best place to choose. The only other Christian kingdom that might have been used as a base was Cyprus, but the low opinion that Othon had formed of the Cypriots in 1271 had only been strengthened by his recent experiences at Acre and on the island itself. The Armenians would make far better allies, and since their king was a vassal of the Persian Il-Khan, he could be instrumental in working for the Mongol alliance, which Othon now felt was necessary to the success of the expedition.

His visit to Armenia also confirmed his earlier conviction that the army should land there in the middle of September. At that time of year, he pointed out, in an unconscious echo of Hesiod, the trip itself would be quicker, for the heat and "infirmity" of the sea have passed and the water is colder, which makes for a safer and easier passage. Men and horses would be fresher when they left, and when they arrived there would still be good pasture to get the horses back into condition after their journey, while the crops would be in and provisions would be easier to come by than at any other season of the year. The Armenian summers are unhealthy, and it would be better for men from overseas, who are born and brought up in a cold climate, to have the winter before them, so that when the hot weather came they would have learned how to adapt themselves to their new surroundings. Then they could march on Acre where they would meet the cargo ships, and once they had reached Jerusalem, they could do what God pleased.

For the moment, Othon looked no further into the future, but more than ten years later, when he and Hayton of Gorigos met again, this time at the papal court at Avignon, they realized that the scope of their plans must be enlarged to include the preliminary financial arrangements and the organization of the kingdom once it had been won back by the Christian armies. By then it was apparent that there was only one ruler left in Europe who still took a real interest in the crusade, but though Pierre Dubois, one of the most outspoken supporters of the French monarchy, was to dedicate his book on the recovery of the Holy Land to the king of England and not to the king of France, no one knew better than Othon that Edward was too old a man ever to hope to see the Holy Land again. There was no other secular ruler in whom he could place any confidence, and when he revised his plans for the third and last time, he put the whole responsibility for carrying them out on the Church. The popes were to see that the crusade was preached and the necessary funds collected, and a new military order was to be formed that would not only reconquer the Holy Land and defend it when it was won but would also administer it under the supervision of the papacy. The kings of Jerusalem, who had weakened the kingdom by their rivalries while they were alive and whose deaths had often been followed by even more harmful interregnums, were to be done away with; in their place, the masters of the new Order, responsible only to the Church and under ecclesiastical discipline, were to give the Holy Land the stable government without which it could not hope to survive.[41]

41 Kohler, *op. cit.* The foregoing is based on M. Kohler's article in the *Revue d'Orient Latin*, X, 406 ff., in which he published two texts on the recovery of the Holy Land, one in French and one in Latin. From internal evidence, he deduced that there had been an earlier text, written before the fall of Tripoli in 1289, which is now lost; that the French text is an expanded version of the original and that it was written by a western European living in the East and within the two years between the fall of Acre and the death of Malik; and that the Latin text is a translation of the first, made early in the fourteenth century, with still more material added, particularly as to the means to be employed in financing the crusade and in organizing the kingdom of Jerusalem after the reconquest.

M. Kohler does not give all his reasons for attributing the project to Othon; his two main arguments are that the writer was in Acre in 1271 where he heard Pope Gregory's farewell sermon, and that the second text, the one written between 1291 and 1293, shows a greater knowledge of Armenia and also has many points in common with the plan that Hayton of Gorigos later drew up in his *Flor des Estoires.* This last was written after Hayton had become a Premonstratensian monk and at the request of Pope Clement V in

Fortunately for Othon, he could not know that six centuries must pass before a Christian commander would recapture Jerusalem, and until his death he continued to hope and work for the crusade. He seems even to have infected his own family with his enthusiasm. At the very end of the fourteenth century, when Philippe de Mézières founded his *Chevalrie de la Passion de Jhesu-Crist,* he appointed four "messengers of God" to stir men to amend their lives and to take the Cross "for the redemption of the holy city of Jerusalem and of the Holy Land." One of the four seemed unlikely material for such an enterprise: Chaucer, who had translated some of his work into English, considered him the flower of French poets, and Christine de Pisan, also an expert in her line, ranked him with Lancelot as the perfect knightly lover. But he was Othon's great-great-nephew and namesake, and his interest in crusading may well have started in his childhood when he heard stories of his famous relative, long before he went into the world to win the reputation that the poets gave him.

If Othon's plans were all to come to nothing, he saw for himself one of the reasons for their failure as he was returning from Armenia to Cyprus. The ship on which he sailed was manned by Venetians, Pisans, and Syrians, and as she lay off Gorigos seventeen Genoese galleys came into port. The loss of Acre and Tripoli had only intensified the war between the Italian cities, for with fewer markets open to them their rivalry narrowed. In the previous year, some Venetians had picked

---

about 1306. Since Othon was also at the papal court at that time, it is possible that he revised his plans then after discussing them with his friend, which would account for the markedly ecclesiastical slant of the Latin text. M. Kohler's principal argument against his own attribution is that Othon was *plus brave peutêtre que lettré.* But after his long diplomatic experience, he certainly knew how to put his ideas in order, especially on a question to which he had given so much thought, and he had clerks in his employ to do the actual writing. From my own point of view, I should also take into consideration the very detailed treatment of the subject, which strikes me as being typically Othonian.

a fight with a Genoese fleet, which would not back its sails, and now, in the spring of 1294, the Genoese, who had been defeated, were out for blood. Since Othon was known to be "a knight from overseas of great renown," they listened to him courteously when he asked them if he might come aboard and try to make peace between them, but they refused his request. All they did was to suggest that he have his galley moved out of the harbor, because in her ". . . were some people who had offended them in the past and for love of him, they did not want to grieve them."[42] Since there was nothing else to do, Othon continued his journey to Cyprus, and he was probably still there when news came of the battle of Lajazzo, in which the outnumbered Genoese had more than revenged themselves on the Venetians.

[42] *Gestes,* pp. 830–31.

Puis qu'Acre fu desheritee
et toute Surie gastee,
est le siecle entalanté
de bonté en grant mavaisté.

. . . .

Car rancure, descorde, haine
entre le gent a fait rasine,
et amour [est] d'iaus departie,
et est cem[e] entre yaus envie,
par coy il sont en grant debat
pour aver chascun meillor part
de ce siecle. . . .

Gestes des Ciprois

vi. War with France: Embassies to France and the Empire

O thon's journey to Armenia had been no mere side issue; it was part and parcel of his original commission, which had not ended with the fall of Acre, to prepare for the day when Edward should come in person to help defend the two Christian kingdoms of the East against the Saracen and perhaps even to lead his troops in the eventual recovery of the Holy Land. But by the summer of 1294 it was clear that that day must be indefinitely postponed, for the quarrel that had been brewing for so long between England and France had at last broken out into open warfare.

Othon had been kept well informed of what was happening at home, for there was always a constant stream of travelers to the Levant. Apart from the more or less reliable news brought by official emissaries from the western courts and the Curia, innumerable rumors reached him. Pilgrims brought some of them, but above all they came through the Italian traders who, even after the loss of the Holy Land, continued to do a flourishing business with the Saracen and added to their earnings whatever they could pick up by acting as secret service agents on the side.

It was probably a messenger sent directly from England who brought him the news that Burnell had died in October, 1292, and it may have been the same messenger who carried back his heartbroken letter to John Langton.[1] The chancellor's death was a great blow to Edward, for although Burnell may have used the treasure and lands that he amassed to endow his so-called nieces when he married them off to young English noblemen and to enrich his so-called nephews, his public life had been irreproachable, and he was a great and loyal statesman. One cannot help hoping that his long years of unwearied service to the king did something to atone for his private failings and that he did not have to spend too long a time in purgatory before being transferred to those regions whose many mansions should prove sufficient even for his land-hungry soul.

The rest of the news from England was almost equally bad. For a moment, indeed, when the jealous Scots intrusted the choice of their king to Edward, and on St. Stephen's Day, 1292, he took Balliol's oath of fealty, his position as the leading mon-

---

[1] A.C., XXVI, 34. Only a fragment survives, but from the relevant passage, ". . . cuer de la mort monseignor l'evesque de Ba, laquele j'avoie entendu, car j'ai perdu le mei[n] . . . ," it is easy to judge what the general tenor must have been.

arch of Europe seemed impregnable. But the very success of his policies had put him in a most difficult position, for his insistence on claiming the suzerainty of Scotland in such definite terms meant that Balliol now stood in the same relation to him as he himself did to Philip of France, and while it was to his interest to encourage the appeals of the Scottish nobles to the courts at Westminster, he could scarcely do that while he was discouraging those of the Gascons to the Parlement of Paris.

The French lawyers were not slow to take advantage of the dilemma in which Edward found himself. In the spring of 1293, one of the sea fights that were endemic in the crowded waters between England and the Continent resulted in the victory of an Anglo-Gascon-Irish-Dutch fleet over the Normans and their French-Flemish-Genoese allies. While the resultant squabble between the French and English lawyers was still going on, the men of Bayonne sacked the town of La Rochelle, and Philip cited Edward to appear before the Parlement of Paris to answer for all the misdeeds of his subjects.

Edward was unable to leave the country, for troubles were crowding in on him from all sides. His borders were threatened, for the Welsh were ready to rise as soon as his back was turned and the Scottish nobles were becoming increasingly restive under the overlordship that they had granted him so unwillingly in the first place. There were also disturbances inside the country, especially among the Lords Marcher, who, now that Wales was conquered and they had lost all their responsibilities and almost none of their privileges, spent their time in fighting one another: only the year before, a Parliament had been held, "in the house of Othon de Grandson outside the king's palace at Westminster,"[2] to hear judgment in the quarrel between the earl of Hereford and Edward's son-in-law, Earl Gilbert of Gloucester.

There was one hope left to Edward; he decided to send

[2] *Rotuli parlamentorum*, I, 76.

Edmund of Lancaster to Paris in his place. From one point of view this was an excellent choice, for as the only brother of the king of England and the stepfather of the queen of France, Edmund stood equally high at both the English and French courts. But for once Edward showed himself to be a bad judge of character. Edmund embodied all the knightly virtues: he was generous, loyal, honorable and magnanimous, and he was therefore the last man in the world to be able to deal successfully with Philip the Fair. When the latter, by a massive piece of double-crossing—there is no more elegant word to describe it—tricked him into handing all Gascony over to the French without their having to lift a finger, he wrote a report of his mission that still quivers with the hurt astonishment of a child who has for the first time met with injustice from his grownups. Against such behavior he had no redress. He had given hostages but taken none, "thinking with simplicity that a royal promise needed no guarantee," and there was nothing for him to do but to go back to England and reproach himself to his brother for a fool and a traitor.

In spite of Edward's consternation over the loss of the duchy that he had held since he was a boy and that three generations of his ancestors had held before him—more than three, if we can trust Langtoft's assertion that King Arthur had given it to Sir Bedivere "as to his butler"—he wasted no time in recrimination. He comforted the heartbroken Edmund and then turned with furious energy to preparing for the war that should win him back his lands. The Parliament of the laity that met at Westminster at the end of May, 1294, backed him up, and on June 20 an embassy left for Paris to renounce his homage for Gascony and to declare war.

Othon must have heard this news on his return to Cyprus, and he immediately set about making plans for his departure. They were not easy to carry out, for he was almost penniless. Even if the vitriolic author of the De excidio was right in saying that he had managed to salvage something from the burning ruins of Acre, that money had long ago been spent, for during the last three years he had not only seen to the needs of his own followers but had also done everything in his power for any of the other stranded crusaders who turned to him for help.[3] He had already run deeply into debt, and by the time that he had made all the arrangements for his return journey, everything that he owned was pledged to the hilt.[4]

He reached Sicily in December, 1294.[5] His return must have brought back vivid and bitter recollections of his other return from the crusade twenty-two years earlier, for little seemed to have changed. A second Angevin Charles was now reigning in Naples, but although he disputed the title of "King of Jerusalem" with the Lusignan ruler of Cyprus like his father before him, his energies were even more wholeheartedly devoted to the business of his Italian kingdom. The War of the Vespers still dragged on, for although Alfonso of Sicily had died in 1291, long before Eleanor of England could come south to marry him, his brothers, James, king of Aragon, and Frederick, still carried on the struggle, backed by the obstinate Sicilians, who refused to observe any of the treaties that would put them back under Angevin rule.

If it was disheartening to return to the stale quarrel that he had left behind him four years earlier, Othon cannot have expected a much more encouraging reception at the end of the next stage of his journey, when he took the road northward to Rome. The newly elected pope, Boniface VIII, was an old acquaintance, for as Cardinal Benedetto Caetani he had for years been one of the most powerful members of the Curia, and Othon had had dealings enough with him to realize that his thoughts rarely turned "to Nazareth, Where Gabriel spread his wings," preferring instead to dwell on those more accessible

[3] *Reg. Bon. VIII*, Nos. 826, 4490.

[4] *Ibid.*, No. 830.

[5] King Charles II issued Othon a safe-conduct on December 18, 1294. Reg. Ang., No. 65, fol. 115, in Digard, *Philippe le Bel et le Saint-Siège*, I, 206, n. 2.

towns near Rome that belonged, or might some day belong, to his own ambitious kinsmen. However, for once, Boniface gave more than lip service to the crusading ideal, and Othon was rescued from his financial straits by a munificent gift of 7,000 silver marks, 4,000 to be paid from the German tenth and the remainder from the English.[6]

This grant was not made until September, 1295, so that if Boniface was following the usual papal practice of not bestowing favors until the very last moment, Othon must only then have been on the point of leaving the Curia, where he probably spent the nine months that elapsed between his return to Europe and his departure for the north in becoming conversant with the manifold difficulties of the situation.

There was no better place in which to learn about them. Boniface, the strongest pope that the Church had seen in a hundred years, outdid even Innocent III in claiming domination over all things, temporal as well as spiritual, and since Christendom was seething with unrest and nothing was too insignificant to escape his rather hectoring attention, Rome, where all these troubles finally converged, was one of the two great diplomatic centers of Europe. The only other capital that might have equaled it as a listening post was Paris, for northward to Edinburgh and southward to Palermo, eastward overland to the German Empire or overseas to the Greek, the Capetian king of France and his Angevin cousin of Sicily were either creating disturbances or making use of those that already existed to further their own interests. Under these circumstances, it is small wonder that during the next nine years Othon was Edward's foremost ambassador, first to the king of France and to the emperor and the princes of the Empire, and later to the

6 *Reg. Bon. VIII*, Nos. 826, 4490. The grant from the German tenth was made on September 13, 1295. The date of the other is uncertain, as the only reference to it is in a letter from Boniface to the collectors in England, written on March 19, 1302, complaining that it had not been paid. However, since the wording of the two letters is almost identical, they were probably both written at about the same time.

Curia and to Paris once again, where he finally put his seal to the treaty that he had been largely responsible for drawing up and that finally brought the war to an end. From his early youth he had been employed on a bewildering succession of errands that seemed to bear little relation to one another, except that whether they sent him to an administrative post in Gascony, on diplomatic missions to Rome, Paris, or the Empire, or to actual fighting in the Holy Land, he sooner or later found his way blocked by French ambition. Now suddenly, as so often happens in the lives of men of great activity and wide interests, the moment came for which it seemed that all his previous experience had been only the preparation. Everything that he had learned could be turned to serve Edward's purpose, and even his position as lord of Grandson proved to have its value as the king sought for allies along the western border of the Empire.

On November 5, 1294, Othon's nephew, Girard de Vuippens, left England on a mission to the Curia, so that soon after his own arrival there Othon could get the latest news from a direct and trustworthy source. Edward had made an alliance with Adolf of Nassau, king of the Romans, which stated that both would fight against Philip of France and that neither would make a separate peace, and Adolf had declared war on Philip and demanded the return of the Arelate and the Crown of Thorns. Bishop Bek, who headed the embassy to Adolf, was also negotiating for a marriage between young Edward of Carnarvon and Philippine, the daughter of Count Guy of Flanders, although the latter was a vassal of France. Negotiations were also under way to enlist Savoyard and Burgundian help on the Anglo-Imperial side. At the same time, Philip had made an alliance with the dauphin of the Viennois, Savoy's hereditary enemy, and also with Count Othon of Burgundy—once Othon de Grandson's prospective father-in-law— who had ceded to him the Franche-Comté. This last maneuver received a check when a league of Franc-Comtois nobles swore that they would never become vassals of France, and most of these later came over to the English side. The English marriage negotiations with Flanders also came to nothing when Philip kidnapped Philippine, who died while she was still a hostage in Paris.

During all this time the popes had been trying to make peace. Celestine V, in the autumn of 1294, had sent Cardinal Bertrand de Got, the future Clement V, on a peace mission to England, and in February, 1295, the new pope, Boniface, sent two cardinals, Bertrand's brother, the bishop of Albano, and the bishop of Palestrina, on another peacemaking mission to the French and English courts. They went first to France, and it was not until August 1 that Edward came back from campaigning in Wales—for the Welsh had risen again—to meet them in London at a parliament especially convened to hear what they should say. Such a gathering proved an irresistible temptation to the various ecclesiastics present, and for the first few days the nobles and commons of England heard little except sermons. Both cardinals preached before stating their business—one of them on the text that always seems so ill-omened in the halls of Westminster, "Give peace in our time, O Lord!"—and William Hotham, Othon's fellow ambassador in 1289, answered them with another sermon before Antony Bek rose to reply to their demands. They had asked Edward to make peace, or at least to agree to a year's truce, and Bek answered for the king that although he was willing to allow an armistice, if Philip would do the same, he could not, by the terms of his treaty with Adolf of Nassau, make a separate peace that did not include his ally. The cardinals had to be satisfied with his promise to send envoys to Germany to see what Adolf would say and with his authorization to conclude in his name a truce with Philip to last until All Saints' Day next.

Edward showed his eagerness for peace by the speed with which he acted. On August 14, the same day on which he wrote to Boniface that his concessions might seem shameful to some people but that he made them out of reverence for the pope, he sent two envoys to Adolf and also wrote to Count Amadée of Savoy and to Othon that their presence might be opportune at the discussions in which the cardinals were engaged and that they were to meet with them wherever and whenever the cardinals saw fit and to be at their orders.[7] Amadée was in his own dominions during most of the spring and summer, so perhaps Othon was there with him when the king's letter arrived. One hopes at least that he had a short time at home, for he was about to start off on an endless series of missions.

Undoubtedly, he and Amadée were supposed to attend the meeting to be held at Cambrai in the autumn, but it was indefinitely postponed when Philip, taking a leaf from his enemy's book, told the legates that he, too, was unable to give them an answer until he knew what Adolf was planning to do. They accordingly left Paris for Germany, and Amadée and Othon found themselves as part of an English embassy to Adolf, which was headed by Walter Langton, bishop-elect of Coventry and Lichfield, and also included Hugh Despenser and John Berwick,[8] formerly Queen Eleanor's treasurer and an "averty ber," according to Langtoft. They found it hard to get Adolf to commit himself to anything definite. His interests and Edward's met at only one point, the stopping of French aggression, and even there they were not agreed on the methods to be used. Edward had to regain Gascony, and that could be done only by fighting; Adolf still hoped to settle his difficulties with Philip by diplomatic means. He was also slow in coming to a decision because he underestimated the scope of Philip's ambitions; in the thirteenth century, it was the Germans who mistakenly believed the French when the latter swore that each territorial aggression would be the last. Finally, there was a difference of viewpoint that must have puzzled all Edward's am-

[7] Rymer, I, 825.   [8] *Ibid.*, p. 832.

bassadors except Count Amadée and Othon, for the dweller on the Atlantic seaboard constantly forgets how much the Germans turn away from the West and toward Vienna. Moreover, Adolf was not only a German; he was king of the Germans, and what he wanted above all else was to be crowned emperor at Rome. All his plans were made with that end in view. At the moment, he was in trouble with Boniface over the French war and because of his treatment of the German clergy; he was also involved in domestic difficulties, for in the eastern part of his kingdom, Albert of Austria, angry at not having been elected to succeed his father, Rudolf, was forming a coalition of the disaffected princes; while along his western frontier, although half his vassals had joined the Anglo-German alliance, the other half sided with Philip. Moreover, none of these alliances was ever very stable. The whole border from the mouth of the Rhine to the mouth of the Rhône was like the Welsh Marches but on a larger scale, and its semi-independent princes, all intermarried and all at odds, could change the pattern of their friendships and enmities with kaleidoscopic thoroughness and with very little warning. Under these circumstances, Adolf continued to play for time, and even after the English ambassadors had persuaded him to agree to the delayed meeting at Cambrai, Edward still found it advisable to urge his ally to send the plenipotentiaries without whose presence nothing could be done.

Spurred on by the Franco-Scottish alliance of October 23, 1295, Edward redoubled his efforts. On January 1, 1296, after having asked his clergy to pray for peace, he again gave the cardinals plenary powers to conclude a truce and appointed a magnificent embassy to meet them at Cambrai. It was headed by his uncle the earl of Pembroke and included the bishops of Winchester and Ely, the duke of Brabant, the counts of Bar, Holland, and Savoy, as well as Langton, Despenser, and Othon, who were already veterans in these negotiations.[9] With them went nine lesser men, some of whom afterward rose to high positions, for "the practical mediaeval mind secured the happy mixture of good breeding and capacity . . . by putting a great nobleman at the head of a foreign embassy, while associating with him a bishop, who had perhaps begun life as a chancery clerk, to help out his intelligence, and a chancery clerk or two still on the make, to supply the necessary hard work and technical knowledge." One of these clerks was Henry Newerk, a future archbishop of York, who took with him for reference four rolls, three dealing with the peace between France and Aragon that had been proclaimed at Anagni in June, 1295, and one—probably rather tattered by this time—dealing with the treaty of 1259 between England and France.

Cambrai was one of the great centers of the cloth trade in the days when industry brought riches without the inevitable modern film of coal dust that has long since turned all the buildings of northern Europe to a uniform gritty black; the towns of the Low Countries were as rich as those of Italy and even more fantastic to look at, for their citizens made up for the sunless skies under which they spent most of their lives by painting and carving and gilding every available surface and then covering most of their handiwork with the tapestries and stuffs that brought them their wealth. Only by imagining the museums of modern Belgium turned inside out, so that their dirty walls are hidden and their brilliant pictures and statues line the streets, can we get a faint idea of how Cambrai looked in the early winter of 1296, even before the princes of the Empire and the princes of the Church, the bishops and knights with their retinues, the lawyers and the bankers, arrived to add any color that might be lacking to the snow-covered streets. Unfortunately, all these splendid preparations led to nothing. The German envoys were adamant when it came to making a truce with Philip,

[9] *Ibid.*, p. 834.

and in March Cardinal Béraud of Albano crossed the Channel to report to Edward that Adolf wanted "neither peace nor any love." He did not go alone, for "Sir Emery de Sauvay, a count of great renown, came in the company, and Otes de Grant-souns. He came out of Cyprus with his companions, who, when Acre was taken, escaped and passed the surrounding seas."[10] Jean de Grailly was there too, and while Amadée and Othon could tell Edward of the progress of negotiations in Germany, Jean could bring the latest news from the other end of Europe, for in October, 1294, he had gone with the mission sent by Celestine V to Aragon to try to make a final peace between King James and Charles II of Sicily.

For the moment, however, there was little time for a discussion of all that had happened in the six years since Othon had left for Acre, for Edward was in camp north of the Border. The Scottish allies of Philip had become increasingly recalcitrant vassals to Edward, and on March 28, 1296, the English army had marched on Berwick. A few weeks later, Scottish resistance was already crumbling, and by May 13 Edward was able to hold his Whitsun court at Roxburgh with the cardinal, the count of Savoy, Jean de Grailly, and Othon.[11] There, perhaps, the two friends were able to talk a little, to condole with one another over the losses and misfortunes of the past years, and to hear those minor details of each other's lives that so rarely get into letters and often seem for that reason so much more vivid than matters of greater importance. Both Othon and Jean must have known that the discreditable rumors about them had reached Europe, and they undoubtedly told Edward their version of the disaster of Acre and, fresh from the battle of Dunbar, where ". . . the terrible sound of the horns penetrated almost to the depths of Hell," compared the ear-piercing Scottish pipes with the Saracen drums as to their alarming effect on both man and

[10] Langtoft, II, 238.   [11] Cotton, p. 312.

beast. But neither Othon nor Edward, although they were both in their middle fifties, had yet reached the age of reminiscence when there was still so much work to be done. On Whit Saturday the king had given Langton, Amadée, and Othon new powers to treat for an armistice, and Othon left on his mission four days later.[12]

Edward also wrote at the same time to Adolf of Nassau. From the English point of view he was still a most unsatisfactory ally, but from the German point of view the same could be said for the English. In his letter Edward admitted that he had granted the cardinals' request for a truce all the more readily since he understood that Adolf had as "great and arduous" business in his kingdom as he himself had with the Scots, and it is true that the Welsh and Scottish risings and the opposition first of the clergy and later of the barons had prevented Edward from coming to any of the long-planned meetings or even from sending any reinforcements to his northern allies. Adolf did not want to find himself fighting alone against Philip, and perhaps even then, despairing of help from England, he may already have opened negotiations with the French.

If he had done so, he was not the first. As early as the year before, Edward had forbidden English merchants to land in Holland, telling them to go instead to the territories of "le duck de Brabant," since there were rumors that Count Florence had gone over to the French, and when these proved to be justified, Edward decided that the only solution was to kidnap him. He would then be brought to England, where he would be forced to abdicate in favor of his son John, who was already there in preparation for his marriage with the king's daughter, Elizabeth. The lord of Cuijk, who was intrusted with the carrying out of this business, rather overreached himself, and on June 26, 1296, the very day that Edward wrote to Adolf complaining of the count's behavior,

12 B.M. Add. MS, 7965.

Florence was murdered by one of his own nobles. This was unfortunate, but it made no difference so far as Edward's plans were concerned. He refused to accede to the request of the Hollanders, who wished their new ruler to come over to take possession of his country, and he suggested instead that they send representatives to England to form the government there and not on the troubled soil of Holland and Zeeland, which had already been invaded on various pretexts by the count of Hainault and by one of the sons of Guy of Flanders. He also did everything possible to hasten the marriage, although his behavior at the ceremony, which took place on January 7, 1297, showed that the nervous strain was telling even on his robust constitution. It takes more than the normal masculine dislike for such occasions to explain the payment entered in the Wardrobe book, "to Adam, the king's goldsmith, for a great ruby and great emerald bought to set in a certain coronet of the countess of Holland, the king's daughter, in place of the two stones that were lost when the king threw the coronet into the fire." However, he quickly recovered his royal composure and redeemed the bridal bed, which Pierre de Champvent, as chamberlain, should have as his fee, for the generous sum of twenty marks.[13]

There is no record of Othon and his colleagues ever having lost their tempers during the months that they spent on the Continent, but if they never did it showed a phenomenal self-control. Not only did they have to deal with the French and German representatives, but by now they were even more deeply involved than before with those of the Church. The two cardinals, after their rebuff by Adolf in the early winter of 1296, had become so discouraged that they had written to Boniface urging him to come north to preside over the negotiations in person as the only way of ending the war. His answer was most affecting. It touched lightly on the fact that he did not dare leave Italy, which was obvious to everyone,

13 Agnes Strickland, *Lives of the Queens of England*, I, 450, n. 1.

for by now he had powerful enemies scattered through the whole length of the peninsula, but put most of the blame for his refusal on his age and debility; the spirit was willing, but the flesh was all too weak to undertake the burden of a long journey when it meant crossing the Alps with their "hollow valleys and mountain precipices." The only solution, he wrote to them later, was for Edward and Philip to send their representatives to Rome, and this was one more factor that the English had to remember in all their discussions.

In addition, it seemed as though they were never allowed to finish one piece of work before they were sent off on another. In July, 1296, Othon and Bishop Langton were in Paris;[14] in August, Othon, by himself, was accredited to Adolf of Germany.[15] In October he was back in Paris;[16] while in November, with Langton and Amadée, both members of the original embassy, Despenser, and Berwick, he was sent to Burgundy.[17] There they were to treat for peace and also to make alliances with the nobles of Burgundy and indeed with anyone else, for they were plenipotentiaries in the fullest sense of the word. In fact, the five ambassadors were described as "the Council of the king of England stationed at Cambrai"[18] and were more or less the arbiters of Edward's continental policy. In February, 1297, Bishop Langton—he had been consecrated by the two cardinals the summer before—Amadée, Othon, and Berwick, besides having all their former powers confirmed, were commissioned on business connected with the alliance that had finally been made with Count Guy on January 7 and empowered to make other alliances with the duke of Lorraine, the counts of Hainault and Guelders, and the bishops of Liège and Utrecht.[19] The next day Amadée, Othon, and Berwick were

[14] G. P. Cuttino (ed.), "Bishop Langton's Mission for Edward I," p. 156.

[15] Rymer, I, 843.

[16] Cuttino, *loc. cit.*

[18] Böhmer, *op. cit.*, VI, 2, 782.

[17] Rymer, pp. 848–49.

[19] Rymer, I, 857–59.

ordered to pay Edward's debts to the archbishop of Cologne, to patch up the archbishop's quarrel with the duke of Brabant and the hot-headed lord of Cuijk, to see that these last two paid back all the money that their people had stolen both from the archbishop and from the dean of the cathedral, and also to assure the dean that Edward's promise to him of a prebend in Dublin still held good.[20] A few days later, with Langton again added to their number, they were given the sweeping and impossible task of allaying all the quarrels between all Edward's allies and friends in the Empire.[21]

Since the count of Holland was fighting the duke of Brabant and, allied with the count of Hainault, was also fighting the count of Flanders, while the duke of Brabant was engaged in quarrels with everyone else besides, Othon must have been overjoyed to have had that mission interrupted, like all the others, by something of an equally political but pleasanter nature. He was to leave at once, taking with him anyone he saw fit, to arrange for the marriage of Joan of Acre with Amadée of Savoy,[22] whose first wife had died in 1294, the year before the death of Joan's husband, Earl Gilbert of Gloucester. Except for Edward's stipulation that the lands that the count would give his bride must lie outside the kingdom of France, there seemed to be no difficulties in the way. Othon had already had a hand in arranging Joan's first marriage as his brother had arranged her first betrothal, so that he knew the procedure to be followed, and Amadée would have no objections to strengthening the ties that bound him to his generous and powerful kinsman. But the discussions had barely started before Othon learned that he had been sent on a sleeveless errand and that an unexpected and irremediable difficulty had arisen. Perhaps Joan, after five years of marriage during which she had borne four children to a man whom she did not love, was averse to the idea of another husband who, although not so old as her first one, was still only ten

---

[20] *Ibid.*, I, 859.   [21] *Idem.*   [22] *Ibid.*, I, 861.

years younger than her father; perhaps she had little faith in political matches, since Earl Gilbert had been just as difficult a vassal after he became the king's son-in-law as before; perhaps she merely fell in love. None of these possibilities offered any excuse for her subsequent behavior. As for the first two, it was no business of hers to have any say in the choice of a husband; as for the third, everyone knew that love and marriage were incompatible, for the logical reason that the lover must always look up to his mistress and once they were married their positions were naturally reversed, so that any further love between them was out of the question. The only people who were unaware of this were the uncivilized Celts, whose lays gave no proof that they knew anything of the complicated structure of courtly life and love, built up so laboriously over the centuries. Young girls, who would never be allowed to stir outside their castle walls without an eagle-eyed guard of mothers and men at arms, neglected their prayer books to hear the stories of those others who traveled only with a fairy tale retinue of maidens riding two by two on white palfreys, each pair more beautiful and more richly dressed than the one before, while the young squires, already pledged by their fathers to the rich lands of some wellborn heiress, saw nothing out of the way when the knight who rescued the spellbound heroine with a kiss married her on the spot without waiting to find out whether she was descended from a line of dragons or from a line of kings, or what properties in Avalon or Lyonesse she brought with her as her dowry. It may be that the youthful countess had let her head be turned by these stories sung by the Welsh minstrels who crossed the nearby border to relieve the tedium of life in the Gloucestershire castles where so much of her short married life had been spent. At any rate, the graybeard discussions between Edward and Othon as to the "many conveniences" that might result from the proposed marriage were suddenly broken off when the twenty-three-year-old widow informed her father that she was already married to Ralph Monthermer, who had been one of the earl's North-country squires. It is true that he was no longer a squire. Joan seems to have been a woman of great forethought, for she had not only got her children out of the way of her intended honeymoon by packing them off with their nurses to Bristol Castle, but she had also induced her unsuspecting father to knight her new husband earlier in the year. She must also have inherited her mother's sweetness as well as her father's strength of character, for although Edward promptly threw Monthermer into prison, he was not only released within a few months but was also recognized as earl of Gloucester in right of his wife and later, because of "his own efforts and industry, he became a great man."

Romance had never been one of Othon's strong points even when he himself had gone wooing eighteen years earlier, and no doubt he shared Edward's indignation at the impulsive behavior of a young woman whom they both still must have thought of as a child. Luckily, Joan's marriage was not the only reason for his journey: he had other business to do as well, for Edward was looking for allies among the smaller feudatories of the great counties of Burgundy and Savoy.[23] Othon was particularly well suited to deal with them, for all of them were his peers, most of them were his neighbors, and many were his relatives. He knew, not by painfully acquired experience but by birthright, what friendships and enmities existed between them, how best to deal with Jean of Joux, whose castle guarded the other side of the Jura passes, and what arguments to use with Gautier of Montfaucon, whose town of Orbe, for which he did homage to the count of Burgundy, made such a large enclave in the territories that Othon held from the count of Savoy.

The Burgundian nobles, incensed by Count Othon's virtual cession of his county to Philip, had already formed an anti-French coalition, and the promise of an English subsidy per-

[23] Cuttino, *op. cit.*, p. 154.

suaded them to join the Anglo-Imperial alliance. On May 10, 1297, four of them, acting for themselves and for their sixteen confederates, met with Langton, Othon, and Berwick at Brussels. They agreed to wage "lively and open warfare in the county of Burgundy and nearby places" against Philip until peace was made between France and England. The English, for their part, promised to pay them 30,000 *livres tournois* before Michaelmas, and an equal amount annually thereafter.[24]

He had other ties with Montfaucon as well, for the latter was not only Edward's ally against France but was also the ally of Bishop Guillaume of Lausanne in his renewed war with Louis of Vaud, the brother of Edward's other ally, Count Amadée. Othon, as head of his family, which included the Champvents, must have been the nominal leader of the coalition of Vaudois nobles who were backing the bishop, even though his missions for Edward kept him from doing any actual fighting, for he was a party to at least two of the truces that interrupted its course. The war was finally ended in an almost royal manner by the marriage of his nephew and heir, Pierre de Grandson-Belmont, the son of his brother Jacques, to Louis' daughter, Blanche of Savoy.

His closest associate on almost all his missions was Count Amadée, and that their relatives were at war with one another seems to have done nothing to interfere with the friendship between them. Indeed, Amadée took so little interest in the difficulties with which his brother became involved on the other side of the lake that when Louis and the bishop grew tired of fighting, they chose him as the impartial arbiter of their quarrels. He was successful in arranging a preliminary truce, which was drawn up at Versoix, near Geneva, on June 29, 1297, but the bishop had to seal it for his cousin, for by

[24] Dipl. Docs. Exch. E 30, 44ª, transcribed in J. de Sturler, "Le paiement à Bruxelles des Alliés franc-comtois d'Édouard Iᵉʳ roi d'Angleterre (mai 1297)," *Cahiers Bruxellois,* V (January–March, 1960), 16–20.

that time Othon was back in England after a mission that had lasted for over a year.

From one point of view, we are well informed about it; the accounts of his fellow ambassador, Bishop Langton, give us a clear idea of how much work it entailed. We know that Othon had been to Paris, to the Low Countries, to Burgundy and Savoy, and even to the wild and inaccessible Auvergne. We also know that all this traveling was arduous, expensive, and sometimes dangerous, especially on the lands of the Empire, where only the year before an English embassy to Rome had been held up and robbed near Basel. The official letters that have survived give the ostensible reason for many of these journeys, and there are hints as to some of the others. In February, 1297, Philip sent messengers to Edward, asking him to free Balliol and the other Scottish prisoners of war, and although we do not know what the English reply was, we at least know, from an entry in the Gascon Calendar of 1322, who made it: "The words in which my lord Ottes de Grandson is to answer to the king of France in regard to the request which the king of France made for the Scots and Bayonnais who are held as hostages in England."[25]

But all these are references only to what appeared on the surface, to the finished product; as to the discussions that lay behind them, little is known now and not much more was known then, except to Othon and his associates and to the constant stream of messengers who passed between Edward and his ambassadors, between them and his allies, and even between the members of the mission themselves when they were separated by the different duties assigned to them. Occasionally these tireless men did odd jobs, as when "Hugh, a courier," brought some hackneys to Othon in Brabant,[26] but in general their business was to carry letters, many of them too secret ever to have been enrolled, or other instructions

[25] *The Gascon Calendar of 1322*, p. 457.

[26] Cuttino, *op. cit.*, p. 175.

and reports, more secret still, that could be delivered only by word of mouth.

Othon enlarged on what they had already told the king when he returned to England in June, 1297, and at the same time he presented his accounts to the Wardrobe. Although he had received several large sums of money from the Frescobaldi[27] while he had been on his embassy, these had all been for incidental expenses, and he was now paid his full salary for 393 days' service at 40 shillings a day, which the royal accountants correctly worked out as coming to £784.[28] He also agreed to accept £1,000 a year to keep his men and horses overseas to fight the king of France,[29] even though at the time he made the agreement it seemed very doubtful whether the proposed expedition would ever sail.

When Philip had heard of the treaty between his vassal, Count Guy, and his enemy, the king of England, he had immediately sent an army against the Flemings, and since Adolf, in spite of urgent and repeated appeals from Edward, was unwilling or unable to send help, the French were winning one victory after another. Edward, who had some outdated ideas about the sanctity of his plighted word, was eager to abide by the terms of the treaty and hasten to the defense of his ally, but once again an obstacle arose to keep him from leaving England. In 1294, it had been the Welsh rising, but Wales was now subdued; in 1296, it had been the Scots, but the Stone of Scone was now safely in Westminster Abbey and Balliol was in the Tower, where, with native frugality, he arranged for the English to pay for the board and lodging of his shield-bearer, huntsman, page, and barber, and of the two greyhounds and ten whippets (*canium currentium*) with which he was allowed to hunt in the king's parks and chases. But in 1297, Edward's enemies were still more dangerous, for they were those of his own house.

---

[27] *Ibid., passim.*   [28] B.M. Add. MS, 7965.   [29] *Idem.*

154

Honor was all very well, but war meant money and money meant taxes, and no one has ever enjoyed paying them year after year, especially for an indecisive campaign that drags on with nothing to show for it. Edward had tried to spare his own subjects as much as possible and in 1296 had ordered the seizure of all French-owned properties in England, especially those of the alien priories, but the main effect of this seems only to have been a wave of indiscriminate xenophobia. Othon's brother Guillaume was kept busy proving that various dispossessed monks were not French but Savoyard,[30] but he could not even protect himself, and when he left England to fight in Gascony his own lands were mistakenly seized as well.[31]

In spite of such measures, even if they had been successful, Edward had to rely on his own people for taxes. He met with opposition not only from the clergy, whose hands had been strengthened by the publication of the bull *Clericis Laicos* in the autumn of 1296, but even from his nobles, and it was not until August 22, 1297, that he finally set sail from Portsmouth.

Othon had been in England during some of those tense summer days when it looked as though civil war might be added to all Edward's other troubles, but he was already back on the Continent by the beginning of August when the king wrote to tell him of his impending arrival. The letter carried an implied but nonetheless heart-warming tribute to all his labors on his master's behalf, for although Edward wrote to innumerable other people in almost the same words, saying that he was shortly coming to Flanders and asking them to meet him there, it was only to Othon that he added, ". . . unless you see that your being elsewhere would be more profitable."[32]

---

30 *C.C.R. (1288–96)*, p. 460, and *passim* for 1296.

31 *Ibid.*, p. 502.   32 Rymer I, 871.

Philip had also come north to lead his army in person, but in spite of the martial behavior of both kings, each of them was more than ready to put an end to the war. Philip, too, had his troubles, for his reaction to *Clericis Laicos* had been even more violent than Edward's, and although, after the Anglo-Flemish treaty, he had patched up his quarrel with Boniface, he still wanted to have his hands free to cope with his clergy at home and with the management of the War of the Vespers abroad, which had broken out again when Frederick of Aragon, "the most illegitimate son" of King Peter, as one chronicler unaccountably calls him, had defied the treaty of Anagni by accepting the crown of Sicily.

On October 7, 1297, at Vyves-St. Bavon, a preliminary truce was made. It afforded only a temporary breathing spell, for it was to last for just two months in Flanders and for three in Gascony[33]—barely time enough to allow the Gascons to get word of it before it expired—and the councilors of both kings immediately set to work to have it prolonged. Philip seems to have made some difficulties, but Edward luckily had with him one of his most experienced and charming diplomats, William Hotham, now archbishop-elect of Dublin, who had the further recommendation that he had been friend-ly with the French king and with many of his nobles ever since the days when he had been studying theology at the University of Paris. Quietly omitting to mention that he had already received a papal dispensation from going to Rome for his consecration, since the war made it impossible for him to reach the Apostolic See, he crossed the lines for the ostensible purpose of asking Philip for a safe-conduct so that he could make the necessary journey. While he was in the French camp, he also took the opportunity of asking the king to send certain "discreet and pacific men" to discuss a peace, or at least a truce, and he worked so well that on November 23 he and Edward's other envoys, Bek, Amadée of Savoy, Pembroke,

[33] *Ibid.*, I, 878–79.

and Othon, met with the French at Groningen Abbey near Courtrai and extended the armistice until the following Shrovetide.[34] Even this meant a respite of only three months, and it is hard to see what either side thought that they were gaining by such inconclusive tactics. However, the arrival of two papal legates, the generals of the Franciscan and Dominican orders, who had come to repeat the pope's request that both Edward and Philip send plenipotentiaries to Rome, led to a second prolongation, which was to last until January 7, 1300,[35] so that there was now some hope of a final peace being made before it ran out. Perhaps it had been Adolf's vacillating behavior that had delayed things up to now, for when the five English envoys once more met with the French, at Tournai on January 31, 1298, and agreed to the more permanent armistice, the document that they drew up, unlike the first two, did not mention the emperor's name.

[34] *Ibid.*, I, 881–82.   [35] *Ibid.*, pp. 885–86.

*Item quod cum guerra graviter invaluisset inter regem
Francie ex una parte et regem Anglie proxime defunctum
ex altera: dictus Bonifacius compromissum partium
ut persona privata in se recepit, ad tractandum
et pacificandum inter ipsos reges, ut se falso velle dicebat.
Item, quod pendente compromisso
huiusmodi contra Deum et contra Ecclesiam honestatem
persui [sic] dolosas inductiones, pecuniarum, auri, et
rerum preciosarum magnas quantitates occasione negocii
huiusmodi ab utraque parte habuit et recepit. Item,
quod dictus Bonifacius cum in potestate sua esset pacem
dare partibus, et inter utrosque reges et regna Francie
et Anglie pacem firmare, receptis dictis
muneribus, seu exactis, maiora sperens ab eisdem
recipere, quendam colorem pacis disposuit, non tamen in
negotio tam gravi, tam periculoso, ex quo
Deo Ecclesia turbatura, finem efficacem dedit,
cum posset.*

GUILLAUME DE NOGARET

vii. War with France: Embassies to the Curia

The discussions leading up to the treaty of Tournai had
made it clear that the English and French envoys between
them had small hope of ever arriving at an agreement that
would lead to a definite peace. It seemed better to accept the
pope's offer to arbitrate the quarrel, and since he still refused

to cross the Alps, alleging that he was too old and infirm, Othon and his colleagues had promised in Edward's name that the king would send "great and suitable messengers, according to the magnitude of the business, to the court of Rome with plenary powers to make treaties . . . by the month of Easter at the latest."

In making this decision the English can have had no illusions that their labors would end at Tournai: all of them, Hotham and Bek, Amadée of Savoy and Aymer of Valence, and especially the ubiquitous Othon, must have been aware that as they knew more than anyone else about the business in hand, they would inevitably be chosen as the "suitable messengers." In fact, when the embassy was finally assembled, only Bek was missing, and only two more envoys had been added to the original number, John Pontissara, bishop of Winchester, the same who had been accused of talebearing by Henri de Grandson sixteen years earlier, and Hugh de Vere, son of the earl of Oxford and husband of the Dionisia de Monte Canisio whose grandmother's charter to hold her lands on sergeanty by the service of a rose had been witnessed by Othon during one of his few quiet periods at Westminster.

Othon was still in Flanders on March 9, 1298,[1] and when he left he seems to have traveled with Hotham and with one of Count Guy's sons, Robert de Béthune, for the three of them were together when they broke their journey at Rivoli, the court of Amadée's nephew, Philippe of Savoy-Piedmont.[2] By that time, at least the frozen passes lay behind them, but they were well aware of the difficulties that still lay ahead: the long journey across the Lombard plain, where, if warmer weather brought a respite from the biting mountain winds, it only added to the danger of the road by melting the snow that flooded the swollen rivers; endless weeks of bickering

[1] *C.D.I. (1293–1301)*, p. 232.

[2] S. Pamperato, "Documenti per la storia del Piemonte (1265–1300)," *Miscellanea di Storia Italiana*, 3d series, IX (XL), 100.

until summer came with the sirocco to tighten nerves already strained to breaking point by Roman intrigue and French intransigence; and always the uncertainty that the arrival of messengers with fresh news might change the whole situation and undo anything that had been accomplished. For by now the original cause of the quarrel, Philip's seizure of Gascony, was only one strand in the spider web of French interests that overlay all western Europe and that had been so well and closely spun that the lightest movement could set it trembling from one end to the other. Even so, Edward's ambassadors can scarcely have foreseen that five years of unremitting work lay ahead of them before peace was finally made and that when it did come the countless embassies that left England for Rome during that period had very little to do with it.

It is hard not to lay most of the blame for their failures on the pope. Nogaret is hardly an impartial witness, and even he did not make his charges against Boniface until the latter was dead, but there is some truth in what he said and more in what he did not say. It was not merely a hunger for "money, gold and precious objects" that delayed the papal pronouncement that could have brought the war to an end; the pope was playing a dangerous game, with so many balls in the air at once that a misstep would bring them all about his ears, and his only hope was to temporize so that he could take advantage of every change in the delicate balance of European affairs. When the negotiations began, his quarrel with the king of France was temporarily in abeyance, and he had no intention of reviving it so long as there was hope that French money would come to pay the troops who, under Charles of Valois, the papal vicar of Tuscany, were so valuable in the crusade against the Colonna cardinals and their Sicilian allies. If his circumspection in regard to Philip's sensibilities went so far that he even refused to grant a dispensation for the marriage of Amadée's daughter, Agnès, to the son of the dauphin of Vienne—a truly peacemaking move, according to thirteenth-century ideas, for Savoy and Dauphiné were as usual fighting on opposite sides—for fear that he might seem to be favoring the anti-French coalition, he would certainly never take the far more drastic step of ordering the return of Gascony to Edward, even though, as he admitted to the English ambassadors, he had been advised that the original cession was invalid. On the other hand, he did not want to offend Edward either, and he found himself in a very difficult position. On the surface, the whole question was purely feudal. The French were now occupying Gascony and Flanders on the technical grounds that their rulers had forfeited them by a breach of the feudal contract. But Edward was invading Scotland for precisely the same reason, and his insubordinate vassal was the ally of the king of France. Boniface had to uphold the sacredness of the feudal contract at all costs, for it was only as suzerain of Sicily and of the Patrimony of Peter that he had any justification for his Italian wars, but in the English-Scottish-French triangle it was almost impossible for him to recognize the claims of any one of the contestants without seeming to invalidate those of the other two.

Because of these involvements in the matter at stake, Boniface lacked the impartiality that is supposed to be an essential qualification for the position of arbiter, and in retrospect that would seem to be sufficient reason why the English embassies to the Curia proved so fruitless. But when the situation was so complicated that even Nogaret, one of the principal actors in the drama, could misinterpret the pope's motives, it is possible that Othon and his companions, equally baffled, attributed their difficulties to a more immediate cause. This was Boniface's monumental tactlessness. "Tact," by its very derivation, implies that its possessor keeps in touch with other people, but the author of *Clericis Laicos* and *Unam Sanctam*, the wielder of the two swords, the papal sun of which the imperial moon was but a dim reflection, the peer of Caesar and vice-regent of Christ, was so high above other human beings that he had forgotten what they were like. He was a learned and brilliant man, one of the best jurists in Europe and with flashes of penetrating insight, and yet in his dealings with other people, particularly when he tried to be ingratiating, he was capable of an abysmal stupidity that can have come only from a complete incomprehension of human nature and human motives.

This lofty disregard for others was not shared by such men as Pierre Flotte and his associates, that "brilliant group of mediocre men," as Powicke calls them, who provided the brains for the French embassy that came to Rome under the nominal leadership of the archbishop of Narbonne, the duke of Burgundy, and the count of St.-Pol. They had risen from humble beginnings by their own diligence and astuteness, they were unfettered by the codes that bound nobles like Othon or even the older generation of clerks like Hotham, and they were working for an end that their opponents had never even visualized. Boniface was later to explain to the English that Robert of Burgundy and Guy de St.-Pol were easy enough to do business with; it was the clerks who caused the mischief and who made him say that the ruling passion of their race was covetousness and that in dealing with them he never knew whether he had to do with a Frenchman or with a devil. To the pope, head of the universal Church, to the duke of Burgundy, taking full advantage of his position on the borders of France and of the Empire, or to Othon, who found it quite natural that he should do homage to Edward for Tipperary and to the count of Savoy for Grandson, Flotte's outspoken nationalism was completely incomprehensible. And yet he made no pretense about it; when the pope, trying no doubt to appeal to his better nature, said to him, "You have already taken Normandy. Do you want to drive the king of England from all his overseas possessions?" the Frenchman's answer was a terse "Vous dites vrai." Loyal and un-scrupulous, with a single-minded ambition to which he devoted all his energies, he outmatched the English diplomats time and time again until, by a kind of poetic justice, he fell at the battle of Courtrai, the victim of the equally nationalistic if less articulate Flemings.

The English, relying on a prejudiced arbiter and confronted with superior diplomatic skill, were also hampered in their negotiations by the events that were taking place at home. The Scots had found a new leader in William Wallace, and Edward's yearly expeditions across the Border called for ever-mounting taxes, which only increased his difficulties with the barons and the clergy. He was unable to send any more help to his allies on the Continent, and during the next few years many of them, left to resist French pressure unaided, surrendered to the inevitable and made their peace with Philip. The defeat and death of Adolf of Nassau at the hands of Albert of Habsburg also worked to the disadvantage of the English, for all the efforts to revive the anti-French coalition came to nothing when Philip made an alliance with the new king of the Romans.

These shifts in alliance and allegiance not only increased the difficulties confronting the English embassy as a whole, but also directly involved the two Savoyards, Amadée and Othon. In spite of the armistice negotiated by Amadée two years earlier, the war between Bishop Guillaume of Lausanne and Louis of Savoy was still going on, and although little is known about it, that little proves that it was yet another phase of the struggle against French expansion and was closely interwoven with the larger conflict. A second truce had been arbitrated in April, 1298, by Jean d'Arlay, lord of Chalon-sur-Saône, the most staunch of Edward's Burgundian allies, and these last were represented in the discussions at the Curia by Gautier de Montfaucon, Othon's neighbor and a member of the Vaudois coalition.

But although in many of these discussions Othon and Amadée might have been tempted to consider their own interests as well as those of the king, Edward's confidence in them was so absolute that they were made the acknowledged leaders of the embassy. Amadée may have owed this partly to his relationship with the king, but Othon, who at sixty seems still to have been a simple knight, merited his position solely by his own character and ability. The younger men, Vere, and Pembroke, who was also Edward's cousin and whose Lusignan blood gave him the swarthy complexion that caused Edward of Carnarvon's irreverent friend, Piers Gaveston, to nickname him "Joseph the Jew," were relatively new to the game of diplomacy, but Pontissara had been on missions to Rome before, and Hotham, a man of great learning, "jocund in speech, agreeable to meet, of honest religion, and pleasing in the eyes of all," and an archbishop to boot, was as reliable and experienced as Othon himself. But all the reports of this first embassy show that the two Savoyards were the heads of it, for they were the only ones who were empowered to swear for the king that he would abide by the pope's decision and who were allowed to appoint deputies in the event that one was unavoidably absent.[3]

This also gave them the unpleasant duty of being spokesmen for the mission, and they could foresee that that would not be easy. Underneath all the high-sounding phrases of royal and papal letters and behind the more down-to-earth instructions to the envoys was the inescapable fact that Edward would have to desert his Flemish allies and leave them to the vengeance of their indignant suzerain, the king of France, in return for being given an equally free hand with the insubordinate Scots. This was a doubly bitter blow to the king. In the eyes of those who still cared for such things, it was a reflection on his honor, and it gave further grounds for complaint to his overtaxed subjects, who were already

[3] Rymer, I, 888.

1 6 4

grumbling—although probably not in Latin—"Non est lex sana Quod regi sit mea lana." Bad relations between England and Flanders brought hard times to the shepherds scattered over the dales and downs as well as to the crowded Flemish cities, and while the English, so far, had done no more than grumble, Othon had seen what the discontent might lead to, for before he left the Low Countries the citizens of Ghent had risen in protest against the expense of supporting Edward and his troops, and the regular soldiers had found it unexpectedly difficult to put down the nasty little riot that ensued.

In all the talk of feudal rights, the knights and bishops must never forget the woolworkers, nor was it easy to do so, for all along the road to Italy they passed the Florentine pack trains going home with their loads of raw wool from England and rough Flemish cloth, the former to be spun and woven by the Arte della Lana and the latter to be refined and dyed by the Arte della Calimala with the pigment recently discovered in Asia Minor by one of their members, Bernardo Rucellai, the secret of which they jealously kept for themselves. These chatty merchants made amusing and instructive traveling companions, for their business took them to all four corners of the globe, and Florentine gossip had already reached a high stage of development as even a cursory glance at the *Inferno* will prove. A northern ambassador, willing to keep his mouth shut and his ears open, could learn a lot that would stand him in good stead at the Curia.

They had other topics of conversation, besides their news from courts and fairs, which were of interest to Othon, the builder of castles in Wales and churches in his native country. Behind him lay the Low Countries, where men were still completing the cathedrals that a later Florentine would describe as "a malediction of little tabernacles, one on top of the other, with so many pyramids and spires and leaves that it is a wonder they stand up at all, for they look as though they were made of paper instead of stone or marble"; the

Low Countries, where the Middle Ages were to last for another two centuries and die out only when Charles the Bold of Burgundy met his first defeat in the fields and forests below the walls of Grandson. Before him lay the Florence of Giotto and of the dawning Renaissance. Later scholars would debate the exact dates of the Renaissance and whether, in fact, there had ever been such a period, but Vasari pinpointed it to the year. Art, he wrote, had gone steadily downhill after the fall of Rome, but then "the spirits of those who were being born, helped in some measure by the subtility of the air, so purified themselves that in 1250 Heaven, moved to pity by the rare talents that the Tuscan soil was producing every day, restored it to its original form."

Fifty years later, the results of Heaven's mercy were already beginning to show. In spite of a century of civil wars, the expanding city had already outgrown its second circuit of walls, and the pride of its citizens was demanding a new cathedral "of such extent and magnificence that nothing more could be desired from the power or industry of man" and a palace from which the Signoria could fitly rule their ever-increasing territories. The moving spirit and the greatest financial backer in all these projects was the powerful Arte della Lana, whose symbol, the Risen Lamb, was already being carved on so many new buildings, and in Arnolfo di Cambio its members had found an architect whose genius was commensurate with their most soaring ambitions. It was he who built the last circuit of walls, who designed Santa Maria del Fiore, the cornerstone of which was laid in September of this same year, and who conceived, although he never lived to see, the slender tower of the Palazzo della Signoria, which bears its four massive columns so lightly above the red-tiled roofs below.

Othon can scarcely have reached Rome before the beginning of May, and he found the Flemings already there and already discouraged. They had been well received by the pope at first but had written sadly to Count Guy, "You should know that the Roman court is very grasping and that anyone who wants to do business here must make many gifts and promises and pledges."[4] They had hired the best lawyers regardless of expense, but Flotte outwitted them as he outwitted everyone else. Philip was still insisting that Balliol be included in the negotiations, and although Edward wrote that Scotland had never been mentioned in any of the three truces and that the request was "new, extraneous and surprising," he was opposed also by Boniface, who had already asked him in reproachful papal prose, to whom did he expect to answer at the last day if he continued to claim Scotland as his fief? The Flemings were very modest in their demands: they asked only that their rights under the treaty of Tournai be respected and that Philippine be sent back to her father's court so that her marriage to Edward of Carnarvon might take place. But while the English held out on the Scottish question, there was no hope of Boniface's yielding on the Flemish. On June 11, when he gave an audience to the English and Flemish envoys, he had nothing better to suggest than that they should leave the whole matter in his hands.

Guy's three sons, Robert de Béthune, Jean de Namur, and Philippe de Thiette, realizing that this would deprive their father of all his defenses by removing his one ally, asked for a day's grace and met with the English the next morning at Hotham's lodging. But all that Amadée and Othon could do was to point out what they already knew, that Edward was in no position to back up Count Guy and that although it was hard to agree to the pope's suggestion it would be even worse to turn it down.[5] That afternoon the Flemings had another interview with Boniface and made one last effort to avert disaster. When the kings of England and France had decided to submit their quarrel to a third person, Edward had agreed

[4] Frantz Kervyn de Lettenhove, "Études sur l'histoire du xiiie siècle," *Mémoires de l'académie royale de Belgique*, XXIII (1854), 31.

[5] *Ibid.*, pp. 42–43.

to abide by the decision of the "sovereign pontiff of Rome and head of the universal Church," but Philip, for reasons that are even now obscure, had given powers to his envoys to choose any arbiter that they saw fit, and the astounding Pierre Flotte had picked "a private individual, Benedetto Caetani," who should by rights have disappeared from history on Christmas Eve, 1294, when he ascended the Throne of Peter. Accordingly, when the Flemings, in this second audience, told Boniface that they would leave the settlement up to him as "judge and sovereign," he turned on them in a rage, accused them of trying to get him into trouble with Philip, and told them that unless they had a more suitable answer he would declare all alliances null and void and proceed to make peace between Edward and Philip on that basis. They had one more meeting with the English ambassadors on the following day, but Othon and Amadée could only repeat what they had already said, and the Flemings were forced to yield.

French diplomacy had achieved its first objective; Count Guy was left defenseless, and Philip would be able to punish him at his leisure. Flotte's victory over the English was equally decisive. Although Edward had given them two detailed sets of instructions as to what to say about Gascony, no doubt leaving it to their judgment to use whichever seemed best under the circumstances, neither those that emphasized the legal side of the question nor those that dwelt more on the concessions that he was prepared to make to recover the duchy were successful against the strong French influence that pervaded the Curia. To the English it had seemed as though there might at last be a chance of setting aside the troublesome Treaty of Paris, and Edward's first demand was that Gascony be restored to him and that he should no longer hold it in fee but outright, as he claimed that his ancestors had done before 1259, in return for which he was ready to cede to Philip such parts of the duchy as should be designated by the pope. If this was not granted—and even the most sanguine can hardly have expected that it would be—the English were then to suggest that Edward hold it as a fief of the Roman Church. But Boniface refused even this tempting bait, and on June 30, when he gave his verdict, the fate of Gascony was, if anything, more unsettled than before. Both the greater part of it, now occupied by the French, and the few towns still remaining to the English were to be intrusted to that private individual, Benedetto Caetani, who was to hold them until he decided whether to award the duchy to Edward or to Philip. Even this was far from satisfactory, but when Boniface ordered the archbishop of Toulouse to receive Gascony from the French and English officials and then to hand it over to the dukes of Burgundy and Brittany and to the count of St.-Pol, it was either a premeditated insult to Edward or one more example of the pope's tactless stupidity. The two ambassadors, Burgundy and St.-Pol, were of course wholeheartedly French in their sympathies, but at least they had no reason to be anything else; the duke of Brittany, on the other hand, had been earl of Richmond as well, and when the outbreak of hostilities forced him to make a choice, he had renounced his allegiance to Edward, and his English county was even now in the king's hands. The idea that something was wrong in this muddle seems finally to have penetrated even the pope's sublime insensibility, for a year later he tried to mollify Edward by explaining to him that he had arrived at his decision only after much thought and that he had been sure that it would be pleasing to the king, since St.-Pol was closely related to him and Brittany was his uncle.

It was also as a private individual that Boniface gave his verdict on the other questions before him, although he declared rather inconsistently that his pronouncement was to have the full weight of papal authority and that if either of the kings failed to observe it he would be excommunicated and his kingdom put under interdict. Except for the declaration that a firm and durable peace was to exist between Edward and Philip and that the truce of Tournai was to be observed—a cart-before-the-horse statement that showed just how little had been accomplished—the remaining clauses were purely financial, with the inevitable accompaniment of a bride or two thrown in as makeweight. Both sides were to pay reparations, and Edward was to get a further 33,000 *livres tournois*, 15,000 as the dowry of his new wife, Philip's younger sister Margaret, and 18,000 as the dowry of his new daughter-in-law, Philip's eight-year-old daughter, Isabelle, who was to marry the Prince of Wales as soon as she was old enough.

Even the French were not satisfied with this solution of the Gascon question, although it was more favorable to them than to the English, but for the moment there was nothing more that could be done, and the ambassadors who stayed on at the Curia did so only to wind up the business that they had been doing for their respective rulers and to gain the usual favors for themselves. The bishop of Winchester wanted to get back his lands in France and also the gold and silver vases, the vestments and books, to say nothing of a "not inconsiderable sum of money," that he had left with various Paris churches and that had been seized at the outbreak of the war, while Amadée wanted for himself permission to have a portable altar, and for his son Aymon, reversion of the next vacant deanery at York, although the boy was still under age and not yet ordained. Only Othon was strangely silent, and this time neither he nor any of his numerous nephews benefited from his trip to Rome.

The two Savoyards may also have stayed on at the Curia to see if they could be of any help to the three Flemish counts, who were by now victims of Roman gossip as well as of French enmity, and who had come to Amadée's lodging in Palazzo Sta. Sabina on the very afternoon of the day that the verdict was proclaimed to assure the English that there was no truth in the rumor that they had been talking against Edward.[6] Their father had also written them a long letter asking them to enlist the help of the English ambassadors in his behalf: they were to tell Amadée and Othon of all the hardships that he was suffering at Philip's hands, so that they in turn could inform the pope "that if the king once gains a firm foothold in Flanders, what is left over will be worth little to me or to my heirs," and also to mention to them that Edward still owed him 25,000 *livres tournois*.[7]

But it is possible that the letter arrived too late to reach the ears for which it was really intended. Amadée and Othon probably divided the rest of the year between their own affairs in the Pays de Vaud and Edward's at the court of France, for they did not return to England, and it is to be hoped that they left Rome with Hotham and were with him when he died at Dijon at the end of August. Othon was already beginning to suffer for his longevity: one by one his old associates were dying, and although the younger generation that now rode with him listened respectfully to his instructive comparisons between Philip the Fair and his recently canonized grandfather or between Boniface and his predecessors, they grew politely restive when he tried to tell them about some trifling experience, which, just because it had been shared by so few, seemed to stand out more vividly with every passing year, while in retrospect every embassy to Rome appeared much like every other. There was no turn of the road without its memories, but Othon learned to keep them to himself. Only at Grandson could he still find people, his brother Jacques and their old servants, who could remember the family jokes and happenings of fifty years ago, for the Vaudois are a long-lived race, and Othon himself was still a mere child by comparison with the ancient and well-born Savoyard who was to go to Rome for Pope Boniface's jubilee in the following year and astound everyone with his accounts

[6] *Ibid.*, p. 49.   [7] *Ibid.*, pp. 35–40.

of that of Innocent III, which he had witnessed just a century earlier. At home, Othon could also discuss more recent events with Jean de Grailly, for although Boniface had confirmed his appointment as governor of the Comtat-Venaissan, Jean had done homage to Amadée for his Vaudois lands in 1295, and his towns of Grilly and Rolle, Villars and Prangins, were little more than a day's ride from Grandson.

But as usual, Othon and Amadée had very little time to enjoy the delights of homecoming, for by February, 1299, Edward had already sent one of his Gascon clerks, Raimond-Arnaud de la Rame, as his envoy to them both about the next move in the negotiations,[8] and by April they were already in Paris with Jean of Bar,[9] making arrangements for the peace conference that was supposed to be held at Montreuil-sur-Mer at the end of the month, although because of the delays in turning Gascony over to the new papal legate, the bishop of Vicenza, it did not actually take place until June. The commission responsible for the transfer of the towns still held by the English was headed by Othon's nephew, Girard de Vuippens, who left for Paris with explicit instructions as to how to make the best of a bad bargain. If the bishop of Vicenza did not keep Gascony in his own hands, Girard was to try to arrange that some neutral person, a subject of neither king, be put in charge of it, and if that were not feasible, that it be committed to young John of Brittany, who had fought on the English side, instead of to his father, or to Amanieu d'Albret, one of Edward's Gascon subjects. Edward can be forgiven for this last transparent suggestion, for the French on their side were even going so far as to seem unwilling to loosen their grip on the duchy at all. The English claimed that they had been perfectly ready to live up to their side of the agreement and had offered to turn their part of Gascony over by May 5, but that the bishop of Vicenza refused to take it because Philip had shown no signs of an equal

[8] C.P.R. (1292–1301), p. 394.   [9] Rymer, I, 903.

willingness to honor his word. A year later, when Girard was at the Curia and explained this to the pope, Boniface, with his customary courtesy, called him a liar to his face, but the English contention is borne out by a letter from the bishop, written June 1, 1299, and complaining of the hopelessness of waiting for Philip to act.

While his nephew was haggling at Paris, Othon took the opportunity to pay a flying visit to England. He was with Edward at Canterbury at the end of May,[10] and he could even look forward to the rare pleasure of sleeping under his own roof at his nearby manor of Sheen, although his enjoyment was marred by the discovery that other people had been doing the same thing. Edward had to issue a stiff warning that no one except the Prince of Wales was to stay there or to use it as a storage place for their belongings, since great damage had been done by people lodging in the houses of the manor.[11]

But even though his properties should suffer for it, there seemed to be no immediate chance of Othon's being anything but an absentee landlord, for naturally he was among the envoys chosen to represent the king at Montreuil. It was a most gorgeous embassy, one for show and not for use, since the hard work had already been done and nothing was left to do but arrange for the marriages of the French aunt and niece to the English father and son. It included the bishops of Winchester and Salisbury, the count of Savoy, who was to act as Edward's proxy in the betrothal ceremonies with Margaret of France, the earl of Lincoln, who was to represent the Prince of Wales, especially in regard to his marriage with Isabelle, the earls of Warwick and Pembroke, Othon, Geoffrey de Joinville, and Jean of Bar.[12] Later, when it appeared that the troublesome Gascon question would inevitably crop up, even at the cost of disturbing such joyful ceremonies, Girard

[10] *C.C.R.* (*1296–1302*), p. 308.
[11] *C.P.R.* (*1292–1301*), p. 418.   [12] Rymer, I, 904–5.

de Vuippens and Amanieu d'Albret were also included, although they do not seem to have contributed much, for the only mention of Gascony in the treaty of Montreuil was completely in Philip's favor, stating that if the marriage between the Prince of Wales and Isabelle did not take place the Gascon towns that were still in English hands would recognize the king of France as their suzerain. So far as the war went, the treaty merely stipulated that the truce of Tournai should be still further prolonged.

The magnificent ceremonies accompanying the betrothals were a hollow mockery to all the participants, who realized just how little had really been accomplished. The French were just as disgruntled as the English, for they had not gained Gascony even if their enemies had lost it, and while their great nobles doubtless hid the displeasure that they felt under the polite language of diplomacy, the more ribald among Flotte's little clerks vented theirs in scurrilous gibes at the English pretensions and in even more galling aspersions on their badly pronounced and ungrammatical French. Their unprintable parody of the treaty[13] shows that although Flotte's articulate nationalism may have been a novelty, *l'esprit gaulois* was already fully developed and, indeed, more than a century earlier, there is something very familiar in the mock humility with which the French are made to boast that, whereas the king of England has everything, "we in France have nothing but good bread, good wine, and *joie de vivre.*" There is something very familiar, too, in French appraisal of the English character. Edward's envoys may have originally stemmed from Normandy like Beauchamp and Lacy or from Geneva like the Joinvilles, they might actually be Poitevin like Valence or Vaudois like Othon and Girard, but their years in England had given to all of them that mentality that has always caused the logical and baffled Latin to accuse the English of perfidy: " 'Walecome' font doucement; Intus sunt pleni

[13] Printed, however, by G. Reynaud in *Romania*, XIV (1885), p. 280.

fraudibus." However, in this case, the joke, at least in part, was on their critics. The native English may have spoken a debased Norman-French, the Vaudois may have intoned their flat vowels with the singsong inflection peculiar to their native land, but whoever did the actual writing of the treaty had learned his mother tongue amid the vines and olives of the South and far from the misty skies and "bon bec" of the Île-de-France.

Most of the other envoys were kept busy during the rest of the summer with the ratification of the treaty and the carrying out of its terms, but Othon, back in England by August, was granted a respite. It is true that Edward did not permit him to remain completely idle; with John Droxford, the treasurer, he was appointed to look into the doings of some of the Frescobaldi bankers who, on their findings, were convicted of bringing into the country "pollards and crockards" in defiance of the new statute, *De Falsa Moneta*.[14] But in general his efforts seem to have been directed to restoring his own fortunes, badly shrunken after almost ten years of ceaseless traveling. He was granted twelve bucks from the royal forests,[15] the right of free warren on some of his Irish lands,[16] and, most remunerative of all, a Wednesday market and a yearly fair for the last two weeks in July at his manor of Acconagh in Tipperary.[17] It must be admitted that Othon was not a good landlord, and in receiving this last mark of royal favor he probably did not give a thought to the adverse effects that it might have on the spiritual well-being of his Irish tenants. But the question was one that preoccupied the hairsplitting preachers of the age, who even went so far as to distinguish between fairs and markets on moral grounds. The former were on the whole preferable; even the most strait-laced could not be blind to the advantage of bringing buyers

---

[14] *C.P.R.* (*1292–1301*), p. 430.   [16] *C. Ch. R.* (*1257–1300*), p. 479.

[15] *C.C.R.* (*1296–1302*), p. 264.   [17] *Idem.*

and sellers from far-off places to the isolated villages, and if there were disadvantages as well, still a fair was generally held only once a year. But a market was a different thing altogether. It was attended only by the villagers and their immediate neighbors, who week after week, since markets were almost always held on feast days, were tempted not only to miss the daily offices and sermons but also to disobey the Church's precept of hearing mass. Disregard for sacred things went even farther; the churchyard often afforded the only open space where booths could conveniently be set up, but even on that consecrated ground men could be heard swearing, "By God! It is not worth as much as that!" or "By God! I will not give so much for it!" There was also much heavy drinking, and perfidy and disloyalty as well, for the lord of the manor was often cheated of his just dues.[18]

This last consideration was probably the only one that worried Othon, but he had chosen his attorneys well, for most of them were fellow Savoyards who could be trusted to see that he was defrauded neither of his market dues nor of any of the other revenues accruing to him from the royal bounty. This last outburst of generosity was probably connected with the wedding of the sixty-one-year-old king to his twenty-year-old bride, which took place at Canterbury at the end of the summer, and it seems that at the same time Edward also recognized Othon's services by appointing him permanently to his Council, for after that date he is frequently mentioned as a member of that body and is also, for the first time in his life, summoned to Parliament and to do his military service in person against the Scots.[19]

But so long as the Gascon question remained unsettled, his new honors and obligations made remarkably little difference

[18] Humbert de Romans, "Sermon XCII, In Merchatis," quoted in Bede Jarrett, *Social Theories of the Middle Ages, 1200–1500*, p. 164.

[19] *The Parliamentary Writs and Writs of Military Summons*, I, 642; Rymer, I, 916–17.

to his way of life, and the final peace still seemed as far away as ever. The pope appears to have thought that once the marriages were arranged, the two kings, now so closely related, would come to an agreement by themselves, but as he told Girard de Vuippens in the summer of 1300, although he had planted, by decreeing a peace, and had watered "with the dew of marriage and espousals," God had not given the increase. Rishanger, the English chronicler, came nearer to the truth when he said that Edward was mistaken if he thought that Gascony was reconquered just because he was Philip's brother-in-law, and although the new queen, with youthful ardor, did her best to improve relations between her husband and her brother by bearing her first two sons within the next two years, the aging Boniface continued to play for time. He put off the date for making his decision on Gascony until Epiphany, 1302, and a request from Edward that he settle the question as quickly as possible only brought a papal blast against the English claims to Scotland. The truce of Tournai had expressly stated that Philip's allies did not include Balliol, and it was in return for that assurance that the English envoys to Rome in 1298 had sacrificed Count Guy of Flanders, but Flotte, having gained his point, had no intention of weakening his master's position. French influence was still strong at the Curia, and when the bishop of Vicenza came as papal legate to England he had insisted that Balliol be released and delivered to him, to be put, like so much else, in the hands of the pope. This had been done in July of 1299, in the presence of Amadée, Girard de Vuippens, and Jean of Bar: for once, Othon was not working with them, and he was probably in the Pays de Vaud, for in June he bought the village and all the territory of Suchy, some five miles from Yverdon, from Jean de Cossonay and his wife, Marguerite de Villars.[20] But in spite of the liberation of Balliol, Boniface, egged on by the French, wrote to Edward that

[20] Bruchet, *op. cit.*, No. 322.

Scotland had never belonged either to him or to his fore-
bears but had always been a fief of the Roman Church, proving his point by examples going back to the reign of Henry III
and the days of the Barons' War.

Edward was besieging Carvaerlock Castle when Archbishop
Winchelsey arrived there toward the end of June, 1299,
bearing the papal bull, and he took the castle and made his
plans for granting the defeated enemy a truce at the request
of Philip—"a friend and amiable compositor but not the ally
of the Scots," as he was careful to point out—and only then
summoned a parliament to meet at Lincoln on January 1,
1301, to discuss the papal claims. He decided to use every
tool at his disposal; he asked the abbeys and cathedral chapters of England to look into the matter and also requested
the universities of Oxford and Cambridge to have lawyers
ready to send to Lincoln when the parliament met there.

There was a university in Rome, too, recently established by
Boniface himself, but it soon became apparent that it had not
had time to develop the great tradition of historical research that
was already well established at the older foundations. If any
body of men enjoyed themselves during the next two troubled
years, it was the monastic historians and the scholars of the two
universities—exception being made for those of Balliol College,
torn between their professional love for abstract truth and
loyalty to the family of their founder—as they delved into the
exceptionally original sources stored up in their libraries and
muniment rooms. Not for them were the slight proofs afforded
by less than a generation of history: they went back to the
very beginnings. Naturally, like all such projects, this one
took far longer than had been expected, and the English
barons meeting at the Parliament of Lincoln had already
drawn up their own refutation of the papal claims before
Rishanger had all his materials on hand and could start work
on the final draft. But when the document was completed,
it was a masterpiece, a standing reproach to the slipshod

scholars of Rome and irrefutable proof of English suzerainty over Scotland.

> In the days of Eli and Samuel the prophets, a certain strenuous and famous man, Brutus by name, of the race of the Trojans, after the fall of the city of Troy, with many nobles of the Trojans, landed on a certain island then called Albion, inhabited by giants.

So it opened, and generation by generation and reign by reign, it went on to back up its arguments with such telling facts as that Anselm of Scotland had carried King Arthur's sword before him at a great feast held in the city of London, that Athelstane had given Constantine the Scottish crown with the words, "It is more glorious to make a king than to be one," and that St. John of Beverly had proved by a miracle the validity of the English claims.

But events, as so often happens, refused to wait upon the painstaking labors of the historians, and long before May, 1301, when Rishanger finished his treatise, Edward found it necessary to send another embassy to Rome. He was more than ever anxious to have the Gascon question settled and the French war over and done with, for neither at home nor abroad did the situation show any signs of improvement. His foreign policy was still hampered by the tax-ridden English, who had never ceased to clamor for renewed confirmations of the Charters and for the perambulations of the forests, and all the subsidies that they grudgingly allowed him had to go toward the expenses of the Scottish war. His son-in-law, the count of Bar, was already veering toward the French alliance, and he could send neither men nor money to help the Flemings, even when, on the expiration of the truce of Tournai in January, 1300, French troops under Charles of Valois occupied Douai. Count Guy, after making one more fruitless appeal to his former ally, was forced to put himself and his three sons at the mercy of the king of France.

In 1300 the Scots had sent envoys to Rome to lay their side

of the question before the pope, and on April 15 Edward hastened to appoint an embassy that would counteract the Scottish influence at the Curia and press once again for a speedy decision on Gascony. It was very different from the glittering mission that had gone to Montreuil; the only great name was that of the bishop of Winchester, and the men under him were almost all clerks, chosen for their competence and not for their rank—Brother William Gainsborough of the Friars Minor, Raimond-Arnaud de la Rame, and Pierre-Aimeri de St.-Sever. The only laymen were Geoffrey de Joinville and Geoffrey Russell. Better men could not have been found for arguing day after hot day with their Roman counterparts on the rights and wrongs of appeals to the Parlement of Paris, but changing circumstances made Edward decide to send some of his greater diplomats as well.

The question of the tenth had arisen once again. Boniface needed the money badly for his crusade against the Colonna and their Ghibelline and Sicilian allies, and fate played into his hands when, on December 23, 1299, the Mongol troops inflicted a savage defeat on the Saracens at the battle of Hims. The pope's letter to Edward, announcing the victory, was written in a bubbling style quite different from that usually employed by the papal chancery, which was more apt to punctuate its correspondence with a melancholy sprinkling of *eheu*'s and *proh dolor*'s: "Great news, my dearest son, joyful news, news certainly to be accompanied with especial rejoicing!" Boniface never lost an opportunity to taunt the kings of Europe for their lack of crusading zeal, and when several noble ladies of Genoa asked papal permission to equip a fleet and sail themselves for the Holy Land, both he and his clerks enjoyed the opening that it gave them to show his scorn and their mastery of invective and allusion:

> O miracles! O prodigies! The women outstrip their
> husbands in going to the help of the said land. It is they who,
> wrapped in the garments of the sun, tread under foot the

temporal things signified by the moon. The kings and princes of the world, even when urged, refuse their aid; weak women, unasked, offer themselves instead.

In writing to Edward, Boniface came more directly to the point. He went on to hint broadly that now it was up to the king to complete the conquest of the Holy Land, but it is possible that some of his jubilation was due to his at last having an unimpeachable reason for calling in the sums amassed by the collectors of the tenth, for all winter and spring orders streamed out to them, in England, in France, in Germany, to send the money in their possession down to Rome.

English compliance with this request would have reduced Edward to bankruptcy. Ten years earlier, to pay the ransom of Charles of Salerno, he had been granted a substantial advance from the English tenth, which he had never found it convenient to refund—nor, to be sure, had Charles—and now, when his financial situation was blacker than ever, Boniface was not only demanding the entire tenth but also reminding the king that the annual tribute was 11,000 marks in arrears. Edward needed his most experienced and impressive diplomats to extricate him from his dangerous position, and on September 26, 1300, he wrote to Boniface that in addition to his earlier envoys he was also sending to Rome the count of Savoy, the earl of Lincoln, Othon, Hugh Despenser, Amanieu d'Albret, and John Berwick, with powers to correct, or to accept and confirm, whatever terms might be agreed on.[21]

Othon had gone back to the Pays de Vaud after Edward's marriage and was there on January 31 and February 29, 1300, to put his seal to agreements between Bishop Guillaume and his allies in the war against Louis of Savoy. Most of these were members of his own widespread family, lords of the small castles and villages lying along the slopes of the Jura and scattered over the Gros de Vaud, but they also included Count Amadée of

[21] Rymer, I, 922–23.

Geneva, a lifelong rival of the House of Savoy, and Edward's ally, Gautier de Montfaucon.[22] Pierre de Champvent, the bishop's brother, had been unable or unwilling to leave England and was represented by a deputy, but he did not have to wait long for a firsthand account of the meeting, for Othon was back in England by the beginning of April. He spent the next few months in attendance on the king and, as usual, in looking after the affairs of his friends. Wherever he went, men of all classes and all countries asked him to use his influence to forward their interests. Guy of Flanders wanted to see justice done to one of his merchants who had been cheated by an Englishman;[23] Earl Thomas of Lancaster and the prior of the Carmelites at York needed some oaks fit for timber from the royal forests;[24] even Queen Margaret, who had promised to ask her husband to return some of the sequestrated French properties to the archbishop of Rouen, found it easier to do so through Othon.[25] Italian bankers who could not collect on their bills,[26] or who were accused of violating the currency regulations,[27] Dover boatmen in trouble with the authorities over a rented house,[28] old servants,[29] and men fined for killing the king's deer[30] or outlawed for killing the king's subjects,[31] all turned to him for a way out of their difficulties.

At the same time, there were always the various odd jobs that Edward found for him to do, such as auditing the accounts of Bishop Langton. Before reaching his present eminence, Walter Langton had been Keeper of the Wardrobe, but in the press of affairs he had forgotten to hand in his accounts to the treasurer, and they were now five years over-

[22] Forel (ed.), *Régeste*, Nos. 2297, 2298.   [23] A.C., XXX, 75.

[24] *C.C.R. (1296–1302)*, pp. 341, 355.   [25] *C.P.R. (1292–1301)*, p. 343.

[26] A.C., XXX, 101; transcribed in Kingsford, *op. cit.*, pp. 189–90.

[27] *C.P.R. (1292–1301)*, pp. 504–5.

[28] A.C., XXXI, 5; in Kingsford, p. 191.   [30] *C.P.R. (1292–1301)*, p. 501.

[29] *Ibid.*, XXIX, 101.   [31] *Ibid.*, p. 446.

due. The treasurer could no longer audit them, for Langton now filled that position as well as his double bishopric of Coventry and Lichfield, and a commission headed by John Langton, bishop of Chichester and chancellor, was appointed to look into them. When the audit was completed, the chancellor, Walter Beauchamp, Steward of the Household, and Othon had the pleasant job of reporting to the Exchequer that their friend's account showed a surplus, or in the exultant language of the Middle Ages, which believed in celebrating that joyful rarity with a suitable wealth of syllables, a "superplusagium."[32]

When Othon and the others did arrive in Rome that autumn, it was to find Girard de Vuippens and his associates on the earlier embassy with their tempers exacerbated by several months of papal conversation. Boniface was still continuing his tactics of blowing now hot, now cold—"à la fie dures, à la fie moles," as the three counts of Flanders had described his words to their father. At one moment he was telling the English that Edward—although he had his faults; everybody had *some,* the pope kindly pointed out—was still the best of the European monarchs; at another, he was inveighing against the king for allying himself with the emperor and with the Burgundians and for going to the help of Count Guy. He would not have criticized him had he led an expedition for the reconquest of Gascony, but Flanders, where his ancestors had never possessed any rights, was a completely different matter. But the patience of the English gained them one diplomatic victory. Although nothing was done about the war except a further prolongation of the truce of Tournai until Epiphany, 1302, Boniface allowed Edward to keep all the money that had been advanced to him from the tenth.

Othon had brought with him a golden cup worth £56 3s. 4d. as a present to the papal Master of Requests for having expedited the king's business—certainly an example of wishful

---

[32] Pipe Roll, 27 Ed. I, m. 21: in Tout, *op. cit.*, II, 91 and n. 2.

thinking on the part of the English—and also gifts amounting to £201 6s. 8d. for the various papal notaries.[33] Edward's officials were most scrupulous in paying him for these, once he got home, but they were equally careful to withhold his salary for the forty days that he spent in "making his pilgrimage."[34] For this was the Holy Year, the Great Jubilee, the climax of Boniface's career, when so many pilgrims thronged into Rome that traffic regulations had to be instituted on the Ponte del Castel Sant'Angelo, so that those going to visit the tomb of St. Peter kept to one side of the bridge and those returning to the other. Othon could gain many advantages for himself in the next world during the forty days that he spent in visiting the basilicas; he could also gain more immediate favors for his nephews in this, and two of them, Thibaut and Othon de Grandson, were given dispensations to hold plural benefices at the request of their indulgent uncle.[35] He may also have been partly responsible for the even greater honor soon to be bestowed upon one of his family. In March, 1301, while the embassy was still at the Curia, Guillaume de Champvent died, and in the following year Boniface ratified the election of Girard de Vuippens, Edward's clerk and Othon's nephew and fellow ambassador, as the new bishop of Lausanne. It was probably also at this time that Othon made arrangements for the union of the priory of Montfavres with that of St.-Jean de Grandson and for the transfer of thirteen monks to the latter foundation, which was agreed to by the abbot of La Chaise-Dieu in the following September.[36]

As well as acting for Edward and seeing to his own salvation, Othon, during his stay in Rome, also took a hand in the affairs of Count Amadée. The count's nephew, Philippe, who ruled over the Savoyard territories south of the Alps, was to marry Isabelle de Villehardouin, heiress of the principality

[33] B.M. Add. MS, 9966a.

[34] *Idem.*

[35] *C. Pap. R. (1198–1304)*, p. 594.

[36] A.C.V., Grandson, C IXᵃ 2.

1 8 4

of Achaea. She was no longer in her first youth, for before her father's death in 1278 she was already married to Philippe of Anjou, one of the sons of Charles of Sicily; she was now the widow of Florence of Hainault, but through her first marriage the Angevins still had claims on her principality. King Charles II had come to Rome to arrange matters. On February 23, 1301, after she married "with a certain ring that the lord king drew from his own finger," he invested Philippe with Achaea, for which the latter did proper homage, "save and except for the homage and fealty done by the said Philippe of Savoy for the land of Piedmont to the illustrious Amadée, count of Savoy and marquis in Italy." Othon was one of the witnesses of the investiture;[37] another, more surprisingly, was Ruggiero da Loria, now the honored subject of a king whom he had once taken prisoner.

Othon's term as ambassador ended officially when he reached Savoy on May 31, 1301, and it was Girard de Vuippens who brought Edward the glad news about the moneys from the tenth. But Boniface was incapable of granting favors gracefully, and his letter to the king was calculated to dispel any good feelings aroused by the "munificence" of which Edward spoke so warmly. The hackneyed tag is inescapable; if the gods, bent on the destruction of Boniface, had not already made him mad, they had nevertheless, using the glories of the Jubilee as their tool, succeeded in depriving him of any shred of tact or even common sense that he might ever have possessed. In answer to Edward's repeated requests that he bring the war with France to an end, the pope retorted that it was all the king's fault that peace had not yet been made, since he despised eternal joys for those that were fleeting and preferred his transitory inheritance to a perpetual one. Specifically, he persisted in his obstinate claim to those fragments (*particulas*) of the kingdom of France. They were

[37] Samuel Guichenon, *Histoire généalogique de la royale maison de Savoie,* II, 103–4.

such little bits (*tam modica*) anyway, and Philip, with youthful fervor, was led astray by the seduction of evil counselors and the malice of flatterers; certainly Edward, who was more mature, more circumspect, and more moderate, could without any reflection on himself content the younger man, until God, who corrects and reforms errors, should see fit to make them both of better counsel, bringing forth more helpful fruits.

Edward's Plantagenet temper had not improved with age, and Othon could count himself fortunate that when this letter reached the king he was safely employed with his own affairs far away in the Pays de Vaud. On July 5, 1300, at Ouchy, the port of Lausanne, Amadée had finally drawn up a peace settlement satisfactory both to his brother and to Bishop Guillaume and his allies,[38] and Othon spent several months at home during the summer of 1301 to see that the provisions of the treaty in regard to the Grandson lands were carried out. His dealings were mainly with the little town of Yverdon, which lies where the waters of the Thiele empty into the southern tip of Lac Neuchâtel only a few miles from Grandson itself, but which in the thirteenth and fourteenth centuries belonged to Savoy and as such had been at war with its northern neighbor. The men of Yverdon had taken prisoner Jean Sautier, Othon's castellan, and some of the troops fighting under him, and they were now to be set free to return to their native villages, at whose towers they had looked longingly during the months of their captivity. There were also reparations to be collected from Louis of Savoy, who in some unstated manner connected with the mill gates of Yverdon had damaged the nearby fields belonging to the lord of Grandson.[39] For Othon, after his years of wrangling over European affairs in Paris and Rome, it must have been a delight to spend a summer in his own castle, acting for him-

[38] Given in Charrière, *Recherches sur les sires de Cossonay et sur ceux de Prangins issus de leur famille*, No. 16. The document has since disappeared.

[39] *Idem.*

self and not for the king of England, subject only to the assured approval of his overlord and friend, the count of Savoy.

But in November he was already back in England,[40] where it looked as though the treadmill pattern of his life were to start all over again, for in August he had been appointed once more with Walter Langton, Amadée, and Girard de Vuippens to go on yet another embassy to Rome.[41] Two months later the other three, without Othon but with the addition of Lacy and John Berwick, were appointed as plenipotentiaries to France and also to make a truce with the Scots. But when the embassy crossed the Channel on February 14, 1302,[42] Othon went with them to Paris instead of continuing on to Rome. He and Amadée had firmly refused to undertake another mission to the Curia. Edward's letter to the pope, announcing his distress at the news, merely says that they had both given many notable and convincing reasons for excusing themselves, even though he had repeatedly sent messengers asking them to reconsider, since they knew more about the business than anyone else,[43] and it was not written until March 5, three weeks after the embassy had sailed. We do not even know whether Othon told the king of his decision before he left Windsor on February 3,[44] still less what his reasons for making it may have been. However, from Edward's reluctance to be more explicit with Boniface, it is quite possible that both Othon and Amadée had realized the hopelessness of waiting for a papal decision and had convinced the king that their time would be better spent in negotiating directly with the French.

The special powers that they had exercised on most of the other embassies were transferred to Langton and Girard de Vuippens, but as usual they returned from Rome without

[40] Stevenson, *op. cit.*, No. 584.

[41] Rymer, I, 935.

[42] *Annales Londonienses*, p. 129.

[43] Rymer, I, 939.

[44] B.M. Add. MS, 8835.

having accomplished anything definite. Girard was hardly more fortunate in his attempt to straighten out the enmities that were still boiling in his new diocese as an aftermath of the Vaudois war. He had asked the pope to grant a dispensation for the marriage of his cousin, Guillemette d'Oron, to a certain Jean d'Everdes, to end the discord between their two families, and this was granted on March 19, 1302, but, like many middle-aged bachelors, he seems to have had difficulty in distinguishing between his younger relatives, for in April, 1303, Boniface had to rescind the earlier dispensation and issue another, since it appeared that it was not Guillemette but her sister, Amphélisie, whom Jean wished to marry. Girard's efforts on behalf of his uncle were more successful, for it was at that time that Boniface wrote to the papal collectors in England, ordering them to pay to Othon immediately the grant of 3,000 marks from the tenth for his crusading expenses, promised to him so long ago and so long delayed.

From February, 1302, to May, 1303, it is almost impossible to keep track of Othon's goings and comings, for he was almost constantly employed on embassies to Paris and came home to report on them only to be sent off once again.[45] But at last there was some hope that the end was in sight, for it was now Philip's turn to be in difficulties. In December, 1301, Boniface had issued the bull, *Ausculta Fili*, rebuking Philip for all his sins, very much in the manner of a nursery governess, and calling for a synod of the Gallican clergy to meet at Rome in November, 1302, to discuss the reform of the realm, as he put it in his usual ingratiating fashion. The only bishops who obeyed the papal summons were those of Gascony, Burgundy, Brittany, and Anjou, for the rest backed up their king, and when the synod did meet there were only thirty-nine Frenchmen present to hear Boniface, in the bull *Unam Sanctam*, enunciate such an uncompromising statement of papal claims that it left Philip no alternative but to submit

[45] Rymer, I, 940 (April 25), 942 (August 15), 945 (October 29).

188

unconditionally or to fight them with every means at his disposal. To the north he was also suffering reverses. On March 17, 1302, the Flemings rose against their conquerors as the Palermitans had done seventeen years earlier, and the Matins of Bruges, although on a smaller scale than the Sicilian Vespers, threatened just as much trouble for the French. The threat was fulfilled in July, when the Flemish militia, watching the chivalry of France leave the field of Courtrai at a dead run, christened their victory "The Battle of the Spurs."

With all these troubles on his hands, Philip was now as eager as Edward to put an end to the difficulties between them, even if it meant relinquishing Gascony, and on March 22, 1303, the bishop of Winchester, Amadée, Lacy, and Othon were appointed on their final embassy to France.[46] They had accomplished so much on their former missions during the last year that when the appointment was made all of them except Pontissara were already in Gascony, preparing for its restoration to English sovereignty, but by April they had all arrived in Paris.

Louis II of Savoy, who had succeeded his father as lord of Vaud, was there as well, for the Savoyards also had their own little war to consider, and on April 27 he and Othon put their seals to the marriage contract between his daughter, Blanche, and Pierre, the son of Jacques de Grandson, which brought the inconclusive Vaudois hostilities to a close. Like all such documents, it dealt mainly with money and lands, and, in addition, Othon promised to make Pierre his heir and to bequeath to him all his English holdings as well as his castle of Grandson. But a final clause was added that seems to show that Othon, at least, had some consideration for the bride's feelings. Making no mention of his nephew's wishes in the matter, he stipulated that if, after his death, Blanche preferred Grandson to her husband's castle of Belmont, she should go there to live.[47]

[46] Rymer, I, 950.   [47] *Minutes of Evidence*, p. 99.

A few weeks later, on May 20, the French and English plenipotentiaries concluded an offensive and defensive alliance between their two kings, and on the same day Lacy did homage for Gascony in Edward's name and took seizin of the duchy. The English diplomats had been outmaneuvered time and time again by the French; time and time again, news of Welsh or Scottish risings and of baronial or clerical opposition at home, of broken alliances and papal equivocations abroad, had undone the patient work of months. But in the end they could congratulate themselves on having won at least the initial victory. The war would not be technically over until the last claims and counterclaims were satisfied, and the more experienced among them must have realized how much wrangling that would still entail. But if they had gained little, they had lost nothing, and after ten years Gascony was once again in English hands.

"Altre chose vous diroms," [dit] *le pape as Fraunceis,*
"qe les Gascoigns ne voudroient mie estre du tut sans
meen [seig]*nurie le Roi Dengleterre sans* [soutz?]
le sovereinte de Rois de France. Ben poet estre
par aventure qe ascunes persones le voudroient par ascune
singulere affeccioun, mais jeo vous parle de [co]*mun.*
Car tele est la manere de soutzmis qi voillent
einsi avoir plusors seignurs qil ne puissent mie
moult estre greveez par un."

Report of the English ambassadors, 1301

viii. Gascony

That Gascony was once again in English hands even the
reluctant lawyers of the Parlement of Paris could not deny, but
the three men who left for the south within a fortnight after
the treaty was sealed knew only too well that the Gascons,
whose character had been so neatly summed up by Pope
Boniface, were in the habit of using legal documents of all
kinds merely as springboards from which to dive into the
sea of troubles that was their natural habitat. Othon and
Amadée of Savoy, to whom was intrusted the responsibility
for taking seizin of all the places that were to be restored to
Edward,[1] and Lacy, who went with them, had all had previous experience of Gascon affairs, even before their few

---

[1] *R.G.*, III, No. 4589.

weeks' stay there during the late winter and early spring of 1303, when they had made a beginning on the job that lay ahead of them and had discovered how many new obstacles they would have to overcome in addition to the ebullient but familiar and unchanging Gascon temperament.

It is true that the main difficulty in their way was also a familiar one, but by 1303 Edward's finances, always the weakest point in his administration, were in a state of such complete confusion that Langton, the treasurer, and Droxford, the keeper of the Wardrobe, were reduced to robbing Peter to pay Paul, for every time that they set aside funds for the settlement of one of the king's debts it meant that they were taking the money away from someone else who had an equally good claim to it. The long-drawn-out French war, with its fruitless but expensive expedition to Flanders, had been an enormous drain on the king's resources, already burdened by the yearly campaigns across the Border, and it now looked as though peace might prove to be just as costly, for his newly recovered Gascon subjects were clamoring for money, and he could not afford to alienate them by refusing prompt payment of all that he owed both to communities and to individuals. The former debts were almost all for direct loans made to him during the war; the latter included both payments of back wages and compensation for damages suffered in the actual fighting. Of the first, his debt to Bayonne was the largest; the Bayonnais had lent him the huge sum of £45,763 14s. 1½d.—the penny-halfpenny gives a convincing touch of verisimilitude—and he was responsible as well for the £2,000 that they had advanced to John of Brittany while he had been in command of the English troops. The money owing to individuals was for more varied reasons, and some of the king's creditors were as hard up as he was himself. Guillaume de Soe, who had been bailiff of the Île d'Oléron, had not been paid either for his services or for the grain and wine that he had had to buy, but as late as 1305 he was still begging for the last twenty pounds owing to him so that he could go home, since it would be honorable neither to himself nor to the king if he returned as he was. Othon and Lacy, who bore the main burden of the Gascon mission, since Amadée, involved again in his perennial quarrel with the dauphin of the Viennois, was frequently absent, satisfied as many of these creditors as possible[2] and then turned to the still more complicated question of war indemnities. Even the Gascons who stayed loyal to Edward had done so at a price, and they now demanded satisfaction; others put in their claims for property lost, damaged, or requisitioned during the fighting. Many of these claims, as might be expected in that region, were for wines, but an item of almost equal importance was horses. A far more differentiated lot than their owners, the great chargers canter by, black, and sorrel, and dapple-gray; some with their legs fired (*coctis*), a bright bay with a darker star on his forehead, and one described by an absent-minded clerk as "bay, with one eye and four white forefeet."

Even during the war Edward had done his best to send help to the Gascons. He had distributed food to the people of Blaye and of Bourg-sur-Mer and, knowing the temper of the Gascon ladies, had spent £409 13s. 4d. for sixty cloths of different colors to make them dresses according to their state. He had pawned some of his own jewels for £2,520 and now, by the agreements reached at Paris, he was free to collect if he could all the debts that had been owing to him in Gascony before the war and was also promised that £900 still due to him by the terms of an earlier treaty would be paid to him by the French. But this was only a drop in the bucket, and he had to turn elsewhere, for even one of his greatest sources of revenue, the export duty on wools, hides, and fells, had already been pledged, as long ago as 1299, to the Bayonnais, who were to keep it until his debt to them

2 *R.G.*, III, Nos. 4794, 4939.

should be completely paid off. In these straits, the triennial tenth granted to him by Boniface was his salvation, and almost as soon as Girard de Vuippens had brought him the joyful news enormous loans were made against it.

And there were always the obliging Italian bankers. Obliging, and discreet as well, at least if they followed the suggestions laid down for them by one of their number, Giovanni de' Frescobaldi. Being a Florentine of his day, he embodied his precepts in a sonnet, and although it is not one of the more sublime examples of the *dolce stil nuovo*, starting as it does with the unfortunate first line, "Memorandum for anyone crossing to England," no exception can be taken to it as a piece of sound business advice.

> Wear quiet clothes, be humble; look rather stupid but act
> craftily. Spend generously so that you do not seem mean,
> pay your bills as you go, and buy things up ahead of
> time if it seems advantageous. As for collecting your debts,
> make your request nicely, and explain that you are compelled
> to do so only by extreme need. Do not get into trouble
> nor ask unnecessary questions, do not get involved with
> courtiers, stay on good terms with the other Florentines,
> and be sure to lock your doors, just in case.

Perhaps some of the untraveled brothers in the English monasteries took at face value the dowdy, well-spoken merchants who came to buy their wools and to collect the money stored up from the tenth, but a man like Othon was not so easily deceived. He had seen the Frescobaldi palaces across the Arno from Santa Trinità, which were so magnificent that Charles of Valois made them his headquarters while he was in Florence, as thirty years earlier Gregory X and the Emperor Baldwin had stayed with the rival family of the Mozzi, and he knew, too, that once out of England the Frescobaldi were more than bankers, that they were fighters, politicians, and builders as well. In fact, remembering Florence as he had last seen it, with the new churches and palaces rising in all parts of the town, he must have had a very shrewd idea of where a great part of the money for all that activity came from. As Christians, the bankers of course could take no interest on their loans, but it was always possible to doctor the accounts a little or to claim extra for the losses that they incurred when these loans were not promptly repaid. A casuist might have argued that last point, but Edward was in no position to haggle. Almost as soon as Othon reached Gascony, he and Lacy handed over to the Ballardi of Lucca the Great Customs on the Bordeaux wines,[3] while in England the customs on wool, already pledged to the Bayonnais for years to come, were to be given to the Frescobaldi, once the former were satisfied, to be held by them until they had recovered all their debts as well as an extra £10,000 to repay them for their losses. Othon had a personal interest in the Italian loans as well, for twice at least the payment of his wages for the work in Gascony and later for an embassy to the Curia had depended on the complaisance of the Florentines.[4] Once, they attempted to defraud him of a thousand marks, and a merchant of the Mozzi was sent to the Tower as he was about to leave England with the money.[5] This was an unfortunate habit of some of the smaller banks; although the Frescobaldi seem always to have been solvent enough to afford the luxury of acting honestly, the Pulci agents in 1306 absconded with such large sums that Edward was forced to write to the Signoria to have them and their ill-gotten gains sent back to England.

Financial worries, both his own and the king's, overshadowed everything that Othon had to do in Gascony, but even so, they were only one part of his job. After ten years during which most of the duchy had been occupied by the French while the remainder had been the scene of intermittent fighting, almost the whole administration had to be reorganized. In addition to making new appointments, he and Lacy also had to disentangle

---

[3] *Ibid.*, introduction, p. xcvii and n. 3.

[4] *Ibid.*, III, No. 4593; Rymer, I, 1014.   [5] *C.C.R.* (1302–07), p. 259.

innumerable claims and counterclaims dealing with the many lands and castles that had changed hands during the war. In Gascony, this would have been an arduous business even under normal conditions, but it was now made doubly difficult, and at times almost impossible, for all the Gascon records kept at Bordeaux had disappeared. In the early days of the war, Robert Leisseth, the constable, had put them all for greater safety in the Dominican monastery there, and later, when he was a prisoner in Paris and heard how badly things were going for the English, he managed to get word to his lieutenant to send them to London. The ship that was to take them was commandeered to guard the Île d'Oléron, but the crew mutinied when their wages were not forthcoming and left their post, having first deposited the records with the Franciscans on the island. Oléron was later captured by the French, and the records disappeared, as well as Leisseth's own books, "which he would not have lost for a hundred pounds sterling." Until copies could be made from the originals in England, Othon and Lacy had nothing to go on except the word of one Gascon against that of another, and they went ahead with their decisions as best they could. Many of their appointments were combined with the payment of debts, and an official position would be given to a man to whom the king owed money, with the hope, no doubt, that somehow or other he would recoup his losses out of the perquisites of his office.[6] Others were mere routine: a controller was named for Bordeaux,[7] a lieutenant for the seneschal of the Agenais,[8] and a member of the Council of Gascony;[9] governors of castles,[10] bailiffs,[11] king's clerks,[12] and a keeper of the royal forests.[13]

[6] This seems to have been true in the case of Guillaume de Soe; *C.P.R.* (*1301–07*), p. 58.

[7] *R.G.*, III, No. 4700.

[8] *Ibid.*, No. 4736.

[9] D.D. Exch. E 30, No. 1712.

[10] *R.G.*, III, No. 4841; *C.P.R.* (*1301–07*), p. 58.

[11] *R.G.*, III, No. 4865.

[12] *Ibid.*, No. 4732.

[13] *Ibid.*, No. 4757.

The various claims to which they had to listen were kept from being monotonous by their infinite ingenuity. Guillaume de "Cortosia" had been robbed of a hundred tuns of wine,[14] and Guitard de Laporte wanted permission to bear arms, as he was being pursued by mortal enemies.[15] An enterprising gentleman, Bertrand de Ravignan, sire de Buzet, wanted letters patent stating that all crimes and "excesses" committed by the king's men during the war should be pardoned. The letters were granted on the advice of Othon and Lacy,[16] who must, however, have been perfectly well aware that Ravignan's request was not quite so altruistic as it sounded, for earlier in his career he had already received a pardon for breaking into and robbing his own parish church.

A more complicated matter was that of the town of Castillonès, which before the war had been under divided jurisdiction, five or six parishes being administered by the English seneschal of the Agenais and eighteen by the French seneschal of Périgord. This arrangement, so satisfactory to the Gascon mind, had been upset by the treaty, which gave the whole town to the English, although still leaving it split between their two seneschalries. The citizens were now demanding to be united under the seneschal of Périgord. John Hastings, the seneschal of all Gascony, was ordered by Othon and Lacy to go to Castillonès and investigate the matter on the spot, but although he assembled the other two seneschals with their councils, the consuls of the town, and forty "good men," no one could come to any decision, and the question was referred to the king, who granted the first part of the request but decreed that the town should form part of the Agenais.[17]

Amadée, Lacy, and Othon were also responsible for receiving back into the royal favor those Gascons who had fought against

---

[14] *Ibid.*, No. 4915.   [15] *Archives historiques de la Gironde*, I, No. 21.

[16] *R.G.*, III, No. 4828.

[17] *R.G.*, III, introduction, p. lxxx and n. 10. See *The Gascon Calendar of 1322* (ed. G. P. Cuttino), No. 82.

Edward during the war, chief of whom were Marguerite, comtesse de Foix and vicomtesse de Béarn, and her thrice-widowed sister, Constance, vicomtesse de Marsan. Their father, Gaston de Béarn, had died in 1290, leaving his lands and his temper to be inherited by his four daughters, but the lion's share of both went to Marguerite and Constance. The property settlements made during his lifetime had done nothing to improve relations between the four sisters, for he was constantly changing his mind and dispossessing one in favor of the others. As soon as he died, a war broke out between Bertrand d'Armagnac, the son of his third daughter, Mathe, and Marguerite de Foix, which was waged on the latter's side first by her husband, Roger-Bernard, and after he died, by their son, Gaston. It had started in a truly Gascon manner by Bertrand's challenging his uncle by marriage to a duel, and it was to keep on for years, being interrupted only when something more exciting turned up to distract the attention of the contestants. One such respite was provided by the Anglo-French war, in which the comte de Foix had commanded some of Philip's troops in Gascony, but after the truce of Vyves-St. Bavon he started once again to build up alliances against his nephew and enemy, Bertrand d'Armagnac. The whole family was involved, for Constance was siding with her sister Marguerite, and in January, 1304, when the king of France held a great parliament at Toulouse, they were all summoned to put in an appearance so that he might bring their quarrel to an end once and for all. Lacy, Amadée, and Othon were there as well, for Philip consulted with them and with his own councilors before handing down his decision.[18] Toulouse, glowing rose-red in the southern winter sunlight, provided a setting worthy of the magnificent assemblage; the king was robed in cloth of gold over purple and gold brocade, sprinkled with the fleur-de-lis, the princes of the blood wore purple cloth of gold, and the constable of France, who bore the king's sword before him, outshone

[18] Claude Devic and Jean Vaissette, *Histoire générale de Languedoc*, IX, 262.

them all, in his robe of state, divided by strips of gold into blue and red squares with the fleur-de-lis in the center of each one. But so far as ending the Foix-Armagnac war was concerned, this glittering mountain brought forth a very small mouse, for all that was decided was that the quarreling family should make peace and obey the new ordinance that once again forbade private warfare. Philip can have had little hope that this would pacify the contentious offspring of Gaston de Béarn, and he was undoubtedly very much relieved when Marguerite did homage to Edward's three lieutenants,[19] for it meant that she would now devote herself to plaguing the English officials instead of the French. In fact, her demands and complaints soon became so tiresome that Edward seems to have lost his patience, for at one point he wrote to John Havering saying that he wished to hear no more about the matter.

Constance was not received back into the royal favor until the following September and then only at the request of Amanieu d'Albret. When she had taken up arms against Edward, her English lands had been granted to Albret, and by this move he lost them. This seems to argue a certain magnanimity of character on his part; but he was not a Gascon for nothing. Six months later, in June, 1305, he became involved in a war with the sire de Caumont that set off a whole series of little struggles between their inflammable fellow countrymen. Havering led a small army from Bordeaux to Casteljaloux, but the whole thing ended only when Caumont was safely imprisoned at La Réole and Albret, Edward's trusted ambassador, in the castle of Bordeaux.

No sooner had that rising been suppressed than Havering got news that Gaston de Foix had once again invaded the county of Armagnac. This second war could not have come at a worse moment for the seneschal, since the newly elected pope, Clement V, was even then in Bordeaux, the city of which he had been archbishop until his elevation to the papacy on June 5,

19 *R.G.*, III, No. 4599.

1305. Othon had been in the thick of Gascon affairs in the autumn of 1303, when the first shocking reports came from Rome that Boniface VIII had been arrested in his palace at Anagni by Sciarra Colonna and Guillaume de Nogaret, who had been Pierre Flotte's right-hand man and was now his successor, and that although the pope's fellow townsmen had quickly rescued him, he had died of rage and heartbreak a few weeks later. Hard on the heels of the first messengers came others to announce that after an unusually short conclave, lasting for only ten days, Boniface had been succeeded by a Dominican, Cardinal Boccasini, who had taken the name of Benedict XI. Othon had been named as a member of the embassy that was to be sent to congratulate the new pope,[20] but before he could leave for Rome, Benedict died, after a pontificate of only nine months.

Although Othon's Gascon mission was officially ended on June 30, 1304, two days after his appointment to the embassy, he seems to have stayed on at Bordeaux, for his wages were paid to his chaplain at Berwick-on-Tweed the following August,[21] and there is no mention of his having returned to England. While in Gascony, he is mentioned as a member of the king's Council, but he was probably kept there chiefly so as to be in readiness to start on his embassy to the Curia as soon as the next pope was elected. This meant a wait of nearly a year, for the cardinals had recovered from the shock that had made them proceed so expeditiously to the election of Benedict, and the conclave was once again rent by quarrels between French and Italians, Black Guelphs and White, Colonna and Caetani. It was not until June, 1305, that they all agreed on Cardinal Bertrand de Got, a choice acceptable to all parties, for as a Gascon he stood comparatively aloof from the local aspects of the Italian quarrels, and where they were colored by sympathy or antipathy to the French he could claim to be

[20] Rymer, I, 964.   [21] B.M. Add. MS, 8835.

impartial, for although he was Edward's subject he was at the same time on very friendly terms with Philip the Fair.

He had not attended that conclave that elected him and was at Lusignan on June 23 when the messengers from Rome arrived. Shortly afterward he set out to revisit his old archiepiscopal see. When Havering heard that he was coming into the duchy, he summoned the Council and on their advice decided to send a deputation to meet him at the frontier and to offer him service and gifts in Edward's name. This entailed a great deal of expense, for not only was there food and wine to be bought for all the people who would accompany him, presents for the various ecclesiastics, and a gold crucifix with a gold and crystal corpus for the pope himself, but also the delegates must be suitably appareled. Havering's first expense seems to have been for four pieces of cloth, two of "cameline" and two striped, and two lengths of green "sindon" for linings, to make robes for himself, his escort of eight knights, and the mayor of Bordeaux. But when they met the pope at Saintes, Havering discovered that an even larger guard would be necessary, for the great retinue that accompanied Clement included men as unpopular with the Gascons as Charles of Valois, who had conquered the duchy for the French in the early days of the war, Louis of Evreux and the archbishop of Narbonne, who had been among the French ambassadors to the Curia during the long negotiations leading up to the treaty, and the duke of Brittany, who had held Gascony during the long and futile wait for the papal award to be made. Accordingly, from Saintes on, Clement was accompanied by an armed guard, so that he might be brought into Bordeaux "benignly, honorably and in quiet," and all the time that he stayed there the town was policed day and night to avert any sudden action on the part of the Bordelais, made nervous by the arrival of so many French magnates, "because of the ill-will that the king of France and the French felt toward them on account of the recent war."

Needless to say, Othon played a great part in all this. He

received some of the wine provided for the entertainment of the guests, and it was also by his advice and by that of others of the king's Council that honors were paid and gifts were made to the unpopular French members of the pope's retinue. He also took part in the deliberations that followed Gaston de Foix's invasion of Armagnac, and he was one of those who advised Havering to lead the two expeditions that resulted in the count's final capture.[22]

There can be no doubt, too, that he was instrumental in obtaining the grant of the tenth that Clement made to Edward before he left Bordeaux, for there had not yet been time for a new embassy to arrive from England, and now that Lacy was back with the king, Othon was by far the most experienced diplomat left in Gascony. Ever since the death of Boniface, the question of the tenth had been a sore subject, for when he died his triennial grant of it still had one year to run, and Edward claimed that the pope had promised that if he should die before the three years were out and if the Sicilian war were over—which it was, the peace of Caltelbellotta having finally ended it in 1302—the whole amount should go to him outright. This claim was laid before Benedict XI both by Bek, who was at the Curia to straighten out his quarrel with his diocese and with the king, and by Bartolomeo di Ferentino, who had been on an embassy to Boniface; but the former was merely laughed at, whereupon "the bowels of his money again gushed out," as the always graphic and scriptural Hemingburgh put it, while Ferentino got an even colder reception. The latter, one of the collectors of the English tenth, was also Edward's clerk, having been long ago appointed to his canonry at St. Paul's, even though, as Peckham had written to his proctors at the Curia, he could not only not speak English but could scarcely speak Latin (*satis literaliter loqui nescit*). When he returned to England in March, 1304, so crippled with gout that it had

[22] Accounts of John Havering in *R.G.*, III, introduction, appendix II, pp. cxciv–cc.

taken him twice the usual time to make the journey from Dover to London, he sent Edward a report of his mission. Benedict had first of all told him that he could not give him an audience since his credentials were not to him but to the dead Boniface, and when Ferentino insisted, the pope demanded to see the bull that would substantiate his claims. "I said that you had been told about it by word of mouth by my lord Othon and myself, and that we would not have said such things from a great lord if they had not been true, but he told me that without the bull he would not believe it."[23] Ferentino then went on to make the ingenuous suggestion that his and Othon's verbal report be put in writing, although what conviction that would have carried it is hard to see. In the meantime, both the king and Benedict's chaplain, Pecorara, whom he had sent to England, claimed the tenth; the pope died; Pecorara was ordered to leave the country; and the whole matter remained in an uncomfortable abeyance until Clement's grant in the summer of 1305 ended the stalemate.

Undoubtedly, it was also Othon's doing that the pope, while he was still at Bordeaux, appointed Walter Langton as one of the collectors of the English tenth. Since Langton was still treasurer, this was playing directly into Edward's hands, but Clement was eager to conciliate him, and there was no better way of doing it than by honoring one of his ministers who had been so harshly handled. The old king's reign was closing under a cloud of disillusionment and suspicion, and by far the least edifying aspect of those bitter years was the quarreling that went on between Edward and his bishops and between the bishops themselves. It is not strange that Edward should have fought with Winchelsey, the archbishop of Canterbury. Relations were never very good between a strong king and a strong primate, and, moreover, the archbishop had led the clerical opposition in 1297 and had also brought to the king Boniface's

[23] Letter to Edward from his "petit clerk, si vous plest," in William Prynne, *Records*, p. 989.

bull claiming the overlordship of Scotland and had upheld its pretensions at the Parliament of Lincoln in 1301. It was because Edward considered that Bek had also taken the papal side at Lincoln that he bore a grudge against him, and in 1303 he used the dispute between his old friend and the priory of Goldingham as an excuse for taking the liberties of the see of Durham into his own hands. This seems to have been only a flash of temper, for a few weeks later he restored them to Bek, but in the acrimonious fight against Winchelsey he used every weapon at his command. The archbishop retaliated by attacking Edward through Walter Langton. Jealousy of Langton may have entered into it, as Edward wrote to Boniface, for the king "loved him like a father" and showered him with favors, until from a poor clerk Langton rose to be a bishop and in charge of "all the arduous business of the kingdom," a task that he fulfilled with imagination and circumspection. He also controlled the three royal households, which was an equally arduous job, for the queen and the Prince of Wales were usually as short of money as was Edward himself, and if, as the latter also told the pope, Langton was treated like a member of the family, his discretion probably merited it. No secrets were kept from him; he was even privy to some of the small subterfuges that kings must hide from their people but to which even they must descend when they fall behind in their correspondence. In one of those moments, Edward had forwarded to him and to John Langton the draft of a letter to the emperor, which should have left a fortnight sooner; he told them to date it from Roxburgh, July 20, instead of from Peebles, August 12, to make any alterations in the contents necessitated by the change of date, and, finally, to have the messenger who took it to Germany say that he had been "disturbed at sea" or give some other excuse to explain its late arrival.

It was through this confidential friend and minister that Winchelsey attacked the king, and he sent Sir John Lovetot to Rome to lay charges against him. Lovetot told the pope that

Walter Langton, both before and after his elevation to the bishopric, had had as his mistress Jeanne de Brianzon, Lovetot's stepmother, and that after they had had her husband strangled to death in his own dishonored bed, Langton had kept her publicly as his concubine and she had followed him all over England; that he had made a pact with the Devil, kissed his rump, and frequently conversed with him; and that he was a simoniac and held plural benefices. There can be no doubt that this last charge was true, as it was of almost every other influential priest in Europe, but Boniface, who was hoping that Edward would reopen hostilities with Philip, absolved the bishop of all the accusations against him, as Langton was able to tell Othon when he passed through Gascony in the summer of 1303 on his triumphant return from the Curia. He was back in England in time to see the complete downfall of his rival, for Clement, in his anxiety to please Edward, suspended Winchelsey and cited him to appear before the papal court. For some incomprehensible reason, the archbishop asked the king to intercede for him with the pope, but Edward answered this request with such a blast of rage, reminding him of all the harm that he had done and of all the trouble that he had stirred up in the realm, that Winchelsey completely lost the little presence of mind left to him and asked the king to give him his blessing. Edward coolly answered, "That is not fitting, father; it is I who should be blessed by you," and the archiepiscopal benediction was accordingly given. But the blessing did not keep Edward from pursuing Winchelsey with his vengeance long after the latter had left England to join the pope at Bordeaux, where he remained until after Edward was dead.

With Lacy, Langton had been appointed to head the embassy to the Curia that had not yet left England when news came of Benedict's death, and in the summer of 1305 he and the other ambassadors were notified to be in readiness to leave for the court of the new pope. Although Othon's name was not mentioned in this second appointment, that can have been only because he was already overseas, for when the envoys left they bore a letter to him from the king, and the royal messenger had great difficulty in delivering it, until he finally caught up with the active sexagenarian somewhere in the neighborhood of Toulouse.[24] Othon had probably left Bordeaux with the pope, surrounded by the armed guard that, on his advice and on that of others of the Council, accompanied Clement to the frontier because of the "tumult of the people," for in October they were together at Lunel and Nîmes,[25] on the way to Lyons, where, at the suggestion of Philip IV, the papal coronation was to take place.

Clement had no intention of braving the turbulent crowds of Rome. By choosing Lyons he could save face for practically everyone, for although the town was still theoretically part of the Empire, French influence was already paramount, and Philip saw a way of increasing it by attending the coronation surrounded by the great magnates of his realm. Clement had also urged Edward either to come himself or to send the Prince of Wales if that were impossible, but the king had written to excuse them both on the grounds that he was worn out, that there was no time to get a suitable escort together, and that it was too late to get a safe-conduct from the king of France. As a matter of fact, this last had already been granted, but whether Edward knew it or not would probably have made little difference to his plans. The Scottish war seemed to be over at last, and Wallace had been executed at London in August, but it was quite true that the aging king was exhausted by all his years on the Border and by the difficulties that he had had to face within his own kingdom. In addition, he had summoned another parliament to meet at Westminster in October. However, he told the pope that he was shortly sending some of his prelates and magnates to dis-

24 Exch. Accts. (K.R.), 309 (9); transcribed in Kingsford, op. cit., p. 157, n. 1.

25 Reg. Clem. V, Nos. 22, 44.

cuss various matters that he had very much at heart, and a few days later he appointed an embassy to treat about the crusade, the final settlement of the French peace, and other things having to do with the salvation of his soul. It was headed by Langton and Lacy and included Hugh Despenser, Amanieu d'Albret, Othon, John Benstede, chancellor of the Exchequer, Robert Pickering, Ferentino, and Philip Martel, all experienced in negotiations at the Curia.[26] Later, the bishop of Worcester was added to it, as well as Brother Thomas Jorz, shortly to be given a cardinal's hat, and Brother John Wrotham.

They left England in October, bearing with them the magnificent set of vessels all of pure gold that Edward, in spite of his financial straits, was offering to the pope, and they arrived at Lyons in time for the coronation ceremonies on November 14. If Philip's parliament at Toulouse had been spectacular, the meeting at Lyons outdid it, for in addition to the handsome king of France and his gorgeously attired nobles, there were all the various grades of the hierarchy, to say nothing of the English laymen, who, out of pride in their master if for no other reason, could not allow themselves to be outshone by either the French or the Roman courtiers. It was a glittering display even for that brilliant age, and the town was full of the devout and curious crowds who had flocked in from all over the countryside and who packed every rooftop and point of vantage from which they could watch the procession pass by. As the pope rode from his coronation, with the duke of Brittany and Charles of Valois walking at his bridle, a wall bordering the street collapsed under its weight of cheering spectators. The pope was knocked from his horse, and the tiara rolled in the dust, losing in the process a carbuncle worth six marks Florentine, as the careful Villani pointed out. Worse still, Charles of Valois and John of Brittany were buried in the rubble up to their waists, the latter being so badly hurt that he

26 Rymer, I, 974.

died four days later, while many of the unfortunate onlookers were also killed or injured.

In spite of the tragedy, no sooner were the ceremonies over than the English embassy got down to work. While they were still at Vienne on their way to Lyons, John Ditton, one of Othon's clerks, had handed over to Langton the transcripts of thirty-six papal bulls with which he had been intrusted by the autumn parliament in London,[27] and armed with these the ambassadors set about presenting their demands to the members of the papal court. They dealt with the crusade and also with Edward's request for the canonization of Thomas Cantilupe, late bishop of Hereford, who since his death had miraculously given "light to the blind, hearing to the deaf, speech to the dumb, and movement of the lame." But they also had a less worthy end in view, and when Langton returned to England he was able to read out the bull of December 29, 1305, by which Clement released Edward from his oaths to observe the Great Charter and the Charter of the Forest, on the grounds that their confirmation had been wrung from him by force and while he was absent from his kingdom. Some of the ambassadors also had business to do with the envoys from other countries, and Othon was one of those who discussed with Jean of Bar and his brother the return to England of their niece and Edward's granddaughter, Jeanne of Bar, and also the disposition of the lands in Scotland assigned to them "in consideration of their past, and as the king hopes, future services to him," which they finally agreed to exchange for £3,000, to be paid to them by the Frescobaldi.[28]

Langton and some of the other ambassadors left for England early in March, 1306, but Othon stayed on, first at Lyons and later at Avignon, well into the following summer.[29] Since there

---

27 *Gascon Calendar*, No. 2029.

28 *C.P.R.* (*1301–07*), p. 386.

29 *Ibid.*, p. 431; *C.C.R.* (*1302–07*), p. 450.

is no record of new powers having been granted to him, it may be that he remained there as Edward's resident ambassador. Although the practice of appointing envoys separately for each mission and even of giving them separate letters of procuration for each detail of their business was to continue in general use for another century at least, "there were semi-permanent English representatives at the courts both of France and of Rome from a very early period. The presence . . . of those in Rome [probably dates] from a time when royal requests for papal privileges and concessions came to be more than occasional demands."[30] Not only was this the case just after the accession of Clement, but also there were papal requests to be dealt with as well, for the pope wished to further the affairs of his own family and friends, and as most of these were Gascons, he needed Edward's help almost as much as Edward needed his. The king willingly granted to one of Clement's nephews permission to fortify his house and to make it strong with "walls, turrets, and ditches," but he made difficulties over the pope's request that Amanieu d'Albret be given the castle of Meillan. Amanieu, who had so often been Edward's envoy to the pope and who later acted as the pope's envoy to Edward, who negotiated with diplomatic patience on foreign soil and fought like a Gascon at home, had by now been released from his imprisonment at Bordeaux, and Edward did not even mention that incident when he wrote to Clement explaining why he was reluctant to comply with his request. What made him really angry was that Pierre-Arnaud de Vic, "not the least of our council," was himself in prison at the moment, and the king more than suspected that it was owing to the machinations of Amanieu, who had always held a grudge against his fellow countryman. He suggested that Vic first be freed, which seems to have been arranged, for the castle was finally handed over after four months of haggling.

As for Edward's requests to Clement, they were both nu-

[30] G. P. Cuttino, *English Diplomatic Administration*, pp. 96–97.

merous and varied enough to require the services of a permanent representative at the Curia. He wanted to be assured that no ecclesiastical sentence should be passed on him without the express consent of the pope—an obvious reference to Winchelsey; he wanted a change in the conditions under which the tenth was granted; and he wanted favors for his subjects both living and dead, benefices for six of his clerks, and the canonization of Grosseteste as well as of Cantilupe. But the most pressing questions were still those of Scotland and France. The northern kingdom refused to stay pacified. Early in 1306 Robert Bruce had murdered his rival, John Comyn, in the Greyfriars' church at Dumfries and, outlawed by the deed, had raised his banner and had himself crowned at Scone, for which sacrilege and rebellion Edward demanded his excommunication. As for the French war, that would not be legally at an end until all the provisions of the treaty had been put into effect, the question of reparations settled, and the Prince of Wales married to Isabelle of France. In 1303 it had still been too early to do anything about this last, for the bride was only eleven, and though before leaving Paris Othon and his colleagues had appointed Robert Burghersh and John Bakewell to meet with two French commissioners to straighten out the claims on either side, the Process of Montreuil, as it came to be called, dragged on and on, each party blaming the other for its lack of success. Clement continued to urge Edward to wind up both matters once and for all, so that the crusade could once more be preached, and Bakewell and Philip Martel were appointed to meet with the French commissioners for a second time, but again nothing came of it.

The Prince of Wales was also learning how useful his father's friend might be to him at the Curia, and it was at his request but by Othon's influence that the pope granted favors to many of his friends and clerks.[31] He was particularly careful to keep

31 Hilda Johnstone (ed.), *Letters of Edward, Prince of Wales, 1304–05*, *passim.*

on the right side of the powerful Frescobaldi and wrote twice to Othon, urging him to see that one of them, who had entered the Order of the Hermits of St. Augustine at the early age of fourteen, be returned "to the world and to his father,"[32] doubtless to follow the more remunerative occupation of banking. Othon gained papal dispensations for other members of the family as well, including the restoration of his benefice in the diocese of Salisbury to a certain Giovanni,[33] who, since he was a clerk familiar with England, may also have been the businesslike poet.

Othon also used his favored position at the Curia to forward the affairs of the Grandsons and their friends. Even before the coronation, he had obtained benefits for three members of his family,[34] and in March, 1306, he was instrumental in getting a grant for the Premonstratensian Abbaye de Joux, where, ever since its foundation by Ebal de Grandson in the twelfth century, all his ancestors had been buried.[35] He must also have been almost as swamped with requests at the Curia as he was whenever he returned to the English court, for now that the fearsome barrier of the Alps no longer lay between the pope and the princes of northern Europe, they or their representatives came to Lyons and Avignon in a steady stream, and hardly a month passed without Othon's seeing the arrival of one or more of his friends. In February, 1306, while the embassy was still at the Curia, his brother Guillaume came south to seek benefits for his two sons, John and Thomas,[36] while Amadée came from Savoy to obtain the pope's arbitration in his war with the dauphin of Vienne. Clement declared a truce and later granted Amadée permission to build a chapel at La Tour-de-

[32] *Ibid.*, pp. 74, 146; *Reg. Clem. V*, No. 457.

[33] *Reg. Clem. V*, No. 454.

[34] *Ibid.*, Nos. 22, 44.

[35] *Ibid.*, Nos. 1284–85. In the grant the monastery is called "Lascurran," a corruption of its early name of "Lacus Cuarnensis."

[36] *Ibid.*, Nos. 285–86.

Peilz outside the eastern gate of Vevey, since "in time of war, there was no sure access to the parish church." Probably before Othon left for England, he saw yet another friend, for in 1306 Hayton of Gorigos, now a Premonstratensian monk, arrived from Cyprus with the report on the Mongols that caused Clement to set plans on foot for a new crusade. Hayton found Europe full of crusading enthusiasm; even such unlikely people as Guillaume de Nogaret and Charles II of Naples were setting down their own notions as to how the Holy Land might be reconquered, and the new patriarch of Jerusalem, Antony Bek, was even then preparing to leave for the East. This meant that his beautiful cathedral, "half church of God, half castle 'gainst the Scot," would have to be left in the hands of an underling, but this glaring example of plural benefices was easily excused by his contemporaries: ". . . the bishop was rich, and the pope was poor."

If this cynical explanation was the right one, Clement was doing his best to remedy its cause. Even when he had granted the tenth to Edward, he had at the same time, "believing that charity begins at home," reserved for himself the first fruits of all English benefices, and in the following year, as he "sweated to collect treasure and to build castles," he appointed the archdeacon of Aran, Guillaume de Testa, who was already in England, to collect all the moneys owing to the Church from whatever source, warning Edward not to treat the new legate as he had treated Pecorara.

Other messengers also came to England from the Curia, among them the Spanish cardinal of Sabina and Amanieu d'Albret, to discuss the crusade and the French marriage, and it may be that Othon traveled north with some of them, for by the autumn of 1306 he seems to have been with Edward at Lanercost. He had to report not only on his protracted stay at the papal court, but also on his negotiations for a marriage between Edward's baby daughter, Eleanor, and a son of the late count of Burgundy.[37] Although the king had been forced to desert, or had been deserted by, most of his continental allies and had been compelled to drive the Flemings out of England and even to provide ships to be used against them by Philip the Fair, he had not lost faith in the value of matrimonial alliances; in the same year, he was trying to arrange another marriage as well, that of young Edward of Bar, the son of his first daughter Eleanor, long since dead, with a daughter of the duke of Burgundy. However, his plans for the latter seem to have been more financial than dynastic, for he had written to the duchess that young Edward was falling more deeply into debt every day as the interest on his loans mounted up and that the sooner he could get the money that would come to him on his marriage the better things would be. This cold-blooded statement of fact does not seem to have put off the prospective bride's parents, for young Edward's marriage, unlike that of his little aunt, who died in infancy, eventually took place.

Othon had not seen the king for almost four years, and he reached Lanercost to find him very ill indeed. It was an illness of some standing, but in the previous summer, owing to the intercession of St. James and the skill of the royal physician, Nicholas Tyngewick—both of whom had been rewarded, the former by an oblation that a special messenger carried to Compostella and the latter by the gift of the rectory of Reculver —Edward had been well enough to preside at the Whitsun festivities at Westminster, where the Prince of Wales and at least a hundred young squires had been knighted at the king's expense and vowed, as did Edward, never to rest until they had taken vengeance on Robert Bruce. In pursuance of his oath, the prince had led an army into Scotland, but there he had behaved with such brutality, ravaging, killing, and burning everything that came in his way, that he drew down on his head a stern rebuke from his father. The king was particularly

37 Rymer, I, 986.

displeased because, as he pointed out, the rich could always take to flight and it was the poor who suffered most. He ordered the new-made knight, who had so soon forgotten his vows, always to be merciful to the lowly and common folk. Edward himself was bitter enough against the Scots and, not content with having captured the Stone of Scone, wrote to the pope that Scone Abbey itself would be better off if it were transferred to a safer place than the perverse nation in the midst of which it was placed. In spite of his illness, he decided to follow his son north, but when he reached the abbey of Lanercost he was so weak that he was forced to winter there.

He did not leave it until March, 1307, when the Easter parliament was to meet at Carlisle. It was attended by the Prince of Wales, who had to submit to seeing his favorite, Piers Gaveston, banished—although he need not leave the country until after the next great tournament—while the prince promised that he would not recall him from his native Gascony without his father's permission. But there were matters of greater moment to be dealt with by the assembled magnates. The first of these was the Scottish question, and once the long preliminary sermons were over Testa robed himself and with lighted candles and clanging bells "terribly excommunicated" Robert Bruce. The next question was that of the papal exactions. Testa's sweeping commission to collect the debts owing to the Church had raised such a storm of protest from laymen and clerks alike that the legate was summoned to appear before the Council, where a group of its members, composed of Langton, Lacy, Despenser, Othon, Albret, Bakewell, and Thomas Fishburn, warned him not to exceed the limits set by the emissaries of earlier popes and informed him that a deputation was being sent to the Curia to lay the English complaints before Clement.[38] In the matter of the French marriage, Edward insisted that he had always been ready to live up to his side of the bargain and that the delay was owing to Philip's refusal or

[38] *Rot. Parl.*, I, 210–11.

inability to take the castle of Mauléon from the French knight who was wrongfully in possession of it and to hand it over to the English. The efforts of the Spanish cardinal finally broke down this last barrier, and an embassy was ordered to be ready by May 22 to cross with the prince to France. From the list of names that composed it, it was clear that it was more than merely the magnificent retinue suitable to such an occasion, for they read like a summary of all the embassies that had left England for the Continent during the last ten years: the bishops of Chester and Worcester, the earls of Lincoln, Warwick, and Richmond, Othon, Despenser, Albret, John Berwick, and John Bakewell.[39]

The embassy was not ready to leave on the date set for it; Othon was not given letters of protection until a month later;[40] and he was still in London when the first rumors of Edward's death reached him. The old king, like so many other people who have been used to seeing to things for themselves, could not think that anything was done right if he were not there to do it, and earlier in the year he had written to Pembroke and to his other commanders in Scotland, complaining that since they had sent him no news of their progress it could only mean that they were making no progress at all. It was the pitiful letter of a man feeling all the helplessness of illness and old age, but when Edward heard that the Scots had indeed won some victories, he decided that the only thing to do was once again to lead his troops in person. By slow stages he started moving northward and on July 6 reached the little town of Burgh-upon-Sands near Carlisle. Here his illness was further aggravated by dysentery, and the next morning, as his attendants were raising him in his bed, he died in their arms.

The news was hushed up until the new king could reach his father's deathbed, and it was not until July 25 that the truth was definitely known in London. In the interval, the chancellor,

39 Rymer, I, 1012.

40 June 21, 1307. *C.P.R.* (*1301–07*), p. 531.

Ralph Baldock, bishop of London, continued to use the king's Great Seal, "on the advice of Lord Othon de Grandson, Roger Brabazon, and others of the king's Council,"[41] and it was only on August 1 that it was sent up to Edward II at Carlisle.

The old king's last wish, that his body should be borne before his army until the final victory over the Scots had been achieved, was not carried out, for his son and successor had no intention of pursuing that troublesome enterprise. Instead, the cortège started southward, to Edward's own abbey of Waltham, where his body, wearing the sacramental dalmatic and stole, the royal mantle of crimson satin fastened at the shoulder by a jeweled clasp, with one hand holding the scepter with the cross and the other the scepter with the dove, lay in state until it was borne up to Westminster. There Bek, with all his rancors forgotten, said the last mass and read the committal service over the body of his friend.

The funeral was held at the end of November. A few days earlier, Othon had been granted letters of protection,[42] and shortly afterward, he left England, never to return.[43]

[41] Rymer, I, 1018.

[42] October 26, 1307. *C.P.R.* (*1307–13*), p. 9.

[43] Murimuth, *Continuatio chronicarum*, p. 11.

Che, dopo lui, verra di piu laid' opra
di ver ponente un pastor senza legge,
tal, che convien che lui e me recuopra.
Nuovo Giason sarà, di cui si legge
ne' "Maccabei"; e come a quel fu molle,
suo re, così fia lui chi Francia regge.

Inferno, xix, 82–87

ix. Avignon

The chroniclers of the reign of Edward II, writing after his deposition and murder in 1327, could not draw too clear a distinction between that unworthy monarch and his great father. They used no halftones; everything was black or white. The wisest prince and noblest knight of Christendom was dead, to be succeeded by a son who was his opposite in every respect. They carried their accusations against the latter so far that even their contemporaries turned against them, and the pilgrims who thronged to Gloucester Cathedral revered his tomb as that of a saint and a martyr. Later historians, striving to keep a just balance between these two extremes, have found much to say in his favor, and so long as they remain on constitutional or administrative grounds their arguments have a solid foundation, for even the first Edward had found it increasingly difficult to stem the tide of baronial opposition that was setting so strongly during the last years of his reign, and it is just possible that it might have succeeded in overwhelming the father as in the end it overwhelmed the son. That it did not do so seems owing to the difference in character between the two men, for after all the excuses for the younger Edward have been made and the blacker charges against him have been explained away, the fact still remains that he was a fool and a weakling. It has been argued that he had not had his father's advantages; that the frequent absence of both his parents and the early death of his mother deprived him of the normal family life that Henry III, for all his faults, had managed to provide for his children; and that in his youth he was never given the responsibilities that so soon made a man of Edward I. The first argument seems open to question if only because the upbringing of an heir to the throne, even in the twentieth century, is so far from normal in the modern sense of the word that it is difficult to know just what it would have implied in the thirteenth. As to the second, it is true that a man of strong character is often loath to relinquish authority, particularly to his own sons, but it is also true that, in general, Edward I proved that he was expert in picking the right man for the right job, and if the story of the prince's expedition into Scotland is correct, it justifies his father's decision to leave him to the frivolous foreigners and trifling amusements that he really preferred to the burden of a leadership for which he was quite unfitted.

We can still pity the man while condemning the king, and even his severest critics would no longer hold him responsible for all the woes of his reign, as did his contemporaries, but although the latter were wrong in attributing to one man the general deterioration that was taking place around them, they were right in their uneasy feeling that the times were out of joint. A strange, unhealthy haze had come over the sun, which a hundred years earlier had shone with such clarity through the freshly glazed windows to color the sharp white carvings below, and in its creeping shadow sickly corruptions were spreading out from the dark corners in which they had hitherto flourished. Accusations of witchcraft were becoming more frequent, not only against old women from the gutters of the towns and from villages forgotten in the folds of the hills but even against members of the court and of the hierarchy itself: the bishop of Troyes, although he was later acquitted, was suspected of having procured the death of Queen Jeanne of France by witchcraft or poison. The wholesale arrest of the Knights Templar in the autumn of 1307 had shocked the princes of Europe into outright disbelief of the charges brought against the Order, but these protests were soon silenced by the incriminating avowals of the prisoners themselves.

The innocent historians of the late nineteenth century, unfamiliar with forced confessions under either physical or mental torture or both, solemnly tried to weigh the evidence that piled up under the endless interrogations; our more experienced generation, aware of the worthlessness of such testimony, finds it interesting for a different reason and stands amazed that neither the great ecclesiastics and shrewd lawyers who conducted the trials nor such responsible and experienced men as Othon's friend, Jacques de Molay, the Grand Master, could think of anything more damning than the few puerile obscenities that, monotonously reiterated, were all that was needed to bring those Templars who had escaped the burning ruins of Acre to die on the pyres of France.

The luxury, which, more than their reputed crimes, had first aroused the cupidity of Philip IV against the Order was not confined to the Templars but was general among all those who could afford it, and although Cacciaguida's comparison between the sober wives of his day and their painted granddaughters in contemporary Florence could be echoed up and down the ages, the sumptuary laws, while increasingly stringent, were becoming increasingly ineffective. Edward's order to the sheriffs of England, regulating the number of courses that might be served at each meal, did little to curtail the lengthy banquets in the great halls or to still the grumbling of the poor, who saw the castle, which had been built to shelter

2 1 9

lord and peasant alike in case of danger, becoming nothing more than the stage on which the former, with his growing army of retainers, could make an ostentatious parade of his riches. With all this came an inevitable decay in sexual morality. Two of Philip IV's daughters-in-law were convicted of adultery, while homosexuality, then as now particularly prevalent among the sciolists—"many were clerks," as Dante noticed when he passed through the region of Hell set apart for their punishment—was spreading to the less lettered classes, until even the king of England was suspected of the vice of sodomy.

Edward's behavior immediately after his father's death did much to substantiate this charge. Although his apologists explain his treatment of Piers Gaveston as natural and even praiseworthy loyalty toward a friend whose companionship had been one of the few fixed points in a lonely and neglected childhood and blame the bias of the chroniclers, it is not only in the pages of the latter but also in official documents that his gifts to the favorite are recorded. He had already incurred the wrath of Edward I by his extravagant generosity toward Gaveston; his attempt to invest him with the county of Ponthieu had led to a bitter quarrel between father and son; and Gaveston's own overbearing behavior and barbed tongue had antagonized the nobles, who concurred heartily in the sentence of banishment passed against him by the Parliament of Carlisle. But now, before the old king was even in the tomb that was to bear his motto, "Pactum serva," Edward had broken his six-month-old pledge, recalled his friend, and bestowed upon him the rich county of Cornwall. In the face of mounting opposition from his barons he was to continue to load the new earl with honors and riches. When he left England for his marriage with Isabelle of France, it was Gaveston who was appointed over the heads of the great nobles to be regent of the kingdom, and on his return it was once again Gaveston, resplendent in purple and pearls, who carried the most precious of all the regalia, the crown of Edward the Confessor, before the king at his coronation.

It is difficult even for the most charitably-minded not to see in this reckless favoritism something stronger than mere friendship, and it also provides an explanation if not an excuse for Isabelle's subsequent behavior. When her uncles, Charles of Valois and Louis of Evreux, returned to France with angry reports that even at the coronation Edward paid more attention to his friend than to his queen, we can still feel that they were making insufficient allowance for the behavior of a young king of twenty-three who, excited and flattered by his new dignity and by the ceremonies that went with it, can easily have overlooked a hitherto unknown twelve-year-old princess. But when within a few years the child who at first had had no weapons against her husband's neglect except tearful complaints to her father turned into the "she-wolf of France," and from her lover's arms hounded that husband to a horrible and brutal death, her unrelenting vindictiveness can be explained only as the fury of a woman whose pride and whose feelings had been unbearably wounded.

It is true that there may be another reason for Edward's insanely thoughtless partiality for Gaveston, but although it does more credit to his morals, it does less to his character. His behavior may have been nothing more than the natural reaction of a weak son against a strong father. After having been dominated all his life, he could now show his independence, and he did so, not by taking positive action as a more forceful man would have done, but by reversing, so far as possible, all his father's policies. Bek was reinstated in the royal favor, and Winchelsey was recalled from his exile at the Curia. At the same time, Edward was no sooner king than he lashed out against his old enemy, Walter Langton, imprisoning him and sequestrating all his properties. Murimuth, writing years after the event, makes it look as though Othon, too, had been a victim of this sudden change:

> Also, the nobles, growing indignant against the said Piers, laid many plots, as the outcome later proved. Also, the count of Savoy, who was the cousin and counselor of [Edward's] father, and lord Othon de Grandson, both took perpetual leave of England.[1]

This ambiguous statement, which might mean either that they were among the indignant nobles and left England in disgust or else that they were driven out by the wave of xenophobia resulting from hatred of the Gascon favorite, is wrong on both counts, and Murimuth should have known better, for he was to see much of Othon during the years that they both spent at the Curia. He was wrong about Amadée, for the latter was soon back in England for the coronation, and although he seems to have been right in saying that Othon never returned, when the latter left in the autumn of 1307 it was only as he had done so many times before, on an embassy to the court of France.

In fact, it was much the same embassy as that to which he had been appointed by the new king's father, and its purpose was also the same—to make the final arrangements for Edward's marriage to Isabelle. There were some changes: since Langton was in prison and the bishop of Worcester dead, their places were taken by Bek and by the bishop of Norwich; the earls of Warwick and Richmond were dropped and the earl of Pembroke put in their place; Robert Pickering was substituted for John Bakewell; but Othon was retained, as were the earl of Lincoln, Amanieu d'Albret, and John Berwick.[2] It was an embassy still made up of the old king's counselors, and Othon was traveling in familiar company. He was also traveling on doubly familiar business: there was nothing that he did not know about arranging royal marriages, and since this one represented one more step in carrying out the provisions of the treaty of 1303, there would also be the inevitable discussions as to the still unpaid war indemnities and reparations and the fate

[1] Murimuth, *loc. cit.*   [2] Rymer, II, 11.

of the disputed Gascon castle of Mauléon. Othon had been over that ground too often to hope for a quick settlement of the questions involved, but so far as the marriage went he and his colleagues dispatched their business speedily, for by December 30, 1307, Edward was writing to Philip that he would agree to the arrangements made and would be at Boulogne by January 21, 1308, in time to be married the following Wednesday.

If, as the Aragonese ambassador to the Curia had written to King James the summer before, Edward was still coming to his wedding "morosely" because of the delay in returning Mauléon, there was no outward sign of it during the tournaments and festivities that went on for two weeks after the wedding ceremony. Now that Philip was by far the most powerful monarch in Europe and could boast that even the center of Christendom lay within his dominions (for the Curia was still moving uneasily from Poitiers to Bordeaux and back again), everyone sooner or later came to France, and the wedding of his daughter to the young king of England brought princes from as far away as the snow-covered mountains of the Tyrol and the orange groves of Naples to joust and feast and dance under the lowering Channel skies, while the stiff gold embroidery of their pennons flapped dismally in the wet squalls blowing in from the sea, and the winter night fell so early that half their merrymaking was lit only by the flaring torches. Othon was undoubtedly present to witness the marriage that he had worked so long to bring about, a hale and dignified gentleman nearing seventy, followed only by his modest retinue of squires and clerks but treated with respect—if Edward's attitude toward him is any criterion—by the princes whose earliest memories were of his arrival at their father's courts at the head of an embassy from the king of England. His experienced eye missed none of the intrigue going on behind the brilliant scenes: it rested with benign approbation on the young and lovely lady of "Ulmeto," whose grace and pretty manners caused her to outshine all the others present but were not enough to keep her husband's affection from straying to the mistress for love of whom he was to murder his wife, by spells or poison, men said, before the year was out; it clouded regretfully at the rumors that the rich gifts that Edward received from his father-in-law —the royal ring, the unimaginably beautiful bed, the pick of the French stud, and others too numerous to mention—were all being sent back to England to be given in turn to Gaveston.

Before leaving for his wedding, Edward had already made plans for his coronation, and he and his new queen returned to find London hung with cloth of gold and looking like the New Jerusalem adorned with bridal finery. Othon did not accompany him; he had other business in hand and a few weeks later was once again at the Curia.[3] More than ever before, the king of England needed a trustworthy and permanent representative at the pope's side. His own country was in a state of perpetual turmoil, his relations with his father-in-law were unsettled and Clement seemed to be the only person in Europe who was honestly trying to conclude a final peace between them, and for both these reasons, as well as for less pressing routine matters, there was an increased exchange of embassies between Avignon and Westminster. Brother Thomas Jorz—now a cardinal—received a pension for looking after English affairs at the papal court, and Edward kept his proctor, Andrea Sapiti, there as well, but to tidy up the threads of business left behind by one embassy and to smooth the way for the next to arrive the king required someone more experienced than the rather inefficient Englishman and more influential than the Florentine. Othon was to spend most of the next ten years at Avignon, where the papal court finally established itself in the autumn of 1308, and the only explanation of his presence there is that he was acting as Edward's resident ambassador. He was not a proctor—at least, he is never described as such—but other ambassadors, coming from England to the Curia on specific business, as was still the usual diplomatic procedure, were fre-

[3] Delaville LeRoulx, *op. cit.*, IV, No. 4792.

quently accredited to him as well as to the pope and to any of
the cardinals who might be of help to them, and all the letters
of protection regularly issued to Othon during that period state
explicitly that he was remaining overseas on the king's service.
If, in deciding to use him in this capacity, Edward was ahead
of his age, he also gave proof of possessing both wisdom and
thoughtfulness, and a post was found for Othon that spared
the weakening flesh, a little wearied by years of unremitting
travel from one court to another, but gave scope to the yet willing spirit to make the best use of all its accumulated knowledge
and experience.

There was no question of the job's being a sinecure, for all
western Europe was drawn into the eddies that swirled around
Avignon, where Philip, usurping his rival's prerogatives, played
the successor of the Fisher of Men with all the skill of an expert
angler, yielding at times but only to draw the line even tighter
immediately afterward. Clement was scarcely fair game, for
during all his pontificate he was an ailing man, forced to ex-
pend a great part of his strength in fighting off the pain that
frequently kept him confined to his room for days at a time and
left him too worn and weary to refuse even the most outrageous
of the demands that were constantly being made upon him. He
was wax in the hands of his Gascon relatives—everyone in the
duchy seems to have been his cousin—and the Sacred College
was soon full of his clerical kinsmen, while the States of the
Church were intrusted to the lay members of his family.
Amanieu d'Albret became rector of all the northern part of the
Patrimony except for the unconquerable Romagna, and Guillaume de Soe was rescued from the poverty of which he had
complained so piteously to Edward I by being made governor
of Viterbo. But the peasants guiding their white oxen through
the fertile valleys of Umbria or forever bending against the
wind that sweeps the dry, brick hilltowns of the Marches never
saw their foreign rulers. Although there was even more fighting
in Italy than in Gascony, it lacked the pungent savor of famil-

iarity, and the Gascons preferred to stay at home and spend the revenues of the lands that they never visited on the local wars in which their souls delighted. Yet in spite of Clement's unblushing nepotism and his often shameful weaknesses, he manages to remain a sympathetic figure, and if the bust of the wracked, haggard man that passes for his portrait is a good likeness it is easier to admire him for his tenacity in ever daring to stand up to Philip and the French lawyers than to censure him for the concessions that they wrung from him by their constant bullying.

There was no longer any possibility of his returning to Rome —Philip was playing his fish too close to the shore for that—but Clement managed to persuade himself that he would stay north of the Alps only until he had arranged the final peace that would enable him to preach a crusade under the leadership of the kings of France and England. He also made a small gesture of independence when he chose Avignon as his residence, for it lay in the Comtat-Venaissin, which had been acquired for the Church by Gregory X, and the town itself was an enclave belonging to Charles of Sicily.

But the Curia was still at Poitiers when Philip arrived there in May, 1308, in an attempt to overwhelm, once and for all, the papal objections that still stood in the way of his ambitions. The first question was that of his vengeance against Boniface VIII. Early in Clement's pontificate, he had forced the pope to revoke the two troublesome bulls, *Clericis Laicos* and *Unam Sanctam,* and to reinstate Boniface's enemies, the Colonna cardinals. He now pressed for the revocation of the sentence of excommunication against Nogaret, the canonization of Celestine V, the posthumous trial of Boniface, and finally—the verdict was naturally a foregone conclusion—the exhumation and burning of the remains of the dead pope. Clement promised to look into the matter, and Philip had to be content with that. He then turned to attack the Templars, who since their arrest the previous year had been lying in the royal prisons of France.

2 2 6

The French canon lawyers preached threatening sermons and the civil lawyers backed them up with bullying harangues, but Clement insisted that the Templars and their properties must first be handed over to the Holy See, and that not until that was done would he look into the question of their guilt at a council summoned to meet in the following year.

There were also discussions about the settlement of the English and French war claims, and in these Othon took an active part,[4] but he must have listened with interest to many of the other deliberations as well, remembering the weary months of argument with Boniface and the last gallant stand of the Templars at Acre, and knowing better than any of the younger men present just how to untangle all the interwoven threads of truth and falsehood. He also had a personal interest in the question of the Templars, since for thirty years one of his steadiest sources of revenue had been the annual grant of £2,000 made to him by Jacques de Molay, then Preceptor of the Order in England, later its Master, and now a prisoner at Chinon. This income was now cut off, "because of certain impediments that have arisen to the aforesaid Master and Order," to use Clement's euphemistic words, but luckily, the "magnificus et potens vir, dominus Othon de Grandissono, miles egregius," as the Master of the Hospital had called him earlier in the year,[5] had influence even with the king of France, and Philip made him an equivalent grant on the confiscated lands of the Order, which was later ratified by the pope when these lands were turned over to him.[6]

The meeting at Poitiers also discussed the wished-for crusade, for Hayton of Gorigos, who had returned to the East after having been at the Curia that winter, had sent back word that the sultan was planning another attack on the Christians

[4] Pierre Chaplais, "Règlement des conflits internationaux franco-anglais au xive siècle," pièce. just., 5: *G.C.*, No. 169.

[5] Delaville LeRoulx, *loc. cit.*

[6] *Reg. Clem. V*, Nos. 2938, 4404.

and was even then preparing a fleet of eighty galleys. The pope and Philip promised to send 400,000 gold florins between them, and on August 11 Clement issued a call for a crusade, but even he must have known that it was little more than a gesture. The only king in Europe who still showed any real interest in such a movement was James of Aragon, whose ambassadors were working on the pope to have the expedition diverted southward to drive the Moors from Spain. The imperial throne was vacant, for Albert of Habsburg had been assassinated by his nephew early in May; the grandson of St. Louis was not the man to leave his kingdom to look after itself while he pursued unobtainable ends in the far corners of the earth; and Edward of England became daily more embroiled in his own domestic troubles.

The king had continued to infuriate the English by his treatment of Gaveston, and his latest move had been to marry him to his niece, Margaret of Gloucester, the daughter of his dead sister, Joan of Acre. The favorite, holding what had been a royal earldom and now connected with the royal family, became increasingly insufferable, and the barons once more insisted on his exile and ordered the English bishops to excommunicate him if he ever dared to return. Edward had been forced to submit to their decision, but his infatuation led him to do so in a way calculated to fan the baronial jealousies to a white heat, for with the sentence of banishment was coupled Gaveston's appointment as the king's lieutenant in Ireland and a grant of castles and lands both in England and in Gascony. At the same time he did everything in his power to have his friend recalled and sent a passionate stream of letters overseas, to Philip, to Clement, and to some of the more friendly cardinals. He wrote also to Othon and to Amanieu d'Albret, urging them to use all their influence to have the pope send nuncios who would restore peace and tranquillity to England and to persuade him to revoke the sentence of excommunication.[7]

7 Rymer, II, 50.

Poor peace-loving Clement was only too eager to do whatever he could, and on August 11, 1308, he wrote to Edward that in answer to his request he was sending Arnaud, bishop of Poitiers, to England. He also gave the bishop letters of credence to Philip so that they might discuss the matter, but for some reason the king detained Arnaud for so long at the French court that he had finally to write to Clement apologizing for the delay. In his letter, he told the pope that he had heard from the earl of Pembroke that Edward had managed to patch things up, and he suggested that Clement write to the king of England, urging him to get rid of the Gaveston faction and restore his barons to the Council. Clement answered this letter on October 5, explaining the steps that he was taking and also informing Philip that he was sending yet another messenger to Edward:

> And also, we charged and urged by our letters our
> beloved son, the noble Othon de Grandson, whom
> we consider most useful in making the aforesaid peace
> according to your and our desires, telling him that putting
> all else aside, he shall not fail to betake himself into the
> presence of the king of England and together with the said
> bishop and with those whom Your Serenity is sending for this
> purpose, that he study best how to work for this peace.[8]

Othon seems to have left Fontcouverte, where Clement was spending the hot summer months, soon after September 8, 1308, for on that date a long list of indulgences and dispensations was issued at his request, to his nephews,[9] to his clerks,[10] and to Filippo Sapiti, the son of Edward's proctor at the Curia.[11] In August he had already gained a forty days' indulgence for all those who, after having received absolution, should visit his Franciscan church at Grandson on certain specified feast days,[12] and now he also procured favors for the Abbaye de

[8] Étienne Baluze (ed.), *Vitae paparum Avenionensium*, III, 87–90.

[9] *Reg. Clem. V*, Nos. 3097, 3154, 3166.   [11] *Ibid.*, No. 3098.

[10] *Ibid.*, Nos. 3162–63.   [12] *Ibid.*, No. 2885.

Joux,[13] permission to found a monastery for thirteen monks, to be attached to the priory of St.-Jean, and the grant of revenues for its support,[14] and the promise of a pension for three clerks who should be present at his obsequies.[15] This last provision and the renewed interest in the churches of his native land sound almost as though he were indeed "wearied by the tedium of living" and was planning to return to the Pays de Vaud and devote his remaining years to good works, but in fact nothing seems to have been further from his mind. In the previous spring he had gained a dispensation for a certain Adam Osgodby to hold plural benefices on the understanding that "before Othon sets out for the Holy Land, Adam shall deliver to him one year's income as a subsidy for the same."[16]

Even though he seems to have gone no farther on his journey than Fontainebleau, where on November 26 Philip made him the detailed grant of a pension on the Templars' three houses of Thors, Epailly, and Coulours,[17] and is next heard of six weeks later at Vevey, it was not fatigue but the pressure of his own affairs that made him disobey Clement's request to let nothing stop him from going to England. The assassination of Albrecht of Habsburg had thrown Europe into confusion. Philip of France saw no reason for delaying the election of a new emperor, and to his mind there was only one possible candidate, his brother, Charles of Valois. But although he used every weapon in his armory, bribing, threatening, and cajoling, the idea of the Valois ruling in Germany and the Angevins in southern Italy, while Capetian France lay in between, having swept all its opponents from the board and able to play its own game unhindered from the Elbe to the Straits of Messina, was too much for even the most Francophile of the electors. In spite of all that Philip could do, the interregnum lasted for only six months, and in November, 1308, Count Henry of Luxemburg was proclaimed emperor.

[13] *Ibid.*, No. 3123.   [15] *Ibid.*, No. 3156.

[14] *Ibid.*, No. 3161.   [16] *Ibid.*, No. 2785.   [17] *Ibid.*, No. 4404.

All these events had their repercussions in the small principalities lying on the western border of the Empire, where French efforts at infiltration had never abated and where the lords of the Grandson lands were constantly involved in the shifting policies of their greater neighbors. Philip had gained one victory when his second son, another Philip, had married the daughter of the count of Burgundy, perhaps one of the very children on whom Othon, more than twenty years earlier, had cast a matrimonial eye, and although the marriage was not ideally happy, for Blanche was one of the two sisters-in-law later convicted of adultery and imprisoned, it was satisfactory to the French, for half the lands of the Franche-Comté now fell into Capetian hands. The various branches of the Grandson family were all more or less affected by the transfers of homage that ensued,[18] as they were by the perpetual quarrels between the count of Savoy and the dauphin of Vienne. However, these quarrels were temporarily allayed by the election of Henry of Luxemburg, since Amadée's hereditary enemies, the Habsburgs, although still holding the lands that had always blocked Savoyard expansion to the east, no longer controlled the Empire as well. In 1309, Amadée made a truce with the dauphin.

One of the arbitrators of the truce was Othon's nephew and heir, Pierre de Belmont,[19] who as the future lord of Grandson was already playing an important part in the tangled affairs of the Pays de Vaud, but who must still have been grateful for the help and advice of his experienced uncle, when Othon, not even heeding the pope's earnest request, turned homeward in the late winter of 1308. Othon's natural inclination to be at Grandson during this period may still not have struck Clement as sufficient reason for his not having undertaken the English mission, but he could give an excuse for his behavior that would satisfy even the pope. During the interregnum, the ashes of discord between Louis II of Savoy, baron of Vaud, and Bishop Girard of Lausanne had once more broken into flame,

[18] Kern, *op. cit.*, No. 183.   [19] Guichenon, *op. cit.*, I, 358.

and yet another Savoyard-episcopal war was raging. It was ended by a truce, "made and given by the hand of the most high and puissant baron, the lord Amadée, count of Savoy, and by the hand of the noble baron, the lord Othon, lord of Grandson," on January 2, 1309, at the house of the Hospitallers (*en lospital*) at Vevey,[20] but evidently from what Othon had seen of both contestants he had very little hope of the peace lasting while Girard de Vuippens still retained the see of Lausanne. When he returned to the Curia later in the year to busy himself once again with Edward's affairs,[21] he must have reported to Clement on just how things stood in the Pays de Vaud, and it was undoubtedly at his suggestion that Girard was transferred to Basel and that his place in Lausanne was taken by the aging Othon de Champvent, the brother of the last bishop but one and Othon de Grandson's first cousin.

Meanwhile, Edward's affairs continued to go from bad to worse. In England, he was leaving no stone unturned to have Gaveston recalled from exile. On his northern border, the Scots were once again in arms, under the leadership of Robert Bruce, who scornfully asserted that it had been more glorious to wrest six inches of land from Edward I than to conquer a whole kingdom from his successor and that the very bones of the dead father were more to be feared than was the living son. In France, the interminable talks designed to settle the claims and counterclaims left over from the war were leading nowhere, and Philip's unyielding position was further strengthened when the quarrel between Amanieu d'Albret and the seneschal of Gascony, John Ferrers, broke out into open fighting, and Amanieu, who in moments of stress always seemed to forget that he had been one of the most trusted advisers of both Edwards, reverted to the old Gascon expedient of an appeal to the Parlement of Paris. Edward's relations with Clement were no better: the annual census of 1,000 marks was, as it had al-

[20] *Recueil diplomatique du Canton de Fribourg*, II, No. 87.

[21] *C.C.W.*, p. 292.

most always been, badly in arrears, and in addition, Edward's resistance to the increasing papal policy of giving English benefices to foreigners was interpreted by the pope as an infringement on ecclesiastical prerogative. All these difficulties ended up sooner or later at the Curia, and Othon had to deal with most of them, for even when he was not actively appointed to an embassy or asked to lend his support to the envoys sent out from England, he was frequently appealed to as an authority on the wars and treaties of bygone years, and when he spoke from his vast experience, with the sureness of an expert and the urbanity of a diplomat, even the lawyers of the Parlement of Paris had to take him at his word.

In March, 1309, he was at Avignon, as a member of the English embassy sent to discuss Edward's difficulties with the Church,[22] and since its business lasted for several months he was probably still there in June when another embassy arrived, this time from Henry of Luxemburg, to ask for papal ratification of his election. This was purely routine business, and the only unusual thing about it was the speed with which it was accomplished, for Clement wished to forestall any objections that might have been forthcoming from Philip IV. What was far more interesting was to see the four men whom Henry had chosen as his principal ambassadors. These were the counts of Flanders, Geneva, and Savoy, and the dauphin of Vienne. It was not surprising to see Amadée associated with his old ally, Count Guy, but when he was working hand in glove with his two archenemies, Jean of Vienne and Guillaume of Geneva, it could mean only one thing: with the election of the Luxemburg candidate, the wind of imperial ambition had veered, and the embassy was a weather vane pointing southward to Italy.

The king of the Germans must become king of the Romans and be crowned with the Iron Crown of Lombardy before seeking imperial coronation at Rome, and between the two kingdoms lay the Alpine passes, controlled on their northern slopes by

22 Rymer, II, 68–69, 97–98.

Amadée himself and on their southern by his nephew Philippe. There was yet a third crown to be gained, that of the Middle Kingdom, the Arelate, still disputed between the king of France and the emperor, but in reality ruled by neither of them but by the majestic Rhône and by the men who held its banks. That alone would have accounted for the presence of the count of Geneva and the dauphin in the embassy that Henry sent to the Curia, but that they were there for another reason as well is shown by the inclusion of Guy of Flanders. All four men came from the western frontier of the Empire, and now that the Franche-Comté was to all intents and purposes a Capetian appanage, their lands were all that kept the frontier from being overrun by Philip.

Even if his flank were secured, Henry would still have to face French opposition once he had crossed the Alps, for the nominal leader of the Guelphs was Robert of Sicily, who had just succeeded his father, Charles of Salerno, and who was supported both by Clement, who was to crown him at Avignon in August, and by his cousin, the king of France. But in spite of that, the chances of a Ghibelline success looked brighter than they had done since the days of the great emperors, for the political map of Italy was changing. A few years earlier, from the southern border of Tuscany north to the Alps, the pattern had been almost invariable; the rising towns had been Guelph, while their less successful neighbors, from whom they were sucking the lifeblood of trade, had been driven into the opposing camp and served as a refuge for the *fuorusciti*, the Ghibelline exiles who waited with bitter nostalgia for the emperor to come and restore them to their own cities. The modern student of Italian, who has been taught that *paese* means "country" in the sense of a national entity, is bewildered on reaching Italy to discover that there the word is more generally used to mean "village," but this apparent confusion of ideas explains better than anything else the aching love of the exiles for their native towns, where the stairs of even the highest tower, from whose summit they could see all that their patriotism could encompass, were never so steep as those in the houses of strangers, and where alone the bells rang to the rhythm of their blood. During the last few years, these exiles had been joined by others, for the victorious Guelphs had split into two factions, the Blacks and the Whites, and those who were only too glad to profit by the resultant anarchy had driven out the others, who, despairing of help from their leader, the pope, now practically a prisoner in French hands, united with the Ghibellines, their erstwhile enemies, in looking toward the Empire to restore order to Italy and her dignity to Rome.

Accordingly, in the summer of 1310, another embassy arrived at the Curia, to announce to the pope that Henry intended to cross the Alps and to ask for the papal support without which the expedition was doomed to failure. It is easy enough to understand why the counts of Savoy and Flanders should again have been chosen for a mission of such importance, for apart from all other considerations they were two of the greatest feudatories of the Empire: it is harder to explain why the only other member of the embassy should have been Othon.[23] Although his influence would extend well beyond the limits of the Grandson lands so long as he could be sure that the see of Lausanne was occupied by members of his family, he was still lord of only a few castles guarding the relatively unimportant passes of the Jura, and even these he did not hold directly of the emperor, so it is clear that his position was not owing to territorial considerations. We can only suppose that Henry, who had spent the greater part of his youth at the French court and who had been at Lyons for Clement's coronation, had been impressed with the ability displayed by Edward's envoy in his dealings with the lawyers of the Curia and of the Parlement of Paris and that perhaps the high opinion that he had formed of the older man was increased by all that he had

[23] Jakob Schwalm (ed.), *Constitutiones et acta publica imperatorum et regum,* IV (i), No. 390.

heard of him from Count Amadée. At any rate, and for whatever reason, Othon was to play a leading part in one of the innumerable series of negotiations in which the emperor was involved.

This dealt with his position in regard to Philip IV. While Clement, with incomprehensible optimism, was encouraging the Italian expedition, in the hope that it would put an end to the strife between Guelph and Ghibelline, even though this would entail the defeat of his own champion and Philip's cousin, Robert, king of Sicily, he apparently saw no contradiction in simultaneously seconding the emperor's efforts to come to an agreement with the king of France. So far, these had not been conspicuously successful, for the latter was playing his usual devious game. Henry's first overtures of friendship, in January, 1309, immediately after his election, had been met with polite irony; by June, 1310, Philip's attitude seems to have changed, and word reached Henry's envoys at the Curia that the French and Imperial delegates had drawn up an agreement that laid the groundwork for a final settlement; but within four months Philip hardened again and reopened all the vexatious frontier questions when he gratuitously insulted the emperor by taking under his protection the city of Verdun. He also continued his efforts to gain possession of Lyons. The town was still part of the Empire, but two years earlier, at the famous meeting at Poitiers where Philip had gained so much, he had recognized the church of Lyons as a county and the archbishop had agreed to recognize the suzerainty of the king of France. Now, on the grounds that the archbishop, Philippe of Savoy, had refused him the oath of fealty, he besieged the town, and Philippe was forced to yield to his versatile uncle, Count Amadée, who within six months of having served as Henry's ambassador in Avignon was commanding some of the French forces that were attacking the imperial city. Feudalism was dying hard, and Philip IV's plaintive remark that he wanted nothing more than to include among his subjects only those who lived within the boundaries of what had once been ancient Gaul, although it has a familiar ring to those who have heard exactly the same arguments used about the *Volksdeutsche,* must have struck Amadée and his contemporaries as mere duplicity. But even if Philip gave more comprehensible reasons for his behavior, neither his unyielding attitude toward Burgundy and the Arelate nor the appointment of some of his most vehemently nationalistic ministers to draw up the proposed treaty with the emperor hastened its completion, and Henry proposed to leave for Italy while the negotiations were still going on.

After Clement had listened to what the imperial ambassadors, Amadée, Guy, and Othon, had to tell him in the early summer of 1310, he sent word to the people of Italy to receive the emperor with rejoicing, and also, as he wrote to Henry, repeated the same thing to the envoys who had come to the Curia from the north Italian towns, "in the presence of our brothers and of our beloved son, Othon de Grandson, a zealous champion of your honor."[24] By the time Henry received this letter, he was already in Lausanne, where on October 11 he swore fealty to Clement. At the same time he also seems to have redeemed the pledge of 1,500 silver marks, made to Othon earlier in the year, by granting to him the castle and town of Laupen, near Bern, in consideration of his "weighty, gratifying, and acceptable services."[25] A month later Othon was at Aiguebelle in Savoy and was sending orders to the inhabitants of his new fief to do homage for it to Jean Sautier, the castellan of Grandson.[26]

If he had left the Curia for Savoy with the idea of going in the emperor's train to Italy, his plans were frustrated by the serious illness that kept him there well into the following winter. He was not at Susa when Henry, getting his first glimpse

[24] Schwalm, *op. cit.,* No. 390.

[25] *Fontes rerum bernensium,* IV, No. 402.

[26] *Ibid.,* No. 413.

of his Italian kingdom, fell on his knees and prayed to be delivered from the factions of the Guelphs and Ghibellines, upon which Amadée gave him the rather belated advice that the best thing to do was to follow his own example and become involved with neither of them; nor was he at Milan, where the emperor was invested with a hastily made copy of the Iron Crown of Lombardy, the original having been pawned to a Jew by Guido della Torre, the captain of the city. This last procedure was a strange one under the circumstances and speaks volumes either for the probity of the pawnbroker or for the avarice of the Milanese, for the piece of metal incased in the crown and which gave it its name was one of the nails used at the Crucifixion.

Othon was finally cured of his illness by the ministrations of a skilled physician whom, in the manner of grateful patients, he repaid with an enduring friendship,[27] but the doctor undoubtedly deserved the more material rewards that he received as well, for Othon cannot have been the easiest of men to nurse. He was not accustomed to being tied down, and once the crisis was past he must have become increasingly restive; it required a practiced bedside manner to keep him quiet, especially when the great ones of Europe were once again clamoring for his services.

In March, 1311, Clement wrote to Amadée, now marshal of the Empire in Italy, to Henry, bishop of Trent and imperial chamberlain, and to Guy of Flanders and Othon, urging them to persuade the emperor to conclude the French treaty so that his crusading plans might once again get under way.[28] At the same time he sent a covering letter to his nuncio in Italy, which shows that Othon must have informed him that the doctor—unreasonably, no doubt—had not felt that a trip across the Alps in midwinter was indicated in the treatment of a seventy-two-year-old convalescent, and which is also in revealing contrast with the more official letters, for it was written by the papal

27 Baluze, *op. cit.*, III, 497.   28 Schwalm, *op. cit.*, No. 592.

chamberlain and its wording differs considerably from the stately terminology characteristic of the chancery. After telling the nuncio that a letter to the emperor is on the way, the pope urges him to use every "opportunity and importunity" to get Henry to agree to the proposed terms,

> and if the king of the Romans is as sapient as we think he is, it would be much to his advantage; and indeed we cannot see that at the outset of his reign, he can prosper in any other way, considering the character of those with whom he now has to deal.

The legate is also to go to the Lord Othon—". . . it will not take you much out of your way'"—and give him the letter addressed to him, asking him to do everything in his power, both by writing to Henry and by sending messengers, to persuade him to ratify the treaty. The instructions close with some helpful diplomatic hints: do not criticize the emperor too much or be too insistent, for great men are often provoked by such things.[29]

This last piece of advice did not keep the nuncio from dropping broad hints that if Henry did not see his way clear to coming to an agreement with Philip, Clement might put difficulties in the way of an imperial coronation at Rome, and these, together with the emperor's difficulties in fighting his way through Italy, forced him to yield: he ratified the treaty on May 8, 1311, at Cremona. Six weeks later, in the presence of the legate, he empowered the bishops of Basel and Novara and a Dominican friar to appoint the arbiters set by its terms, and, considering the presence of Girard de Vuippens on the commission, it is not surprising that one of these should have been Othon, together with the archbishop of Cologne and Guy of Flanders.[30]

But the treaty was never implemented. The Italian towns along the way stood out for so long that Henry had to send Bishop Girard up to the Curia to explain that because of the

[29] *Ibid.,* No. 594.

[30] Paul Fournier, *Le royaume d'Arles et de Vienne,* p. 367, n. 1.

opposition that he was encountering and especially the pertinacity of the Brescians—they withstood the imperial troops for six months—he could not reach Rome by the Assumption, the date originally set for the coronation. By March, 1312, he was still no farther than Pisa, whence he wrote to Philip, Clement, various cardinals, and Othon—the messenger received three florins for his expenses[31]—and it was not until the end of June that he was crowned at the Lateran. Within a little over a year he was dead, at Buonconvento in Tuscany, killed, so the rumor went, by a poisoned wafer administered to him in Holy Communion, and all the high hopes for the pacification of Italy died with him. Indeed, if the Italian expedition had any effect, it was precisely the opposite of what had been intended. In an effort to provide a more stable government, Henry appointed imperial vicars for life instead of only at the emperor's pleasure as had formerly been the custom, but such men as the Visconti in Milan and the Scaliger in Verona, once in the saddle, were hard to unseat. Henry's new policy laid the foundations for the success of those princely houses who for the next two centuries were to be the artistic blessing but the political bane of Italy.

From Clement's instructions to the legates, it sounds as though Othon must have stayed in Savoy at least through March, 1311, so that he was probably not at Avignon to receive the letters of credence brought to him by Brother John Wrotham, who had left England for the Curia in February. Wrotham also brought letters to the pope and to ten of the cardinals,[32] and although none of them say anything more specific than that he was coming on a matter very close to the king's heart, his business can only have had to do with Gaveston, who had been banished once again, this time out of all the king's lands, for the barons were taking no chances on another exile like the last one, which had proved to be more of an honor than a disgrace. It is hard to believe that Othon felt any deep sympathy for the favorite or that he looked with anything but

---

[31] Schwalm, *op. cit.*, IV (ii), No. 1151.   [32] Rymer, II, 128.

repugnance on Edward's almost hysterical pleas for his reinstatement, and although in this matter as in all others he did his duty and served the king to the best of his ability, he must have been glad, on returning to the Curia in May, 1311,[33] to find that other business of a more savory character awaited him. It was also a business on which he could be completely sure of his ground, for it dealt with the meeting at Périgueux, where for five months the English and French commissioners had been endeavoring to reach a decision that would lay once and for all the ghost of the war that had supposedly been brought to an end by the Treaty of Paris eight years earlier. At least, that was the ostensible purpose of the meeting, but the English claimed that the French were using the talks only to strengthen their own position and had no wish to conclude a settlement. It is true that ever since Edward, in the previous summer, had sent John of Brittany and the bishop of Norwich to France to ask Philip to send his commissioners to Gascony, most of the delays had come from the French side.

The first of these was as expected as the opening move in a game of chess: Philip, when the English envoys met him near Chartres, replied to their demands with the well-worn royal excuse that he could do nothing, as he did not have his Council with him, and he told them to go to St.-Denis and await his answer there. The answer, when it came, was also not very surprising, at least to anyone who had studied the methods of the Parlement of Paris: the ambassadors were told that their credentials were not in order. The English commissioners had been empowered to settle all the outstanding claims between their country and France; now Philip insisted that they should have been appointed to deal only with those arising directly from the war, since as suzerain of Gascony he alone had the right to give judgment in all disputes that had taken place before the outbreak of hostilities in 1293. Apart from the illegality of Philip's claim to suzerainty, the English saw at once that this

33 *Reg. Clem. V*, No. 7020.

would put them wholly in his power; almost all the questions at issue had to do with Gascony, and the French lawyers would have no trouble—or only such trouble as they throve on—in tracing each one back through the maze of conflicting jurisdictions to some event that had taken place before the war, leaving Philip as arbiter in each case. They therefore objected strenuously, pointing out that when the two kings had met at Boulogne they had agreed that the commissioners should settle all claims and that no time limit had been fixed, and furthermore, that at Poitiers, when Othon and Geoffrey de Joinville had made the same request, Philip had granted it. There was another meeting of the French Council, after which the archbishop of Narbonne—the same who had headed the embassies to the Curia in the days of Boniface VIII—told the English that he knew of no agreement ever having been made in Clement's presence and repeated that since their credentials were invalid there could be no further discussions until Edward issued others in conformity with the French understanding of the case.[34]

All this, John of Brittany and the bishop of Norwich wrote to Edward, and since they could do no more at Paris, went down to Gascony to await fresh instructions. Edward copied his father-in-law's delaying tactics; he was not satisfied with the justice of Philip's claims, and he too would have to get advice, not from his Council, but from Lacy, Valence, and Othon, who had drawn up the original treaty. Since he was busy on the Border—he wrote from Berwick—and they were all far away, this would take time.[35] But whatever Othon and the others could tell him did not stave off another diplomatic victory for the French. When the commissioners did finally meet at Périgueux in January, 1311, they discussed with each other only the treaties, infractions of truces, and claims for damages arising from the war, while in the talks about matters dating from before 1292 the English were represented only by a proctor.

[34] Chaplais, *loc. cit.*   [35] Rymer, II, 122.

These halfhearted negotiations could lead nowhere, and in June, soon after Othon had returned to the Curia, the talks broke off.

Edward still had hopes that another meeting with Philip might settle all these difficulties, and in May, 1311, he wrote to the bishop of Norwich and to the other commissioners, telling them to try to have things postponed until that could be arranged. In the same letter he also told them to be ready to go to the general council that was to meet at Vienne in the autumn, since the question of Gascony was sure to come up and no one knew more about it than they did. He was probably correct in assuming that Gascony would be on the agenda, for the council had been convened to discuss the fate of the Templars, the reform of the Church, and plans for a crusade, and as Clement never ceased to reiterate, no crusade was possible until the kings of England and France were at peace with one another.

As to the first item, the council had been prorogued once already because the investigation of the Templars had not been completed in time. Although it had originally been supposed to meet in 1310, it was not until June, 1311, that Edward was able to notify his ambassadors of their appointment. He also sent to his chancellor, asking him to write to Philip for letters of safe-conduct for them,

> so that they may pass through his realm with their jewels,
> vessels of silver, and expenses, without disturbance, and
> make the king's letters so hastily that his messengers may
> have the letters patent of the king of France before they
> pass the sea to the council; also, as the king wills that
> Sir Othes de Grantson be named one of his said messengers,
> to request him by letters under the Great Seal to charge
> himself with the message, with the other messengers, and
> meet them a day or two on this side of the pope's court to
> inform himself from them on the points touching the
> message, and to deliver these letters to the treasurer to
> send to Sir Othes, wherever he may be found, without delay.[36]

[36] *C.C.W.*, p. 367.

This last phrase shows that it was still as difficult as ever for his contemporaries to keep up with Othon's movements, and the chancellor sent the two letters off at once. The one to Othon was couched in the most friendly and considerate terms; he was asked to help the others, "according to the ripeness of your healthful counsel," and was told to meet with them wherever he found it most convenient to do so.[37] Edward also wrote to the pope and to the papal chamberlain, asking them to be sure to assign comfortable lodgings to the English mission, so that "refreshed by fitting quarters," they might the better go about their business, but this request did not affect Othon, since he was now a papal knight,[38] and with the innumerable other members of the household, from the chamberlain himself down to cooks and carters, was lodged at the pope's expense.

The council opened on October 16, 1311—Edward's letters of credence for the archbishop of York, the bishop of London, Othon, Amanieu, and Adam Orleton were dated six days earlier[39]—and after an opening sermon on the text, "I will give thanks to the Lord with my whole heart; secretly among the faithful and in the congregation," it settled down to business. The large English mission originally appointed had been cut down to five men, but even they must often have wondered why they had come, for from the beginning it was clear that the pope was running things as he wished to, "and it scarcely deserved to be called a council for he did everything out of his own head."

The opening question was that of the Templars, and here it seemed at first as though the voice was the voice of Clement but the hands were the hands of Philip. Already the latter had had his own way in the matter of Boniface; it is true that the dead pope had not been exhumed and burnt, but he had stood

37 Rymer, II, 136.

38 *Reg. Clem. V*, No. 5528.

39 Rymer, II, 145. Othon was still at Vienne on December 26, 1311 (*Fontes rerum bernensium,* IV, No. 455).

posthumous trial, the chief prosecutor being the excommunicated Nogaret; all his acts and those of his successor, Benedict XI, that were prejudicial to Philip or to the French had been annulled and the king declared innocent of all complicity in the "Terrible Day"; Nogaret was absolved as well and given no heavier penance than a pilgrimage; and proceedings had been started for the canonization of Celestine V, which took place two years later. Under these circumstances, it came as a surprise when the council stood up to the French delegates and over their objections voted that the Templars had the right to defend themselves. Philip, taken aback by this unforeseen check to his plans, summoned the States General to meet at Lyons in February, 1312, and he followed this up by arriving at Vienne on March 20 with his brothers, Charles of Valois and Louis of Evreux, and a large armed following. It is scarcely surprising that the secret consistory that was held two days later suppressed the Order. But his victory was not complete. He had hoped to make one of his sons king of Jerusalem and have the goods of the Templars adjudged to him, but on this point Clement remained adamant, and a few days before the closing of the council in May, 1312, he granted them instead to the Hospitallers.

If the condemnation of the Templars on the ostensible grounds of heresy was in reality a political and economic maneuver of Philip's, both politics and economics also played their part in the discussions about the crusade. The English and the Imperialists were working for another expedition to the Holy Land and for the grant of a sexennial tenth. The Spaniards, insisting that there could be no united crusade until Granada was in Christian hands, wanted financial help against the Moors but preferred to do the fighting themselves and were therefore against the grant of the tenth to the kings of France and England, since even if the crusade did come their way, that would only mean that foreign armies would overrun the peninsula. In January, 1312, when the Aragonese envoys to the council wrote all this to King James, Philip, delaying as usual, had not yet made up his mind as to which course to pursue, but by April 3, when the crusade was officially declared, he too had promised to take the Cross.

No one understood better than Othon what lay behind these various discussions. He knew all too well what the kings of France and England were apt to do with the tenth, once it was granted to them; the long months that he had spent as a hostage in Aragon had made him familiar with the fanatical pride of the Spaniards; and his sojourns at Acre had taught him just what to expect, should the armies of the Italian trading towns ever pour along the roads that led to Constantinople and to the riches of the Eastern Empire. Aware of all this, he must have been all the more impressed by the vigor and intelligence of the missionary friar, Raymond Lull, who came to lay his own crusading plans before the council. He and Othon did not always see eye to eye: it had probably never occurred to the latter that the Saracens might be conquered not by armed knights but by unarmed friars preaching the Gospel to them in their own tongue; and they did not agree as to the advantages of basing the expedition on Armenia, since Lull, unlike Othon, thought that that kingdom was short both of food and of horses. But in other respects, the ideas expressed by Lull in his *Libre de Fine* tallied closely enough with those drawn up by Othon and Hayton of Gorigos a few years earlier.

The only practical result of Lull's impassioned sermons was that the council decided to set up schools for the study of Hebrew, Arabic, and "Chaldean" at Rome and in the universities of Paris, Oxford, Bologna, and Salamanca, but Othon was quietly making his own plans. He had taken the Cross, perhaps during his illness of the autumn before, straightened out his financial affairs,[40] and by the summer of 1312 was preparing to leave for the Holy Land. Being a seasoned campaigner and seventy-four into the bargain, he knew enough to make himself

[40] *C.P.R.* (*1307–13*), p. 453.

as comfortable as possible, and when he left the Pays de Vaud for Avignon to receive the papal blessing he decided to go by boat down the Rhône instead of making the hot and tiring journey by road. But at "Ponte Duvino" in Bresse, he was attacked by a mixed band of Savoyards and Dauphinois, led by Aymon de la Palud, who held him prisoner for several days, robbed him of 20,500 gold florins and of the other goods that he had with him, killed some of his men, and seriously wounded his squire. Retribution was swift, and Clement wrote at once to the archbishop of Lyons and to his suffragans:

> The enormous gravity of the crime recently perpetrated on the person of our dear son, the noble Othon de Grandson, our knight and a member of our household, disturbed us the more deeply and still shocks us to the depths of our heart, because of the great love that we deservedly bear to him for his devotion and probity. . . . Considering the pious work on which he was engaged and all his other acts, so fruitful in good, and that he is liked by all and that no one has ever received harm at his hands, we are not a little astonished that Aymon has chosen to wreak his impiety on him.

Unless within two weeks the offender had returned all that he had stolen and made full satisfaction for all the injuries that he had committed, he was to be excommunicated and his lands put under interdict, and the sentence was to be read out on every Sunday and feast day in the churches of all the archbishop's cities and dioceses, with tolling bells and lighted candles.[41]

Whether the money was ever refunded or not, Othon relinquished his crusading plans for the time being and returned to the Pays de Vaud, where the death of the elderly bishop of Lausanne had plunged the region into yet another civil war. During the last forty years there had been only three occupants of the see, Othon's two first cousins, Guillaume and Othon de Champvent, and in between them his nephew, Girard de

[41] *Reg. Clem. V*, No. 8205.

Vuippens, and this family tradition seemed bound to continue unbroken, so long as Othon stood in such high favor at the Curia and the cathedral chapter was full of his relatives. When he left on his doomed voyage to the Holy Land, he may well have thought that the election of yet another nephew, Pierre d'Oron, was a foregone conclusion, but the Lausannois, still regretting the vanished privileges that none of the Grandson bishops had ever restored to them, rebelled once again, and Louis II of Savoy, the baron of Vaud, followed his father's example in giving them support. The fighting lasted for a year and a half, and its first phase ended in a complete Grandson victory, for not only was Pierre d'Oron installed as bishop but also Othon's crusading nephew, Pierre d'Estavayer, who had gone with him to Acre, was made *bailli* of Lausanne. The lull was only temporary, however; the revolt broke out again, and it was not until June, 1316, that peace was finally made.

During these four years, Othon was frequently at home. He was at Lausanne with his nephew, the bishop, in April, 1314;[42] as one of the arbiters of the treaty, he took part in the negotiations leading to its completion and was also present to seal and witness it; and even while the fighting was still going on, he seems to have exerted a moderating influence, for it was to his intervention that Michel Guerri, one of the ringleaders of the insurrection, owed his life.[43]

At this time he also crossed the Alps on a peacemaking mission and on October 29, 1313, was at Alpignano near Turin, where with Louis II of Vaud, the bishop of Parma, and the sire de Beaujeu, he arranged an arbitration in the difficulties that had arisen between Amadée and his nephew, Philippe of Achaea.[44]

His own affairs also claimed a great deal of his attention. The details of his transactions are involved and wearisome, for

[42] *Fontes rerum bernensium,* IV, 567.

[43] A.C.V., C IV 166.

[44] A.S.T., Principi del Sangue, Mazzo 2, No. 12.

the acquisition of land, which was his principal interest, was a complicated affair. Before he could take possession of a certain village, he would have to buy its mills and furnaces from one neighbor—who was probably a relative as well—its fishing rights from another, and a stretch of nearby woodland from a third, and then arrange for the homage due on his new lands. But once all this was concluded, another corner of the Grandson properties had been neatly rounded off. The marriage of his nephew to Blanche of Savoy also increased the family holdings. To raise money for her dowry, Louis of Vaud had pawned to Othon and Pierre the castles of Belmont, Grandcour, and Cudrefin, and although he later redeemed them, he then gave them back to Pierre to be held for liege homage.[45]

But the most mysterious of these exchanges was that of April 5, 1315, by which the sons of Jean de Cossonay sold to Othon for nine years the revenues of four of their castles for 6,454 *livres lausannois*. This sum was to be paid to their mother, Marguerite, now the wife of Aymon de la Palud, for the dowry of their sister, who was married to Aymon's son.[46] Since the young Cossonays were probably the grandchildren of one of Othon's sisters,[47] one wonders whether Aymon's attack on Othon, which had so aroused Pope Clement's wrath and astonishment, did not have its origins in a family fight and whether this last transaction may not have had something to do with the restitution of the stolen goods.

The expansion of the Grandson properties was a slow business spread over the years and constantly interrupted, and once again Othon was called away by the king of England. In spite of all Clement's efforts and his repeated instructions to his nuncio in England, neither the barons nor Edward would

---

[45] A.S.T., Baronnie de Vaud, Mazzo 16, Nos. 5, 6.

[46] A.S.T., Baronnie de Vaud, Mazzo 13, No. 41.

[47] However, the *Dictionnaire historique . . . du canton de Vaud*, art. Cossonay, says that Jordane de Cossonay-Grandson was the daughter not of Pierre de Grandson but of Henri de Champvent.

listen to reason. The barons refused even to look at the papal letters, boasting that they were erudite not in reading and writing but only in the use of arms, and that, besides, if they needed the help of the literate there were plenty of noble and well-educated prelates in England who could give them good advice, so that they did not need the help of any meddling foreigners. As for Edward, his infatuation for Gaveston had brought him to the nadir of humiliation, and the English were reduced to seeing their king, with the favorite still under his protection, chivied from one castle to another, up and down the kingdom, in an effort to escape from the rage of the infuriated barons. The chase ended only with Gaveston's capture and execution in the summer of 1312.

The birth of a prince to Isabelle a few months later did something to allay Edward's mourning for his friend: "his sorrow abated as his love for his son increased, and he began to go along more humbly with the wishes of his barons." But even this did not bring to an end his troubles in England or to those in his dominions overseas, where the interminable wranglings of the commissioners still went on, and where Gascony had been thrown into a turmoil by Amanieu d'Albret's private war against the seneschal. However, for the moment, things were sufficiently quiet so that Edward might leave his kingdom, at least for a short time, and the knighting of Philip's three sons, which was to take place at Whitsuntide, 1313, seemed a favorable occasion for the meeting between the two kings that had been postponed so many times. Accordingly, Othon, who was once again at the Curia,[48] was summoned to join the king, wherever it would be most convenient for him to do so before the latter reached the French court, "considering that our company would be honored by your presence and since we wish to have your deliberation and counsel on matters touching us."[49]

He had witnessed many royal festivities before, but never

[48] Rymer, II, 197. [49] Ibid., p. 211.

one so magnificent as this turned out to be. All Paris was hung with silks and precious cloths, and at night it became, perhaps for the first time in its history, *la ville lumière*, when all the streets glittered with an infinite number of lights. The knighting of the three princes took place on Whitsunday; during the following week the kings with their queens and nobles took the Cross; and in between these events there was a succession of banquets—Philip and his eldest son, the king of Navarre, each gave one, as did Edward—for which all the French who were there changed their clothes three times a day. After that it was the turn of the tradesmen and workers, who went in procession through the town, each guild dressed in its own special costumes and each mounting a different pageant; one represented Hell, another, Paradise, while yet a third showed a wilderness full of wolves and other wild animals. But to the French chronicler the best spectacle of all was afforded by the English, who gaped in amazement that any one city could contain such a multitude of men so richly adorned.

After a week of this, the two kings moved to Pontoise, where they finally held their long-wished-for interview. As might have been expected, it did little to clear up the difficulties between them, and even here Edward's bad luck held, for a fire broke out in his wardrobe and he and his queen were forced to flee, wearing only their nightshirts.

Othon was still with the king at Pontoise on June 26, 1313,[50] but when Edward sailed for England a few days later it was the last time that the two men were ever to see each other. Although Edward was to have one more meeting with his father-in-law and one with Philip's son and successor, Othon was summoned to attend neither of them.

[50] *C.C.R.* (*1307–13*), p. 585.

I cannot rest from travel: I will drink
Life to the lees.

TENNYSON

x. The Last Journeys

Othon probably spent the greater part of the next three years in the Pays de Vaud. He had every reason for remaining there, since to the difficulties arising from the Savoyard-episcopal war were added those of the fifteen months' interregnum that followed the death of the emperor, and there was little for him to do at the Curia, for the Holy See was also vacant. The sky had been blazing with portents, the most significant of which was the simultaneous appearance of three moons, each marked with the sign of the Cross. Since those who had stood nearest to Jacques de Molay as he mounted the pyre had clearly heard him arraign the two men responsible for his death, the pope and the king of France, to appear before the throne of God within the year, it came as a surprise to no one who could put two and two together when both Clement and Philip duly followed Henry VII to the grave, the former in April, 1314, and the latter six months later.

Philip was succeeded by his eldest son, Louis X, the first of the three brothers who were to follow their father and to die without heirs male in such quick succession that Othon, whose memories went back to the days of their saintly great-grandfather, lived to see the extinction of that Capetian dynasty against whose ambitions almost his whole life, as crusader, as seneschal of Gascony, as the ambassador of both Edwards, and even as lord of Grandson, seemed to have been one long struggle.

The succession to the papal throne proceeded less expeditiously, and Louis X was dead and Philip V was reigning in France before a new pope was chosen. Once again, the Sacred College was split into an Italian and a French faction, and the French started with the scales already weighted in their favor, for the conclave sat not at Rome but at Carpentras, near Avignon, within easy reach of the trenchant arguments of the French lawyers and the equally sharp swords of Clement's Gascon relatives. These last, who in the indecent scramble for the dead pope's possessions had let his corpse remain unburied for several days, had no intention of losing the even greater riches that their generous kinsman had bestowed upon them, and they realized that the election of an Italian pope and the return of the Curia to Rome would mean the end of those lucrative posts in the Patrimony of Peter to which so many of them had been appointed. In an attempt to stave this off, two of Clement's nephews decided to take matters into their own hands and swept into the town at the head of a force of their fellow countrymen, crying "Death to the Italian cardinals!" and killing several of the hated foreigners before being driven off, but in spite of these high-handed tactics, it was not until August, 1316, that the French faction had its way and elected Cardinal Jacques Duèse, bishop of Porto, as John XXII. He was "not great in stature, but great in learning and of virtuous life," an experienced politician, for he had been chancellor to King Robert of Sicily and vice-chancellor to Pope Clement, and, above all, a hard-headed financier, for he was a native of Cahors, a town famous for its bankers. This last was a particularly necessary characteristic, as things stood at the beginning of his pontificate, for Clement's generosity toward his relatives had almost emptied the papal treasury, and the ceaseless Italian wars soon took not only the little money that was left but even ate into John's private fortune as well. In these straits, nothing less than the most drastic measures would suffice, and he took the unprecedented step of reserving for himself the annates of the entire Church for the next five years.

Murimuth, who was then at the Curia, remarked bitterly that "no one in Germany paid any attention to this, but the English, like patient asses who will put up with anything, bore it as they bore other heavy burdens." They did not do so without grumbling, and the embassy that left England in December, 1316, was empowered to do far more than merely carry the king's congratulations and gifts to the new pope. Even though Edward was in financial difficulties himself, these gifts were still magnificent; very few people could afford to seem penny-pinching when they were courting papal favor. Even fewer could take such a strong stand as did old Marguerite de Foix. Her fiery sister, Constance de Marsan, had died in 1309, after having become so old and feeble that she could scarcely get to church, but Marguerite still survived, and she seemed to think that one of her talismans, "a serpentine horn, made like a penknife, which is said to be very good against hidden poisons," was partially responsible for her longevity. At least, when she lent it to John XXII she demanded his written promise that he would return it, a pledge that was solemnly drawn up by the papal chancery. The English could claim no such guarantees; they could only hope that the presents that they brought for the pope and for various members of his court and household might smooth their way for the business that lay before them. Their first financial experience at Avignon made even that hope grow faint; to begin with, they were given a bad exchange when they bought florins from the Bardi with their English money, and then the recipients of Edward's generosity refused to accept their pensions at the lower rate, so that before matters were even under way the Wardrobe had already lost over six pounds on the transactions.

One of those who stood out so firmly for his rights was Othon,[1] although he himself was a member of the embassy, having been appointed with Amadée on December 16, 1316, together with the bishops of Norwich and Ely, the earl of Pembroke, and the usual number of rising clerks and knights.[2] The two Savoyards received none of the separate powers granted to other individual envoys for dealing with specific matters: they were clearly there in the rôle of elder statesmen, experienced in negotiations at the Curia. In fact, on December 6 Edward had already written to each of them, asking them to meet with the others in Paris so that the latter could have the benefit of their advice before continuing their southward journey. Amadée was urged to do this "because of your friendship to us" (*amicitiam vestram*), but in the letter to Othon, Edward appealed to his affection (*dilectionem*) and showed that this affection was not one-sided by considerately adding, "if perhaps you cannot get to Paris, then by all means meet with them within the octave at the Curia . . . so that we may benefit by your experience and benevolence."[3] Whether the seventy-eight-year-old Othon braved the wintry roads of northern France or not, he was at Avignon in March, 1317, for the Aragonese ambassador wrote to King James: "There is a big English embassy here, one bishop, one count, and other knights, among whom is Miser Otes de Grançp, who asked me for news of you."[4]

[1] Thomas Stapleton, "A brief summary of the Wardrobe Accounts of the tenth, eleventh, and fourteenth years of King Edward II," *Archaeologia*, XXVI (1836), 324.

[2] Rymer, II, 303.   [3] *Ibid.*, pp. 302–3.

[4] Heinrich Finke, *Acta Aragoniensia*, III, No. 152.

By that time, the embassy was preparing to leave, judging by the list of indulgences and dispensations granted to its members at the end of the month, and it seems to have accomplished its business more or less successfully. The most pressing question had been that of the Scottish war, for almost two years earlier, on June 24, 1314, Bruce had won his great victory at Bannockburn and, since then, had proclaimed himself king of Scotland. The English ambassadors had been instructed to ask for the excommunication of the Scots and for the grant of the tenth for four years, basing their requests on the unhappy argument that the pope owed Edward this support since England was a fief of the Church. The papal lawyers were quick to take advantage of the opening thus presented to them and retorted that not only was the annual census, as always, badly in arrears, but also that Edward had never done homage to the pope for his kingdom. Neither had the first Edward, it is true, and Pope John's predecessors had been content to let the matter rest, so long as he tacitly acknowledged their suzerainty by paying the census at more or less regular intervals, but his son now agreed to do so, and satisfied by this promise and by Edward's reiterated expression of his willingness to take the Cross, John granted some of the English requests. He remitted the census for one year and gave Edward permission to pay the remainder in instalments, and he also granted him the tenth, but again only for a year and only as a loan. But he decreed the excommunication of the Scots, should they ever attempt to cross the Border, and he sent two nuncios to England to try to put an end to the war.

They were also to try to bring about a reconciliation between the king and Earl Thomas of Lancaster, who was now the leader of the English baronial party, but although Othon had no doubt taken part in all the discussions about the tenth and the census, as he had been doing for the last thirty years, and had probably also done his best to recover for Edward those Gascon rents that the latter had pledged to the late pope—or rather, to Bertrand de Got, a private person—as security for a loan, he had by now been so long out of England that the king's quarrels with his barons or with the Church over an appointment of an archbishop of York must have begun to seem almost as remote to him as the struggles of the Dominicans against the masters and scholars of Oxford, which the embassy had also asked the pope to settle.

He could leave such matters to the men who knew more about them, and although in June, 1317, he was still in Edward's service,[5] the letters of attorney issued to him in November of the same year, and all subsequent ones,[6] merely state that he was "staying beyond the seas." He was at last free to devote himself wholeheartedly to his own affairs, which, no less than those of the king of England, stood in need of papal intervention, for in spite of the peace drawn up in the previous year between Bishop Pierre d'Oron and Louis II of Savoy, the corner of the world where the Grandson lands lay was still far from pacified. Count Guillaume of Geneva had joined the fray as an ally of the bishop, although he left himself a loophole by stating that the agreement should be binding only so long as Pierre held the see of Lausanne, but to balance this, Count Raoul of Neuchâtel had adhered to the Savoyard faction. This was natural, for relations between the counts of Neuchâtel and the lords of Grandson had always been strained, since their lands marched with each other, and neither the frequent interchanges of properties nor the equally frequent marriages between the two families had ever succeeded in allaying their dissensions. Indeed, the latest marriage threatened to aggravate these and even to split the Grandsons themselves, for Jean de Champvent, who had returned to the Pays de Vaud after the death of his father, Pierre, and had married Count Raoul's daughter, Cathérine, now sided with his father-in-law instead of

[5] *C.P.R.* (*1313–17*), p. 661.

[6] *Ibid.* (*1317–21*), p. 52; (*1321–24*), p. 362; (*1324–27*), pp. 187, 192, 319; (*1327–30*), p. 24.

2 5 7

with his cousins when any disputes arose. On his marriage he had granted to Cathérine, among other lands and privileges, the lifetime tenure of his castle of Champvent, and this meant that Othon was directly involved in the armed clash that soon broke out, for as lord of Grandson he claimed the homage of his nephews for all the holdings that had come to them by inheritance. Even Girard de Vuippens, whose diocese of Basel bordered on the county of Neuchâtel to the north, took sides in this acrimonious family fight, and there can be little doubt that while Othon was at the Curia he asked the pope to use his influence to bring it to an end, for in June, 1317, John threatened to excommunicate Girard unless he immediately laid down his arms and indemnified Count Raoul for any damages for which he had been responsible. Othon must also have discussed the matter with Amadée, for in August the latter turned his practiced hand to trying to arrange a settlement. Having first persuaded his nephew, Louis II, to prolong the pledge that he had taken not to attack Pierre de Belmont, he then enlisted his services as a peacemaker, and between them they arbitrated the various differences that had arisen between Pierre and his brother, Thibaut, on the one side, and Raoul de Neuchâtel and Jean de Champvent on the other.[7]

For the time being, Othon's various nephews were to live at peace with one another and with their neighbors, and this gave him time to turn to other matters that he had very much at heart and that he must also have discussed while he was at Avignon, since both of them required ecclesiastical approval. In 1317, he endowed an altar in the cathedral of Lausanne, to be dedicated to St. George and served by two chaplains,[8] and in the same year his plans for an even more ambitious undertaking were well under way. Since 1303 he had been a Carthusian oblate,[9] and he now set about founding a house for thirteen

[7] Matile, *op. cit.*, I, No. 352.

[8] A.C.V., C V^b 37.

[9] *Dictionnaire historique . . . du canton de Vaud*, art. La Lance.

monks of the Order, near the fountain of La Lance, a few miles from Grandson. With this in mind, he approved the sale of some rights by his nephew Pierre to the mother-house of La Grande Chartreuse and sealed the transaction at Grandson on October 17, 1317:[10] both he and Pierre gave other lands as well, including half the grange of Villars-Luczon, which he had bought from the Abbaye de Joux in 1318; and the cornerstone of the monastery was laid on April 18 of the same year.[11] It adjoined a church that was already standing, which must have been built soon after Hugues de Grandson, in the closing years of the twelfth century, had given the "place called La Lance" to the Premonstratensians of Fontaine-André, a daughter-house of the Abbaye de Joux. The church, with its round-headed western door surmounted by a circular window, was already long out of date, but Othon was either too pious or too frugal to tamper with the work of his ancestors. He left the older structure as it was and concentrated on hastening the completion of his own building. Judging by the small but enchanting cloister, which still remains untouched,[12] this must have drawn expressions of delight from even the most silent of Carthusians. Two years later, when he attended the chapter-general of the Order, Othon must have been sure of the prior's final approval of his foundation. But it was well that he had gone to the Grande Chartreuse with such a charitable purpose in mind, for his visit ended in catastrophe for his hosts. It can be cold in the mountains in May, and since Othon was by then eighty-two, it is not surprising that his servants left a fire for him in the room in which he was sleeping. Unfortunately, it was not well-guarded; some sparks flew out, and the entire monastery burned to the ground. However, there seems to have been no loss of life, and the chronicler was able to see a bright

[10] J. Grémaud, *Nécrologie de la Chartreuse de La Lance*, No. 2.

[11] *Ibid.*, No. 3.

[12] The monastic buildings proper now form part of a private house, while the church has lost its vaulting and has been divided into a two-story barn.

side even to this disaster and to rejoice that all the buildings, which had previously been of wood, were now rebuilt in stone.[13]

Othon does not seem to have suffered either, for he was back at Grandson by July with the final charter, by which he gave to La Lance the remaining lands and rights of Villars-Luczon, thereby completing his donation.[14]

Even with all this on his mind, he had still not forgotten his nieces and nephews, and while he was at Avignon in 1317 he had also procured a dispensation for his great-niece, the daughter of Pierre de Grandson, to marry Louis de Cossonay, her cousin within the prohibited fourth degree,[15] and had seen to it that Thomas, the son of Guillaume de Grandson, received papal permission to study civil law for the next three years, during which time he could continue to hold his benefices without being ordained.[16] The ordination never took place, however, for Thomas died a few months later, and his canonry and prebend at Lincoln went to his brother John. John was clearly destined for a bishopric, for he was by far the most brilliant member of his family. Both his father and his uncle had been unwearied in their efforts in his behalf, but Othon must sometimes have wondered what the younger generation was coming to, as he compared his nephew with the hard-bitten prelates with whom he had traveled and worked in his early days. As bishop of Exeter, John was to become a famous administrator, builder, and liturgist, but his letters show only too clearly that he was also a self-conscious intellectual, more than satisfied with his own prose style and with a barely concealed scorn for men who did not share his interests. Years later, when the Black Prince was riding through the diocese on his way to Plymouth and had summoned the bishop to meet him and to

[13] *Brevis historia ordinis Carthusiensis*, p. 181.

[14] Grémaud, *Nécrologie . . . La Lance*, Nos. 1, 4.

[15] *John XXII: Lettres communes*, No. 3316.

[16] *Ibid.*, No. 3311.

furnish him with horses and supplies, the latter, with evident relish, wrote him a witty and condescending letter, which left no doubt that he considered such material exertions unworthy of notice. After pointing out that the state of the Devonshire lanes in early March made them almost impassable even for oxen, let alone horses, he continued:

> And it may please you to know, most beloved lord, if you please, that I can vaunt myself that there is no other bishop in England and France so bad on horseback as I am, for these three years since I came from the court of Rome, I have not ridden twenty leagues around Exeter nor mounted any horse since Michelmas until now, forasmuch as I do not greatly love to have horses or grooms or dogs or falcons; but, sire, of chaplains, clerks, and books, I have sufficient for my estate.[17]

Undaunted by this, the sixteen-year-old warrior went on to gain his spurs and undying glory at Crécy: the bishop returned to his studies.

Othon had his chaplains and clerks, too, as well as his books, some of which he had borrowed from his learned nephew;[18] he, too, had administrative talents for which he could still find scope in dealing with the tangled affairs of his own family and lands; and undoubtedly, since his passion for detail remained unabated, as much careful thought went into the building of La Lance as into that of the magnificent nave of Exeter Cathedral. But unlike the younger man, he had energy left over for other things as well, and by 1323 the stay-at-home existence that he had been leading for so long had begun to grow wearisome. Five years earlier, he seems to have had another illness, for rumors of his death had reached England,[19] and in 1319 he had paid 10,000 gold florins to be absolved from his cru-

[17] A.C., lxvii, 14, given in F. Rose-Troop, *Bishop Grandison*, p. 21.

[18] *Register of John of Grandison*, I, 173–74.

[19] T. W. M. de Guérin, "Our Hereditary Governors," *Transactions of the Guernsey Society*, VI (1909–12), p. 221.

sading vow on the grounds of old age and bad health,[20] but this must have been only a passing indisposition, and now that spring had come again the white roads winding through the whiter cherry orchards proved irresistible, and soon the eighty-five-year-old lord of Grandson was off on his travels once more.

For the first time, it is almost possible to visualize him, for he cannot have changed very much in the five years that were to elapse before his death, and the effigy on his tomb in Lausanne is an unmistakable portrait. It is tempting to suppose that he may even have sat for it during some of the quieter moments of the last few years; even on his deathbed, he gave such precise instructions for his funeral that it seems only natural that he would have seen to the ordering of his tomb as well. All his fighting had not marred his features: even the small and not unbecoming scar that twists his lower lip may well have come from a childhood fall, for the blow that caused it had not been strong enough to knock out any of his teeth, and his lips close firmly over them, with a tight little quirk at either corner that shows that he was used to having his own way. The marble image of the dead reveals all too little, but even in the flesh and with his eyes open he must have had the reticent face of a man capable of keeping his own counsel, obstinate but good-humored, willing to listen but immovable once he had reached a conclusion. For the rest, a spare, closely-knit frame, with only the slightest suggestion of the paunch that comes to men who have been forced to slow down after a physically strenuous youth.

What the sculptor does not show is the joy that Othon must have felt at being alive to see one more spring and to feel the sun warm once again between his shoulder blades after a winter of confinement within the four walls at Grandson, where the *bise* roared in gusts down the chimneys to fill the drafty

[20] *John XXII: Lettres communes*, No. 9566.

rooms with smoke as chilly as the raw fog that not all the shutters could quite keep out. His delight was increased by the prospect of the journey before him, for once he had crossed the Jura nothing but easy country lay ahead of him, the rolling hills of Burgundy, the pleasant valleys of the Loire and the Seine, and at the end, the blossom-starred pastures of Normandy. He was going to one of the few parts of Europe that he had never visited, to those Channel Islands of which he had been warden for almost fifty years.

The duties of a warden, even when he was appointed only at the king's pleasure, were sufficiently onerous in themselves, for he was the chief administrative, judicial, financial, and military authority in the Islands; when the appointment was for life, he became to all intents and purposes an independent ruler, and Othon, who styled himself "Lord of the Islands," held almost the same position as Edward's ancestors had done in the only lands that remained to the English kings of their erstwhile duchy of Normandy. In addition to all this, the administrative difficulties were doubled because of the anomalous position of the Islands: politically under the English crown, ecclesiastically in the Norman diocese of Coutances, geographically within sight of the Norman coast, they were also a port of call for English shipping bound for Gascony, so that their defense was necessary to safeguard trade and communications between England and the duchy overseas. The Islanders, like the Gascons with whom they had much in common—Othon was only one of the seven men who, during the thirteenth century, held the posts of both warden and seneschal —took full advantage of the situation, claiming to be English or Norman as best suited their convenience, thus assuring for themselves many legal loopholes. They further increased the number of these by their insistence on being judged by their own ancient laws and customs, and since these differed from island to island, no one could be quite sure just what they were. Edward I, with his lawyer's mind, had ordered them to be put into writing, but the only result of this was to start a quarrel that dragged on for thirty years.

For all these reasons, the warden should have been a man who could have given undivided attention to the task, but Edward had expressly stated that his grant to Othon was in recognition and repayment of his services, and the latter had never for a moment looked on his wardenship as anything but a source of revenue. All during his tenure of office, the Islands had been administered by deputies, eight of whom were Vaudois, including his brother Guillaume and several nephews; even when Edward had taken them back into his own hands at the outbreak of the war, since Othon was still in the Holy Land, he had protected his friend's interests by appointing as subwarden Henry Cobham, Othon's associate on the Roman embassy of 1285; and when the indignation of the Islanders became so vehement that the king was forced to appoint justices in eyre of oyer and terminer to hear their complaints, two of these, John Ditton and William Russell, were Othon's own clerks. This meant that several of the charges to which the justices had to listen were against their own extortions and oppressions, so that it is not surprising that the Islanders asked for other justices to be appointed, who were not allied to "the said Sir Othon and his people."

They had always been restive under the misgovernment of their absentee warden, and with reason, for the man who had used all his influence to quash the efforts of his own countrymen to set up a commune in Lausanne would be even less sympathetic to the aspirations of some unknown and remote fishermen, but their discontent came to a head after the Islands had been handed back to him following the truce of 1298. They were impoverished by the war; their principal harbor, St. Peter-Port, had twice been taken and burnt by the French; and the trade and fisheries by which they lived had suffered severe damage. Othon, whose own purse was feeling the strain of his innumerable embassies, made no attempt to alleviate their lot, and one of their most frequent complaints was that although their coinage had been debased as a result of the war he would accept payment both for the Crown and for himself only in "good money of France," which was worth three times as much.

It was at this time that they first protested against the infringement of their ancient customs, but although during the next twenty years several different commissions were appointed to look into their complaints and also into any encroachments on the rights of the Crown, to investigate the charges of oppressive behavior on the part of Othon's bailiffs, and to find out whether the original grant had given him the power to name sheriffs and other officials for Jersey or not, nothing was ever settled. Finally, in 1319, other justices were appointed who for the first time decided various questions in favor of the Islanders, but Othon proved how justified their claims had been by immediately having these judgments set aside.

In addition to all these difficulties, there were also disputes with the bishop of Coutances and with the powerful and neighboring abbot of Mont-St.-Michel, which had been intensified by Edward I's sequestration of the alien priories during the war. Even when these were more or less settled, there always remained the question of the bishop's right to cite the Islanders before his own court on the mainland, a right that Edward II forbade Othon to recognize, and above all, there were the never-ending claims of either side to the *vraic*, the local seaweed which when cut and burnt provided the most valuable manure for the Islanders' tiny fields. Othon, who was such a stickler for his own rights that he disputed even wreckage with his unfortunate subjects, seems to have given in to the others only once, when, in 1316, and at the end of a two years' quarrel with the abbot over the Island priories of Valley and St. Clement's, he remitted to the monks certain taxes that they had incurred in Jersey and Guernsey, "for the devotion that I have to the monastery of Mont-St.-Michel and for the soul of the good King Edward, whom God assoil."[21]

It must be admitted that both Edwards, in spite of their constant preoccupation with the Islands, seemed more anxious to defray the expenses of their "belovèd and faithful" Othon out of the pockets of others than to do anything to improve the condition of the Islanders, for if it had been otherwise Edward II would never have appointed yet another nephew, Girard d'Oron, as subwarden, as he did in June, 1320. Although probably Girard did not leave England until March, 1321, within two months of his arrival he seems to have made himself so unpopular that he was forced to flee from the larger islands to the comparative safety of Sark, and when he did return to Guernsey under the protection of a writ of *de intendendo* it was only to be thrown into prison when he attempted to oust the bailiff, Jean le Marchant. Still Edward had not learned his lesson, for in February, 1323, when he appointed two more commissioners to report on the continued disorders, Girard was one of them. Whether Edward also wrote to Othon or whether it was Girard who appealed to his uncle for help, it must have been at this time that Othon set plans afoot for his journey, for by June 6, 1323, he was in residence at the castle of Jersey.[22]

He passed the summer and autumn in the Islands, but his stay there did nothing to improve matters, for the Islanders, now that they had finally seen their warden, disliked him even more than they had before. Instead of using his undoubted diplomatic talents to placate them, he added fresh extortions to those of which they already complained, and when they once more petitioned for a new inquiry, saying that if they and the king had their rights Othon would be driven from the Islands, they were probably not overstating their case.

Edward paid no attention to this and left Othon in undis-

21 *Cartulaire des Îles Normandes,* No. 104.

22 *Ibid.,* No. 60.

turbed possession, but he did find other work for the unpopular subwarden, and Girard was sent on a mission to the Empire. He left Guernsey in December for the Pays de Vaud—he wrote a little later to Hugh Despenser from "my house of Oron, which is three leagues from Lausanne"[23]—and it is probable that he and his uncle traveled eastward together. Even if Othon left earlier, it cannot have been before the middle of October; the Norman hedgerows were gray with clematis, pale ghosts of the flowers through which he had ridden in the spring, and the autumn rains had turned to snow on the mountains before he was back at Grandson. It must have been a trying journey for a man of his age, but there was little inducement for him to winter among the storm-swept Islands and tempestuous Islanders, and besides, he had a third generation of the House of Savoy standing in need of his diplomatic talents.

In October Amadée had died at Avignon, and his son, Édouard, from the very beginning of his rule, found himself caught up in a whirlpool of interests that centered round Savoy. John of Bohemia, the son of Henry VII, taking advantage of papal opposition to the emperor, Louis of Bavaria, hoped to gain the imperial crown for himself, and in return for French support he promised that if he were elected he would give the kingdom of Arles to Charles IV of France. Charles, seeing no reason why he should not become emperor himself, promised in his turn to Duke Leopold of Austria that if he were elected with Austrian support he would enrich the Habsburg holdings by the gift of ten imperial towns, including Basel, Constance, and Zürich. The success of either of these plans would have spelled the doom of Savoy, and it is no wonder that there was a flurry of Savoyard diplomatic activity or that Édouard should have called on the most experienced of his subjects. The meeting between Charles and Leopold took place at Bar-sur-Aube in July, 1324, and a few months later two of Édouard's messengers were

[23] A.C., lviii, 11, in Kingsford, op. cit., p. 195.

paid for the expenses they incurred "in going to Bar, to the Lord Othon de Grandson, sent there by the lord [count]."[24]

At a distance of centuries, the image of Othon on his last embassy is a very appealing one. One imagines him dressed in the fashion of a bygone time; a little lost in the discussions of Marsiglio di Padova's *Defensor Pacis*, which came out in that same year, and of Ockham's philosophy, so unlike that of Aquinas; secretly comparing Louis of Bavaria with the *Stupor Mundi* of his youth and Charles of France with his sainted great-grandfather; and returning with relief to Grandson, where he could dream undisturbed about the past.

What he did do was to go home and continue to plan for the future. Already in June, 1323, his successor had been named to the wardenship of the Islands when they should revert to the king on his death and, considering everything, this was only prudent. But taken in connection with the two financial trans-actions in which he was involved during the summer, it looks very much as though he were about to leave on another and longer journey. By August, 1324, he already had transferred his rights over Laupen to "Perrod" de La Tour, the young lord of Châtillon in the Valais, who then sold them to the Bernese for 30,000 pounds of silver,[25] and in the same month Pope John confirmed a donation of certain rights and rents that he made to the abbey of St. Bénigne of Dijon. At some earlier time, the abbot had granted these to him for life, "at a certain price and because of urgent necessity," and now Othon was returning them as a gift,

> in consideration of the loyal services that the late Hugues de "Ensgreto," knight, of the diocese of Besançon, father of the said abbot and companion-in-arms- of the said [Othon] had rendered to him, both in Europe and against the perfidious Saracens in parts beyond the seas.[26]

[24] F. Gabotto, *Asti e la politica sabauda*, pp. 419–20, 420, n. 2.

[25] L. de Charrière, *Les Sires de La Tour*, pièce. just., 52.

[26] *John XXII: Lettres communes*, No. 20017.

The mention of "the perfidious Saracens" may perhaps give us a hint as to what his plans were, but no subsequent events cast any further light on them. Inexplicably, he vanishes for over three years. There is no further mention of him in the archives of any of the countries in which he had lived and worked for so long. The king of England, in spite of the increasing opposition that confronted him, both at home, where it led to his deposition and murder in 1327, and in Gascony where it was to lead in the following year to the outbreak of the Hundred Years' War, never called on him again for his "experience and benevolence"; the pope and the emperor, at daggers drawn, appointed him to no more embassies, nor did the count of Savoy; and even his numerous clerical nephews, in their far-flung bishoprics and canonries, and Pierre de Grandson, in his renewed war with the count of Neuchâtel, had to get on as best they could without his help.

Epilogue

The puppet-show is over; the lights are darkened; and they will go up again for only one brief moment, to show Othon taking his final curtain and making his solemn exit from the stage on which he has played his part for almost a hundred years. It has been a spectacular production, involving countless changes of scene and a large cast of richly costumed supporting characters, but it has been a pageant rather than a play, for the protagonist rarely emerges from the background. In fact, he has only two speeches of his own. "I am heartbroken at the death of the lord bishop of Bath," he says at one time, "for in him I have lost my greatest friend"; and at another, "I have taken the Cross, and because of what I hope to achieve overseas, I trust that the Blessèd Virgin and St. John will intercede for me, so that once I have put off this garment of flesh, I shall rest in Abraham's bosom."

Revealing as these lines are, they afford little to go on in determining just how the part should be played, and not much more help is provided by the other characters, for the occasions on which they speak directly to or of Othon are disappointingly rare. We hear two kings of England: "You have served me diligently and well since we were both young. . . . I could not see to the business better myself. . . . I am as anxious for your well-being and honor as for my own." "Because of your love for me, undertake this embassy, and if the journey is too tiring for you, meet the ambassadors wherever best suits you."

And three popes: "We have shared the burden of this business together." "He did all that he could to help the other crusaders stranded with him on Cyprus." "He has never harmed anyone . . . he is unwearied in well-doing . . . he is beloved by all."

A chronicler's voice is heard: "He is a coward who tried to buy off the enemy, and when that failed, he deserted his men and fled from the battle." But another quotes a Genoese sea captain: "We knew that he was a knight of great renown from beyond the seas, and we did not want harm to come to him." A third says, "He was a good and holy man and a most strenuous knight in arms . . . he preferred to be rewarded by God rather than by man, and he held earthly riches as vanities"; while the disgruntled Channel Islanders complain, "He is grasping and dishonest . . . he defrauds us and the king, and if he had his just deserts, he should be driven from the Islands."

And running through the play, there is a ceaseless chorus of lesser voices, trustful and rarely disappointed: "Lord Othon, ask the king—ask the pope—to grant me this."

All these speeches add up to a mere handful, but, except for the accusations of cowardice and corruption, the former of which is disproved by subsequent events, they at least have the merit of consistency; and they give us the sketch for a portrait that we recognize at once when we see the outlines filled in by an artist who, although he lived too late to have known Othon I de Grandson, knew and admired his namesake and great-great-nephew, Othon III:

> A knyght ther was, and that a worthy man,
> That fro the tyme that he first bigan
> To riden out, he loued chiualrye,
> Trouthe and honour, fredom and curteisye.
> Ful worthy was he in his lordes werre,
> And ther to hadde he riden (no man ferre)
> As well in Cristendom as in hethenesse,
> And euere honoured for his worthynesse.
>
> . . . .
>
> And euere moore he hadde a souereyn prys.
> And though that he were worthy, he was wys,
> And of his port as meke as is a mayde.
> He neuere yet no vileynye ne sayde
> In al his lyf, vn to no maner wight.
> He was a verray parfit gentil knyght.

In addition to all these qualities, the speeches make it clear that Othon was gifted as well with a special ability for making friends, and knowing this, we can go on to infer that he also possessed a certain amount of charm, for he obviously had the vitality that is the one essential ingredient in that otherwise undefinable characteristic.

When we turn from words to actions, the light that these throw on his character bears out the estimate of it that we had already formed. He was the most trusted servant of Edward I in all matters requiring diplomatic ability, whether he was sent to restore order among the wild Welsh or the irrepressible Gascons, to make alliances with the touchy princes of the Empire, or to wring concessions from double-dealing French kings or haughty Roman pontiffs; by the next reign, his reputation stood so high that Edward II made what was practically an innovation in the conduct of foreign affairs by keeping him for ten years as his resident ambassador at the Curia; and even in his old age, Pope Clement V and the Emperor Henry VII were glad to make use of his ability and experience by employing him in their dealings with those most redoubtable of their adversaries, Philip IV of France and the lawyers of the Parlement of Paris. Worthiness and wisdom, courage and courtesy, loyalty and humility—the virtues that shine through his own words and through those of his contemporaries when they speak of him are borne out by his actions.

Unfortunately, in his case, these virtues remain as conventional as their unvarying representations carved on the cathedral porches; we know too little of how he actually went about his business to see just how he exemplified them and colored them by his own individuality. He is still a puppet, and all that our researches have been able to do for him is to lift him from the throng of his contemporaries and give him one descriptive line in the cast of characters: *Othon de Grandson, a successful diplomat.*

This estimate of his accomplishments is not invalidated by his failure to attain the end for which he strove, a lasting peace between England and France, for it was not his fault that he was waging a battle that was already lost, with weapons that were already out of date. If he and his fellow ambassadors had been successful in their efforts to have Pope Boniface set aside the Treaty of 1259 and recognize Gascony as an allod and not as a fief, the Treaty of 1303 might once again have put the French and English kings on an equal footing. But while the earlier treaty stood the situation was hopeless, for so long as the kings of England were also vassals of the kings of France defeat was inherent in their very position. To stave off this defeat, the English were relying on the armory bequeathed to them by their forefathers; they neither used nor understood Philip's new weapon, self-conscious and secular nationalism, which blocked Othon's advance time and time again, whether he was dealing with the Capetians along his own borders or in Gascony, with the Angevins in the Holy Land or at the Curia. In 1294, when Edward handed Gascony over to the French, he saw the cession as a step in hastening "le voiage doutremer"; Philip, on the showing of his own ambassador, saw it as a step in driving the English king from all his overseas possessions and in retaking France for his fellow countrymen. The rift between the two countries was too wide to be bridged by the most painstaking diplomacy, but that Othon worked and fought on the losing side does not detract from the value of his efforts or from his claim to be regarded as the most experienced diplomat of his day.

Thus, the task that looked so hopeless at the outset has been accomplished, if not altogether successfully, at least better than might have been expected; if, from his recorded words and actions, we have succeeded in piecing together only a skeleton, it is a skeleton with certain definite characteristics. It is tempting to reverse the procedure, to use these characteristics in trying to ascertain what he may have been doing and saying during those rare moments in which there is no mention of him, and above all, to try to discover how he passed the last three years of his life.

The normal supposition is that he spent them at Grandson and that he no longer appears in the Vaudois documents only because his heir had assumed all the responsibilities that had grown too heavy for his aged shoulders. The only difficulty is that this leaves too much unaccounted for. It does not explain the business transactions of the summer of 1324; it does not explain why he should have stored with the chapter of Lausanne Cathedral so many "ornaments, vestments, and silver vases," including "the little gold cross and the image of the Blessèd Virgin that I always carry with me";[1] it does not explain why he put off making his will until, in full possession of his faculties, he lay on his deathbed; and most puzzling of all, why he should have died not at home, but at the house of Prior Barthélemy at Aigle, fifty miles from Grandson, on the road that leads to the passes and to Italy.

The only alternative supposition is so improbable that it

[1] A.C.V., C V^b 53 (excerpt from Othon's will).

could be entertained only by a writer of historical fiction—or by someone familiar with Othon. On his return from the Islands, he must have felt at least as full of life and energy as he did four years later, when he lay dictating the will that expressed his hope that he would still live long enough to carry out some of its provisions himself, and yet at home, his nephew was clearly capable of getting on without him, while in the courts of Europe a new generation was growing up that no longer knew him. But the habits of a lifetime die hard, and although the living seemed to stand in no need of his services, he could still serve the dead: Edward I and Eleanor, Antony Bek and Vescy, Burnell, whom he had loved, the friends of his youth, and the others with whom he had worked in his later years, Lacy and the Langtons and Amadée of Savoy, to say nothing of the crowds of lesser men who had fought beside him and served him and lent him money, some of whom, once he was dead, would undoubtedly fall into the pitiful category of "those who have no one to pray for them." It would be a meritorious work to gain for them some respite from the pangs of Purgatory; the merit could be increased and combined with enjoyment it he made one last voyage to the Holy Land, and if he died on his pilgrimage, so much the better: no bed was stranger to him than his own, and a pilgrim's road to Heaven was shorter than that of other men. Moreover, he could be sure of not dying unattended; John XXII was the greatest of the missionary popes, and there was a constant stream of travelers headed for the East, bishops on the way to their far-off Chinese dioceses, friars bound for their convents in Egypt and Armenia, and members of the newly reorganized *Societas Peregrinantium propter Christum.*

There is, of course, not one atom of proof that Othon was one of these last, but there is also no proof to the contrary, and for his sake we can only hope that he was on his way back from the Holy Land when he came to Aigle in the spring of 1328. He made his will there on April 4 and, according to the necrology of the Chartreuse de La Lance and to the list of anniversaries in the Grandison Book of Hours,[2] he died on the following day. The necrology of the cathedral of Lausanne puts his death on April 12, but it seems more probable that this was the date of the funeral for which he had planned so carefully.

During the intervening week, the cortège must have made its slow way from Aigle to Villeneuve and thence along the shores of the Léman, past Chillon to Montreux and Vevey, through the vineyards of Lavaux, and finally to Lausanne. The news of his death went before him, and in each of the towns where the coffin was to spend the night, the priests came out in procession to meet it and to escort it to the church where it would lie in state on the high bier surrounded by candles, until one more mass was said for the repose of Othon's soul and his body started once again along the road. As it passed, the lakeside boatmen and fishermen, the vinedressers and cowherds in the country, and the tradesmen in the towns paused in their work to watch the cortège pass by, for the lord of Grandson, an almost legendary figure to many of them, traveled with as much dignity in death as he had done in his lifetime. The more literate among them must have been reminded of the illuminations in their manuscripts, for the brilliance of the procession was enhanced by the clear spring sunlight that filled the whole blue space between the surface of the lake and the snow-covered mountains beyond and was scarcely dimmed by the still unfolding leaves and blossoms of the fruit trees.

But the citizens of Lausanne, his ancient enemies, were afforded the best spectacle of all as the body was carried on the last stage of its journey up the steep hill that leads to the cathedral. According to the terms of his will, two mounted men were to precede him there, both wearing his colors and one carrying his pennon; the horses on which they rode were to be magnificent beasts, for each was worth 100 *livres lausannois;* they were to have trappings bearing his arms and one of them

[2] B.M. Roy. MS, 2, A, xviii.

was to carry his armor; and both horses, with their accouterments, were to be given to the cathedral chapter.

The mass that followed was only one of the many that were to come, for in his will he had set money aside to pay for others *in perpetuum* and to go to the clerks of the choir who should assist at those said on his anniversary. He had also left to the cathedral all the vestments and plate that he had stored with them, except for his little crucifix and the image of the Virgin, and these probably included the objects of which the compiler of the necrology speaks so feelingly: ". . . many good jewels, so that the office on feast-days might be more worthily celebrated; to wit, very good copes, three noble crosses and golden tablets, some clasps, several chalices, and golden cloths for the adornment of the high altar."[3] Among the vestments belonging to the cathedral and embroidered with the Grandson arms was one black set, which Othon, with his passion for detail, may well have provided in anticipation of his funeral.

But perhaps, at last, he was free from such preoccupations, and by the time that his body was lowered into the crypt and long before his tomb could be completed he was enjoying the rest in Abraham's bosom to which he had been looking forward for so many years.

The life of "long, laborious, and faithful service" was ended.

Ly prince ke pur nous suz Pilate fu punye

.   .   .   .

Relese a l'alme face des forfetes en sa vie,
En reyal mansion la mene a compaignye,
Ou service n'i ad fors joye et melodye.

3 J. Grémaud, *Nécrologie de l'église cathédrale de Lausanne*, p. 130.

Bibliography

(Except in a very few cases, I have given references only for statements that refer directly to Othon, and the works that include them are the only ones listed in this bibliography.)

i. MANUSCRIPT SOURCES

Most of the unpublished English documents mentioning Othon de Grandson have to do with the various embassies on which he was sent by Edward I. Letters of appointment and those dealing with the business of the embassies are in the Public Record Office under Exchequer, Treasury of the Receipt, Diplomatic Documents (E 30), and Chancery Miscellanea (C 47), while records of the payments that he received are in Exchequer, Kings Remembrancer, Various Accounts (E 101) and Exchequer, Treasury of the Receipt (E 36), as well as in the Wardrobe Accounts in the British Museum Additional MSS 7965, 7966a, and 8835. The classification Ancient Correspondence (SC 1), a collection of letters both to and from the Chancery, also has some which deal with his embassies, others of a less official nature, and several addressed to him as Warden of the Channel Islands.

The Archives Cantonales Vaudoises have very little material, since so many local records were burnt by the *Bourla Papey* in 1802. They did not touch ecclesiastical records, however, and most of these have been published in the various volumes devoted to the cathedral of Lausanne, the priory of Romainmôtier, and the abbey of Lac-de-Joux in the series *Mémoires et Documents* of the Société d'histoire de la Suisse Romande. The few remaining documents dealing with Othon and with contemporary members of his family are in the Archives Cantonales Vaudoises, Layette 349 (Grandson). The Archivio di Stato, Turin, Principi del Sangue, Mazzo 3, has one document that he witnessed, and Mazzo 16, Baronnie de Vaud, has references to the Grandson properties. In the Sezioni Riunite are all the surviving Savoyard rolls of accounts and some references from these have been published incidentally to other studies. None of the rolls of his period has been published in its entirety.

ii. PRINTED SOURCES

Annales Londonienses. Edited by William Stubbs. Chronicles of the Reigns of Edward I and Edward II, Vol. I. Rolls Series. London, 1882.

Archives historiques de la Gironde, Vols I, XVI. Bordeaux, 1855, 1876.

BALUZE ÉTIENNE (ed.). *Vitae paparum Avenionensium.* New edition by G. Mollat. 4 vols. Paris, 1914–22.

BERNOULLI, JOHANNES (ed.). *Acta pontificum helvetica,* Vol. I. Basel, 1892.

BÖHMER, JOHANN FRIEDRICH (ed.). *Die Regesten des Kaiserreichs unter Rudolf, Albrecht, Heinrich VII, 1273–1313.* Innsbruck, 1898.

Brevis historia ordinis Carthusiensis auctore anonymo. Martène and Durand, *Veterum scriptorum collectio,* Vol. VI.

BRUCHET, MAX (ed.). *Inventaire partiel du trésor des Chartes de Chambéry à l'époque d'Amadée VIII.* Chambéry, 1900.

Calendar of Chancery Warrants, 1244–1326. London, 1927.

Calendar of the Charter Rolls. London, 1903–27.

Calendar of the Close Rolls. London, 1900–1939.

Calendar of Documents relating to Ireland. London, 1875–1910.

Calendar of Entries in the Papal Registers relating to Great Britain and Ireland; Papal Letters, Vols. I, II. London, 1893–95.

Calendar of the Fine Rolls. London, 1911–49.

Calendar of Letter-books of the City of London, edited by R. R. Sharpe, 2 vols. London, 1899–1900.

Calendar of the Patent Rolls. London, 1906–38.

Calendar of Various Chancery Rolls, 1277–1326. London, 1912.

Cartulaire des Îles Normandes: Recueil de documents concernant l'histoire de ces îles conservées aux Archives du Département de la Manche et du Calvados, de la Bibliothèque Nationale, du Bureau des Rôles, du Château de Warwick, etc. Société Jersiaise. Jersey, 1918–24.

CHAMPOLLION-FIGÉAC, J. J. (ed.). *Lettres de rois, reines, et autres personnages des cours de France et d'Angleterre depuis Louis VII jusqu'à Henri IV.* Documents inédits de l'histoire de France. Paris, 1839–47.

Chronicle of Lanercost. Edited by J. Stevenson. Bannantyne Society, Edinburgh, 1839.

Close Rolls of the Reign of Henry III. London, 1902–38.

COTTON, BARTHOLOMEW. *Historia Anglicana.* Edited by H. R. Luard. Rolls Series. London, 1859.

CUTTINO, G. P. "Bishop Langton's Mission for Edward I, 1296–1297," in *Studies in British History presented to H. G. Plum.* University of Iowa, 1941.

De excidio urbis Acconis Libri II. Martène and Durand, Amplissima Collectio, Vol. V.

DELAVILLE LEROULX, J. (ed.). *Cartulaire générale de l'ordre des Hospitaliers de St.-Jean de Jérusalem en Terre Sainte (1100–1310).* 4 vols. Paris, 1894–1906.

DEPUTY KEEPER OF THE PUBLIC RECORDS. *5th and 6th Reports.* London, 1845–46.

FINKE, HEINRICH (ed.). *Acta Aragoniensia: Quellen zur deutschen, italienischen, französischen, spänischen Kirche- und Kulturgeschichte aus der diplomatische Korrespondenz James II (1291–1327).* Berlin, Vols. I, II, 1908; Vol. III, 1922.

Fontes rerum bernensium. Bern, 1877–83.

FOREL, FRANÇOIS (ed.). *Régeste soit repertoire chronologique de documents relatifs à l'histoire de la Suisse Romande.* Mémoires et documents publiés par la Société d'histoire de la Suisse Romande, 1ère série, Vol. XIX. Lausanne, 1862.

(The) Gascon Calendar of 1322. Edited by G. P. Cuttino. Camden Society. London, 1948.

(Les) Gestes des Ciprois. Recueil des historiens des croisades, documents arméniens, Vol. II.

GRANDISON, JOHN OF, bishop of Exeter. *Register* (edited by Rev. F. C. Hingeston-Randolph). 3 vols. London, 1894–99.

GRÉMAUD, ABBÉ J. *Nécrologie de l'église cathédrale de Lausanne.* Mémoires et documents publiés par la Société d'histoire de la Suisse Romande, 1ère série, Vol. XVIII. Lausanne, 1862–63.

——. *Nécrologie de la Chartreuse de La Lance.* Mémoires et documents publiés par la Société d'histoire de la Suisse Romande, Vol. XXXIV. Lausanne, 1879.

HAYTON, COUNT OF GORIGOS. *La Flor des Estoires de la terre d'Orient.* Recueil des historiens des croisades, documents arméniens, Vol. II.

HEMINGBURGH, WALTER DE. *Chronicon de gestis regum Anglie,* ed. H. G. Hamilton. 2 vols. English Historical Society, London, 1848.

HISTORICAL MSS COMMISSION. *Report on MSS in Various Collections,* Vol. I. London, 1901.

JOHNSTONE, HILDA (ed.). *Letters of Edward, Prince of Wales, 1304–05.* Roxburghe Club. 1931.

KERN, FRITZ (ed.). *Acta Imperii Angliae et Franciae ab anno 1267 ad annum 1313.* Tübingen, 1911.

KOHLER, CHARLES (ed.). "Deux projets de croisade en Terre-Sainte composés à la fin du xiiie et au début du xive siècles," *Revue de l'Orient Latin,* Vol. X (1903–4).

LANGLOIS, CH.-V. (ed.). "Notes et documents relatifs à l'histoire du xiiie siècle," *Revue historique,* Vol. LXXXVII (1900).

LANGTOFT, PIERS. *Chronicle.* Edited and translated by Thomas Wright. 2 vols. Rolls Series. London, 1866–68.

LAON, HERMANN OF. *Gesta Bartholomaei Laudunensis.* Bouquet, Vol. XII.

(The) Ledger-book of Vale Royal Abbey. Edited by J. Brownbill. Lancashire and Cheshire Record Society, Vol. LXVIII, 1914.

MATILE, GEORGES AUGUSTE (ed.). *Monuments de l'histoire de Neuchâtel.* 2 vols. Neuchâtel, 1844–48.

Minutes of Evidence taken before the committee for privileges in the Grandison peerage case. London, 1854.

MUNTANER, RAMON. *Chrónica catalana.* Edited by A. de Bofarull. Barcelona, 1860.

MURIMUTH, ADAM. *Continuatio chronicarum.* Edited by E. M. Thompson. Rolls Series. London, 1889.

NAPLES, THADDEUS OF. *Historia de desolacione et conculcacione civitatis Acconensis et tocius terre sancte.* Edited by Comte Paul Riant. Geneva, 1874.

NEOCASTRO, BARTOLOMEO DE. *Historia sicula.* Muratori, RIS, Vol. XIII.

PALGRAVE, SIR FRANCIS (ed.). *The Parliamentary Writs and Writs of Military Summons.* 2 vols. Record Commission, London, 1827–37.

PAMPERATO, S. "Documenti per la storia del Piemonte (1265–1300)," *Miscellanea di storia italiana,* 3d series, Vol. IX (XL).

Papal Registers in the Bibliothèque des Écoles françaises d'Athènes et de Rome. *Régistres de Boniface VIII.* Edited by Georges Digard, Maurice Faucon, Antoine Thomas, and Robert Fawtier, Paris, 1884–1939. *Régistres d'Honorius IV.* Edited by Marcel Prou. Paris, 1888. *Régistres de Nicholas IV.* Edited by Ernest Langlois. Paris, 1886. *Jean XXII: Lettres communes.* Edited by G. Mollat. Paris, 1904–46.

Papal Registers: *Registum Clementis Papae V.* Edited by the monks of the Order of St. Benedict. 9 vols. Rome, 1885–88.

PECKHAM, JOHN, archbishop of Canterbury. *Registrum epistolarum.* Edited by C. T. Martin. Rolls Series. London, 1882–85.

PRYNNE, WILLIAM. *The history of King John, King Henry III, and the most illustrious King Edward I.* ("Records") London, 1690.

Recueil diplomatique du Canton de Fribourg, Vol. II. Fribourg, 1840.

REYNAUD, G. (ed.). French parody of the Treaty of Montreuil in *Romania,* Vol. XIV (1885).

RISHANGER, WILLIAM. *Chronica.* Edited by H. T. Riley. Rolls Series. London, 1865.

Rôles Gascons. Edited by Charles Bémont, Vols. II, III. Paris, 1900–1906.

Rotuli parliamentorum; ut et petitiones et placita in Parliamento tempore Edward R. I, Vol. I., n.p., n.d.

RYMER, THOMAS (ed.). *Foedera, conventiones, litterae et cuiuscunque generis acta publica,* Vols. I, II. Record Commission, London, 1821.

SANUDO, MARINO. *Liber secretum fidelium crucis.* Bongars, Gesta Dei per Francos, Vol. II. Hanover, 1611.

SBARALEA, J. H. (ed.). *Bullarum Franciscanum.* 4 vols. Rome, 1759–68.

SCHWALM, J. (ed.). *Constitutiones et acta publica imperatorum et regum,* Vol. IV, 1298–1313. Monumenta Germaniae Historica, series ii, part ii. Hanover, 1906–11.

STAPLETON, THOMAS (ed.). "A brief summary of the Wardrobe Accounts of the tenth, eleventh, and fourteenth years of King Edward II," *Archaeologia,* Vol. XXVI (1836).

(The) *Statutes of the Realm,* Vol. I. Record Commission, London, 1810.

STEVENSON, JOSEPH (ed.). *Documents illustrative of the history of Scotland, 1286–1306.* 2 vols. Edinburgh, 1870.

YPRES, JEAN D'. *Chronica sive historia monasterii Sancti Bertini.* Martène and Durand. Thesaurus novus anecdotorum, Vol. III.

2 8 2

iii. BOOKS AND ARTICLES

BURNAND, AUGUSTE. "La date de la naissance d'Othon Ier, sire de Grandson," *Revue historique vaudoise*, 1911.

———. "Othon Ier, Sire de Grandson," *Revue historique vaudoise*, 1910.

CÉRENVILLE, BERNARD DE, AND GILLIARD, CHARLES. *Moudon sous la régime savoyarde*. Mémoires et documents publiés par la Société d'histoire de la Suisse Romande, 2ième série, Vol. XIV. Lausanne, 1929.

CHAPLAIS, PIERRE. "Règlement des conflits internationaux franco-anglais au xive siècle (1293–1377)," *Le Moyen Âge*, Vol. LXII (1951).

CHARRIÈRE, LOUIS DE. *Recherches sur les sires de Cossonay et sur ceux de Prangins issus de leur famille*. Mémoires et documents publiés par la Société d'histoire de la Suisse Romande, 1ère série, Vol. V.

———. *Les Sires de La Tour*. Mémoires et documents publiés par la Société d'histoire de la Suisse Romande, 1ère série, Vol. XXIV.

(The) Complete Peerage. New edition by the Hon. Vicary Gibbs. 10 vols. London, 1910–45.

CHIAUDANO, MARIO. *La finanza sabauda nel secolo XIII*. 3 vols. Turin, 1934.

COULTON, G. C. *Mediaeval Panorama: The English Scene from Conquest to Reformation*. Cambridge, 1945.

CUTTINO, G. P. *English Diplomatic Administration, 1259–1339*. Oxford, 1940.

DEVIC, CLAUDE, AND VAISSETTE, JEAN. *Histoire générale de Languedoc*, Vol. IX. Toulouse, 1885.

Dictionnaire historique, géographique, et statistique du canton de Vaud. Lausanne, 1914.

DIGARD, GEORGES. *Philippe le Bel et le Saint-Siège de 1285 à 1304*. Paris, 1936.

DIXON, W. H. *Fasti Eboracenses*, Vol. I. London, 1863.

FOURNIER, PAUL EUGÈNE LOUIS. *Le royaume d'Arles et de Vienne (1138–1378)*. Paris, 1891.

FRASER, C. M. *A History of Antony Bek, Bishop of Durham, 1283–1311*. Oxford, 1957.

GABOTTO, FERDINANDO. *Asti e la politica sabauda in Italia al tempo di Guglielmo Venturi*. Pinerolo, 1903.

GUÉRIN, LT.-COL. T. W. M. DE. "Our Hereditary Governors," *Transactions of the Guernsey Society*, Vol. VI (1909–12).

GUICHENON, SAMUEL. *Histoire généalogique de la royale maison de Savoie.* Lyons-Turin, 1660.

JARRETT, BEDE. *Social Theories of the Middle Ages, 1200–1500.* Boston, 1926.

KERVYN DE LETTENHOVE, FRANTZ. "Études sur l'histoire du xiiie siècle," *Mémoires de l'académie royale de Belgique,* Vol. XXVIII (1854).

KINGSFORD, C. L. "Sir Otho de Grandison, 1238?–1328," *Transactions of the Royal Historical Society,* 3d series, Vol. III (1909).

LANGLOIS, CH.-V. *Le règne de Philippe III, le Hardi.* Paris, 1887.

LUNT, WILLIAM E. *Financial Relations of the Papacy with England to 1327.* Cambridge, Mass., 1939.

MORRIS, JOHN E. *The Welsh Wars of Edward I.* Oxford, 1901.

ROSE-TROOP, FRANCES. *Bishop Grandison, Student and Art-Lover.* Plymouth, 1929.

STELLING-MICHAUD, S. AND S. "Étudiants vaudois à l'université de Bologne de 1265–1300," *Mélanges d'histoire et de littérature offerts à M. Charles Gilliard.* Lausanne, 1944.

STRICKLAND, AGNES. *Lives of the Queens of England,* Vol. I. Second edition. London, 1851.

STURLER, J. DE. "Le paiement à Bruxelles des Alliés franc-comtois d'Edouard Ier roi d'Angleterre (mai 1297)," *Cahiers Bruxellois,* Vol. V (January–March, 1960).

TAYLOR, A. J. "The Castle of St.-Georges d'Espéranche," *Antiquaries' Journal,* Vol. XXXIII (1953).

——. "A Letter from Lewis of Savoy to Edward I," *English Historical Review,* Vol. LXVIII (1953).

TOUT, T. F. *Chapters in the Administrative History of Mediaeval England.* 6 vols. Manchester, 1920–33.

TRABUT-CUSSAC, J. P. "Itinéraire d'Édouard Ier en France, 1286–89," *Bulletin of the Institute of Historical Research,* Vol. XXV (1952).

Finito libro sit laus et gloria Christo.
Manus scriptoris salventur omnibus horis.

Index

and attempted assassination of Edward, 28–30

Bakewell, John: (1303, 1306) appointed to settle Gascon claims, 210; (1307) at Parliament of Carlisle, 214; appointed on embassy to France, 215

Baldock, Ralph, bishop of London: (1307) as chancellor, 215–16; (1311–12) on embassy to Council of Vienne, 244

Baldwin II, Latin emperor of Constantinople (1228–61), 194

Ballardi, bankers of Lucca, 195

Balliol, John. *See* John, king of Scotland

Bannockburn: (1314) battle of, 256

Bar, Edward of, 213

Bar, Henri, count of: (1296) on embassy to Cambrai, 143; (1300) deserts English alliance, 179

Bar, Jean of: (1299) on mission to Paris, 172; on embassy to Montreuil, 173; witnesses liberation of Balliol, 177; (1306) at Curia, 208

Bar, Jeanne of, 208

Barbarossa, Frederick, 3, 59

Bard (Aosta), castle of, 34

Bardi, bankers of Florence, 254–55

Barons' War (1264–65), 13–14

Bar-sur-Aube (Aube), 267, 268

Barthélemy, Prior: Othon dies at house of, 274

Basel, 267

Basel, bishop of. *See* Vuippens, Girard de

Baumaris Castle (Anglesey, Wales), 72

Bavaria, Louis of, 267

Bayonne, citizens of: (1299) export duties pledged to, 193–94; (1303) Edward's debt to, 192; mentioned, 66, 136

Bazas (Gironde), barons of, 54

Béarn, Constance de. *See* Marsan

Béarn, Gaston, vicomte de: (1270) and crusade, 17; (1278) received back into Edward's

grace, 54; (1288) at Canfranc, 95; (1290) death of, 198; mentioned, 33, 58

Béarn, Marguerite de. *See* Foix, Marguerite de

Beatrice of Provence, queen of Sicily, 20, 21, 58

Beauchamp, Walter, Steward of the Household, 183

Beaujeu, Guichard, sire de, 248

Beaujeu, Guillaume de, Master of the Temple: (1290–91) at Acre, 118, 119; killed during siege, 122, 123

Bek, Antony, bishop of Durham, patriarch of Jerusalem: (1272) named executor of Edward's will, 31; (1274) as Keeper of the Wardrobe, 49; (1275) on mission to Paris, 47; (1277) as peace commissioner in First Welsh War, 51; (1285) as Edward's proctor at Paris, 84; (1294) on mission to the Empire, 140; negotiates for marriage of Edward of Carnarvon and Philippine of Flanders, 140; (1295) at Parliament of Westminster, 141; (1297) on truce commission at Groningen Abbey, 156–57; (1298) at Tournai, 157; appointed on embassy to Curia but recalled, 159; (1303) at Curia to straighten out quarrel with Edward, 202, 204; (1306) named Patriarch of Jerusalem, 212; (1307) says Edward's funeral mass, 216; reinstated by Edward II, 221; on embassy to France, 222

Belfaux (Fribourg), 68

Belmont, Pierre de; Thibaut de. *See* Grandson-Belmont

Belmont (Vaud), castle of, 249

Benedict XI (Niccolò Boccasini), pope (1303–4): 200; and English tenth, 202–3

Benevento: (1266) battle of, 5

Benstede, John, Chancellor of the Exchequer, 207–8

Bérard, Thomas, Master of the Temple, 29

Berwick, John: (1296) on embassy to Empire, 142; (1296–97) on King's Council at Cambrai, 148–49, 152; (1300) on embassy to Curia, 181; (1301) on embassy to Paris, 187; (1307) appointed on embassy to France, 215; on embassy to France, 222

Béthune, Robert de: (1298) on Flemish embassy to Curia, 159, 166–68, 170–71

Biarritz, whalers of, 66

Black Prince, 260–61

Blanche, queen of Navarre, countess of Champagne and Brie, 60

Blyborough, William, Edward's clerk, 53

"Bonevill" (Bonvillars), Ralph de, Othon's servant, 74 and n. 69

Boniface VIII (Benedetto Caetani), pope (1294–1303): (1294) elected, 138; (1295) sends legates to England, France, and the Empire, 141; confirms Jean de Grailly as governor of the Comtat-Venaissin, 172; makes grant from crusading tenth to Othon, 139; (1296) asks Edward and Philip to send envoys to Curia, 147–48; refuses dispensation for Savoyard-Viennois marriage, 160–61; (1297) again asks that envoys be sent to Curia, 157; (1298) dealings with embassies to Curia, 167–70; (1299) claims Scotland as papal fief, 177–78; (1300) and Great Jubilee, 2, 184; postpones final decision of Gascony, 177; and crusading tenth, 180–81; and Girard de Vuippens, 173, 177; (1301) writes to Edward on Gascon claims, 185–86; his re-

lations with Philip, 188–89; (1303) absolves Walter Langton of charges against him, 205; death of, 2, 200; his place in the *Inferno*, 62; (1311) posthumous trial of, 226, 244–45; character of, 161–62

Bonvillars (Vaud), 74, n. 69

Bordeaux: (1269) revenues pledged to Louis IX, 17; (1283) and disputed episcopal election, 74–75; duel at, 78, 79–80

Bordeaux, Simon de Rochechouart, archbishop of, 49

Brabant, Jean, duke of: (1278) betrothed to Margaret of England, 52; (1290) his marriage, 112–13; (1296) on embassy to Cambrai, 143; (1297) his quarrel with archbishop of Cologne, 149

Brabazon, Roger, 216

Brainwashing, 219

Brescia: (1311) siege of, 240

Brianzon, Jeanne de: reputed to be Walter Langton's mistress, 205

Brie, Simon de. *See* Martin

Brittany, Jean, duke of: (1272) named executor of Edward's will, 30; (1294) renounces allegiance to Edward, 169; (1298) named to administer Gascony pending final decision, 169; (1305) with Clement V at Bordeaux, 201; dies of injuries at Clement's coronation, 207–8

Brittany, John of. *See* Richmond, John of Brittany

Bruce, Robert. *See* Robert I

Bruges: (1302) Matins of, 189

Brunswick, Otto of, 4

Buonconvento (Siena), 240

Burghersh, Robert, 210

Burgh-upon-Sands (Cumberland), 215

Burgundy, Blanche of, 55, 231

Burgundy, Charles the Bold, duke of, 166

Burgundy, county of. *See* Franche-Comté

Burgundy, duchy of, 54

Burgundy, Othon IV, count of: grants pension and lands to Othon, 55, 105, 113; (1294) makes alliance with Philip and cedes him Franche-Comté, 140

daughter of: (1278) and Othon's plan to marry her, 54–56

daughter of: (1279) betrothed to duke of Burgundy, 55

daughter Blanche marries Philip V, 55

son of: (1306) negotiations for his marriage to Eleanor (II) of England, 212–13

Burgundy, Robert, duke of: (1279) betrothed to daughter of count of Burgundy, 55; (1298) on French embassy to Curia, 162; named to administer Gascony pending final decision, 169

daughter of: (1306) and negotiations for her marriage to Edward of Bar, 213

Burnell, Robert, bishop of Bath and Wells: (1272) named executor of Edward's will, 31; (1277) consecrates Vale Royal Abbey, 50; (1278) treats for return of the Agenais, 52; (1278–79) in Gascony with Othon, 40, 52–54; grants manor of Sheen to Othon, 57; (1287) on commission that sentenced Jean de Grailly, 110; at Oloron, 93; (1288) at Canfranc, 95; (1289) with Edward in Gascony, 97; granted papal favors, 105; (1290) in charge of livings under Othon's patronage, 111; named Othon's attorney in Channel Islands, 112; (1292) death of, 135; character of, 135; mentioned, 87, 88

Caetani, Benedetto. *See* Boniface VIII

Cambio, Arnolfo di, 166

Cambrai. *See* Anglo-French War

Canfranc. *See* Sicilian Vespers

Canterbury: (1275) citizens punished for attack on Othon, 42; archbishops of. *See* Peckham; Winchelsey

Cantilupe, Thomas, bishop of Hereford, 208

Carlisle, Parliament of, 214–16

Carmelites at York, prior of, 182

Carnarvon, Edward of. *See* Edward II

Carnarvon Castle (Wales), 72

Carpentras: (1314–16) conclave of, 253

Castillonès (Lot-et-Garonne), 197

Catalan nobles, 77

Caumont, sire de, 199

Celestine V (Pietro Morrone), pope (1294): sends Bertrand de Got on mission to England, 141; sends Jean de Grailly on mission to Aragon, 145; (1308) his canonization demanded by Philip, 226; (1313) canonized, 245

Chaise-Dieu, La, abbot of, 184

Champagne, Thibaut IV, count of, 75

Champagne and Brie, Blanche, countess of, queen of Navarre, 60

Champvent, Guillaume de, bishop of Lausanne: (1273) elected, 34; and difficulties with his diocese, 35; (1281–84) and war with citizens of Lausanne, 68; (1289) granted papal favors, 104–5; (1297–1300) and war with Louis I of Vaud, 152; (1298) and truce, 163; (1300) and agreement reached, 181; and treaty of Ouchy, 186; (1301) death of, 184; mentioned, 89

Champvent, Henri de: Pierre of Savoy's lieutenant in the Pays de Vaud, 12

Champvent, Jean de, 257–58

Champvent, Othon de, bishop of Lausanne: (1289) granted pa-

Despenser, Hugh: (1296) on embassy to Empire, 142; on embassy to Cambrai, 143; (1296–97) on King's Council at Cambrai, 148; (1300) on embassy to Curia, 181; (1305–6) on embassy to Curia, 207; (1307) at Parliament of Carlisle, 214; (1307) appointed on embassy to France, 215; (1324) and letter from Girard d'Oron, 267

Diplomatic practice, 101, 209

Ditton, John, Othon's clerk, 208, 264

Ditton (Cambridgeshire), manor of, 126

Dover, boatmen of, 182

Drayton, William, 112

Droxford, John: (1299) investigates Frescobaldi bankers, 175; (1303) Keeper of the Wardrobe, 192

Dublin, archbishop of. See Hotham

Dubois, Pierre, 131

Duèse, Cardinal Jacques. See John XXII

Dunbar: (1296) battle of, 145–46

Durham, bishop of. See Bek

Edmund of Lancaster. See Lancaster and Leicester

Edward I, king of England (1272–1307): (1266) defeats Simon de Montfort, 8; (1268) takes the Cross, 16; (1269) pledges revenues of Bordeaux to Louis IX, 17; (1270–72) on crusade, 17–32 passim; (1272) attempt on his life, 28–30; makes his will, 30; returns to Sicily and hears of his father's death, 32; (1273) at Capua, 33; at Curia, 33–34; in Savoy, 34; (1275) leases Channel Islands to Othon, 56; summoned to Parlement of Paris, 48; (1276) writes to John XXI about crusading vow, 61; declares war

on Llewellyn, 50; (1277) makes life grant of Channel Islands to Othon, 13, 56; at consecration of Vale Royal Abbey, 51; (1278) attempts to seize crusading tenth, 81; empowered to arbitrate between Rudolf I and Philippe of Savoy, 67; letter to Othon and Burnell on Gascons, 52–53; letter to Othon on his intended marriage, 55–56; (1279) in France, 57–58; (1280) letter to Charles of Salerno about Guy de Montfort, 64; (1282) difficulties of his position in War of Sicilian Vespers, 79; forbids export of money, 81; and crusading tenth, 81–82; (1283) peacemaking efforts, 80; letter to Charles I on duel at Bordeaux, 78; (1284) summoned as duke of Aquitaine for Franco-Aragonese War, 82; (1285) continues peacemaking efforts, 83; (1286) empowered to make truce, 91; leaves for Gascony, 110; (1287) at Oloron, 93–94; takes the Cross, 108; (1288) at Canfranc, 95–96; (1289) preparations for crusade, 108–9; (1290) loses bet to the queen's laundress, 113; makes financial arrangements for Othon on crusade, 112; (1292) settles Scottish succession, 135; (1293) cited to appear before Parlement of Paris and sends Edmund of Lancaster, 136–37; (1293–94) foreign and domestic difficulties, 136; (1294) renounces homage and declares war on Philip, 137; alliance with Adolf, 140; (1295) sends envoys to Adolf, 142; appoints Amedée of Savoy and Othon to meet with papal legates, 142; (1296) and Scottish rising, 145; ap-

Frederick II, Holy Roman Emperor, king of Sicily (1212–50): 3, 4; his book on falconry, 22–23

Frederick I, king of Sicily (1296–1377), 138, 156

Frescobaldi, bankers of Florence: (1296–97) payments to Othon, 154; (1299) convicted of importing currency illegally, 175; (1303) customs pledged to, 195; (1306) make payments to Jean of Bar, 208; palaces of, 194

Frescobaldi, Giovanni de' (cleric), 211; (poet), 194

Gainsborough, William, bishop of Worcester: (1300) on embassy to Curia, 180; (1305–6) on embassy to Curia, 207, 208; (1307) appointed on embassy to France, 215

Gascony, administrative problems: the Agenais, 48, 52, 58; appeals to Parlement of Paris, 48

Gascony, seneschals of. See Ferrers; Grailly; Hastings; Havering; Thanney

Gaveston, Piers: (1307) banished, 214, 220; created earl of Cornwall, 220; (1308) appointed regent, 220; is sent Edward II's wedding presents, 224; at Edward's coronation, 220–21; married to Margaret of Gloucester, 228; second banishment, 228; (1311) third banishment, 240; (1312) captured and executed, 250; mentioned, 164

Geneva, Amédée, count of, 181–82

Geneva, Aymon de Grandson, bishop of, 12

Geneva, Guillaume, count of: (1309) on Imperial embassy to Curia, 233–34; (1317) an ally of Pierre d'Oron, 257

Genoa, ladies of, 180–81

Genoese merchants in Levant, 24, 132, 133

Ghent: (1297) rising at, 165

Giez (Haute-Savoie), church of, 105

Giffard, Godfrey, bishop of Worcester, 66

Giotto, 166

Gloucester, Gilbert de Clare, earl of: (1268) takes Cross, 16; (1277) at consecration of Vale Royal Abbey, 51; (1283) betrothed to Joan of Acre, 74; (1290) his marriage, 112–13; (1291) his quarrel with earl of Hereford, 136; (1295) his death, 149; mentioned, 17

Gloucester, Margaret of, 228

Gorigos, Hayton, lord of: (1291) reorganizes Armenian government, 128–29; (1306) at Curia, 130, 131, n. 41, 212; becomes Premonstratensian monk, 131, n. 41; his project for crusade, 130–31; mentioned, 227

Got, Béraud de. See Albano

Got, Bertrand de. See Clement V

Grailly, Jean de: (1272) left in command at Acre, 32, 109; (1277) at consecration of Vale Royal Abbey, 51; (1278) at Mâcon, 110; made seneschal of Gascony, 52; (1283) and duel at Bordeaux, 79–80; (1287) negotiates for marriage of Eleanor and Alfonso, 93, 110; at Oloron, 93; dismissed as seneschal of Gascony, 104, 109–11; (1289) commanding French forces in the Holy Land, 104; (1290) returns from Curia to Holy Land, 111, 116; (1291) at siege of Acre, 118, 122; accused of cowardice, 123; (1294) sent on mission about War of Sicilian Vespers by Celestine V, 145; (1295) confirmed as governor of Comtat-Venaissin, 172; does homage to Amédée, 172;

in Gascony with Burnell, 40, 52–54; plans to marry daughter of count of Burgundy, 54–56; granted manor of Sheen by Burnell, 57; on mission to Curia, 61–65 *passim;* returns to England, 65–66; on mission to Savoy, 66–68; and Second Welsh War, 70–71; contracts joint debt with John de Vescy, 73–74; appointed justiciar of Snowdon and later of all Wales, 71; and castle-building in Wales, 72–73; swears to marriage contract of Joan of Acre and Gilbert of Clare, 74; services requested by Edmund of Lancaster, 74–75

Missions connected with War of Sicilian Vespers (1285–89): as Edward's proctor at Paris, 84; on mission to Curia, 83–91 *passim;* obtains papal favors for Vale Royal Abbey, 89–90; at Oloron, 93–94; on commission that sentenced Jean de Grailly, 110; at Canfranc, and remains as hostage in Aragon, 95–97; with Edward in Gascony, 97; named executor of John de Vesey's will, 113; on mission to Curia, 97–106 *passim;* his speech to Nicholas IV, 100–101; at siege of Gaeta, 101–2; at Naples, 102–3; illness of, 103; granted papal favors for St.-Jean de Grandson and permission to build a Franciscan church, 105

Crusader (1291–94): takes Cross, 113; puts affairs in order, 111–12, 113–14; makes second grant to St.-Jean de Grandson, 113–14; gains indulgence for William Burnell at Curia, 115; com-

mander of English troops at Acre, 116–23 *passim;* accused of cowardice, 123–24; at Cyprus, 123–33 *passim;* in financial straits, 124, 137–38; orders altar-frontal for Lausanne Cathedral, 124–25; his pilgrimage to Jerusalem, 125–27; in Armenia, 128–29, 132–33; his friendship with Hayton of Gorigos, 129; returns to Italy, 138; his letter to Langton on Burnell's death, 135

Missions connected with Anglo-French War (1294–1303): at Curia, 138–39; receives grant from crusading tenth, 139; appointed to meet with papal legates, 142; on embassy to Empire, 142; on embassy to Cambrai, 143; at Roxborough with Edward, 145; empowered to treat for an armistice, 146; on King's Council at Cambrai, 148–54 *passim;* negotiates for marriage between Joan of Acre and Amédée, 149–51 *passim;* returns to England, 154; on truce commissions at Groningen Abbey and Tournai, 156–57; on embassy to Curia, 159–71 *passim;* on mission to Paris, 172; returns to England, 173; on embassy to Montreuil, 173; in Pays de Vaud, 177; returns to England, 175; appointed to King's Council and summoned for military service, 176; investigates Frescobaldi bankers, 175; in Pays de Vaud, 181; returns to England, 182; audits Walter Langton's accounts, 182–83; on embassy to Curia, 2, 181, 183–85; obtains papal grant for St.-Jean de Grandson, 184; wit-

Grandson, Othon de—*Continued*
Missions connected with Anglo-French War—Continued
nesses marriage of Isabelle of Villehardouin and Philippe of Savoy, 185; returns to Pays de Vaud, 186–87; appointed on embassy to Curia but refuses, 187; his crusading grant paid in full, 188; last embassies connected with war, 188; becomes a Carthusian oblate, 258; on embassy to Paris, 189; helps draw up treaty of Paris (1303), 242; seals marriage contract of Blanche of Savoy and Pierre de Grandson-Belmont, 189

Last years of Edward's reign (1303–7): on King's Council in Gascony, 189–200 *passim;* appointed on embassy to Benedict XI, 200; at Parlement of Toulouse, 198–99; and Mozzi bankers' attempt to defraud him, 195; on embassy to Clement V on his election, 205–6; with Clement V, 201–3 *passim;* on embassy to Curia, 207–8; remains at Curia, 208–13 *passim;* negotiates for marriage between Eleanor of England and son of count of Burgundy, 212–13; at Lanercost with Edward, 212; at Parliament of Carlisle, 214; appointed on embassy to France, 215; in London at Edward's death, 215, 216; on embassy to France, 222

At Curia (1308–17): his position, 224–25; is made a papal knight, 244; appointed by Clement V on mission to England, 229; granted permission to found Chartreuse de La Lance, 230; arbitrates truce between Louis

II of Vaud and Girard de Vuippens, 232; on English embassy to Curia, 233; on Imperial embassy to Curia, 235, 236; granted Laupen by Henry VII, 237; illness of, 237, 238; appointed arbiter of French-Imperial treaty, 239; consulted on terms of treaty of Paris (1303), 241–42; on embassy to Council of Vienne, 243–46 *passim;* takes cross and prepares to leave on crusade but attacked on way to Avignon, 230, 246–47; returns to Pays de Vaud, 247–49; arbitrates treaty between Louis II of Vaud and Pierre d'Oron, 248; arbitrates in differences between Amedée and Philippe of Savoy, 248; with Edward II at Paris and Pontoise, 250, 251; on English embassy to Curia, 255; last mentioned in service of king of England, 257

Last years (1317–28): involved in Vaudois quarrels, 257–58; endows altar in Lausanne Cathedral, 258; founds Chartreuse de La Lance, 258–59; illness of, 261; absolved from crusading vow, 261–62; visits Grande-Chartreuse, 259–60; visits Channel Islands, 266–67; makes grant to Abbey of St. Bénigne, 268; grants rights to Laupen, 268; as Edward of Savoy's envoy to Bar-sur-Aube, 267–68; stores objects with Lausanne Cathedral, 274, 277; death of, 276; his funeral, 276–77; his will, 275, 276–77; effigy of, ix, xi, 262

Miscellaneous: annuity granted him by Jacques de Molay, 57, 227; his character, 40–

41; his diplomatic training, 139–40; as expert in Gascon affairs, 13, 49; favors granted him at Curia, 90, 229–30; and Grandson properties, 68, 177, 248–49; his house in Westminster, 66, 136; his influence at Curia in behalf of relatives, 88–89, 104–5, 184, 211, 260; his influence at English court in behalf of friends, 182; Irish grants made to him, 56–57, 75, 111, 175; his pension from count of Burgundy, 55, 105, 113–14; his project for crusade, 17, 27, 129–31, 245; and his family's relations with counts of Neuchâtel, 257; his relations with diocese of Lausanne, 34–35; is represented on Queen Eleanor's tomb, 126

Grandson, Othon III de, 132, 271–72

Grandson, Othon de, Othon's nephew, 184

Grandson, Pierre de, Othon's brother, 13

Grandson, Pierre de, Othon's father: Pierre of Savoy's lieutenant in the Pays de Vaud, 12; (1252) granted pension by Henry III, 12; castellan of Moudon, 13; (1285) death of, 13 and n. 9; mentioned, 10

Grandson, Thomas de, 211, 260

Grandson-Belmont, Pierre de: (1303) betrothed to Blanche of Savoy, 152, 189; made Othon's heir, 189; (1309) arbitrates truce between dauphin of Vienne and Amedée, 231; (1317) and dispensation for marriage of his daughter to Louis de Cossonay, 260; sells rights to Grande-Chartreuse, 259; (1318) grants some lands to Grande-Chartreuse, 259; mentioned, 258

Grandson-Belmont, Thibaut de, 184, 258

Grandson (town):
Franciscan church: (1289) Othon given papal permission to build it, 105; indulgences granted those visiting it, 114, 229
St.-Jean, priory of: (1288) Othon makes grant to, 105; (1289) papal favors for, 105; (1290) Othon makes second grant to, 113–14

Great Interregnum (1254–73), 5

Great Jubilee (1300), 2, 184

Greenfield, William, archbishop of York: (1311–12) on embassy to Council of Vienne, 244

Gregory IX (Ugolino di Segni), pope (1227–41), 4

Gregory X (Tealdo Visconti), pope (1271–76): (1268) takes Cross, 16; (1271) elected, 26; sends Polos to Kublai Khan, 27; his farewell sermon at Acre, 27; (1273) excommunicates Guy de Montfort, 34; (1274) authorizes crusading tenth in England, 81; acquires Comtat-Venaissin, 226; and laws governing conclaves, 63; (1275) consecrates Lausanne Cathedral, 67; (1276) death of, 61; mentioned, 5, 194

Groningen Abbey. See Anglo-French War

Grosseteste, Robert, bishop of Lincoln, 210

Guelders, Reynaud, count of, 148

Guerri, Michael, 248

Gümmenen (Bern), 67

Habsburg, Albert of. See Albert I

Habsburg, Clementia of, 76

Habsburg, Hartmann of: (1276) and negotiations for his marriage to Joan of Acre, 59–60;

(1282) drowned, 60; mentioned, 74

Habsburg, Rudolf of. *See* Rudolf I

Hainault, Florence of, 185

Hainault, Jean, count of, 148

Harlech Castle (Merionethshire), 72

Harley, Malcolm, Othon's deputy in Wales, 73

Hastings, John, seneschal of Gascony, 197

Havering, John, seneschal of Gascony, 199, 201

Hawarden Castle (Flintshire), 70

Hayton II, king of Armenia, 127, 128

Helinand, bishop of Laon, 11

Hemingburgh, Walter de: quoted, 89, 123–24, 202

Henry VI, Holy Roman Emperor (1190–97), 3

Henry VII, Holy Roman Emperor (1303–13): (1308) election of, 230; (1309) sends embassy to Curia, 233; (1309–10) and negotiations for agreement with Philip, 236; (1310) represented by Othon at Curia, 236; grants Laupen to Othon, 237; swears fealty to Clement V, 237; (1310–13) and Italian expedition, 237–40; (1311) ratifies treaty with Philip, 239; (1312) crowned at Lateran, 240; (1313) death of, 240

Henry II, king of Cyprus and Jerusalem (1285–1324): (1291) at Acre, 121, 123; mentioned, 124

Henry II, king of England (1154–89), 6

Henry III, king of England (1216–72): (1252) grants pension to Pierre de Grandson, 12; (1272) death of, 32; reign of, 6–8; and upbringing of his children, 218

Henry of Almain. *See* Almain

Hereford, Humphrey de Bohun, earl of: (1290) marries Isa-

belle de Vescy, 113; (1291) and quarrel with earl of Gloucester, 136

Hims: (1299) battle of, 180

Hohenstaufen, Constance of. *See* Constance of Hohenstaufen

Holland, Florence, count of: (1296) on embassy to Cambrai, 143; deserts English alliance, 146; murdered, 147

Holland, John, count of, husband of Elizabeth of England, 146–47

Holy Ghost, Commander of the Order of the, 118

Holy Trinity (London), prior of, 101

Honorius II (Cencio Savelli), pope (1216–27), 4

Honorius IV (Giacomo Savelli), pope (1285–87): (1286) lays interdict on Sicily and excommunicates James and Alfonso, 86; grants English crusading tenth, 85; forbids marriage of Eleanor and Alfonso, 91; and grant to Vale Royal Abbey, 90; (1287) death of, 93; his friendship for Othon, 84; mentioned, 83

Hospital, Order of the, 24, 245

Masters of the Order: Villaret, Foulques de, 227; Villiers, Jean de, 118, 128

Hotham, William, archbishop of Dublin: (1829) on mission to Curia, 99; on mission to Curia with Othon, 97–106 *passim;* his estimate of Charles II's character, 106; (1295) at Parliament of Westminster, 141; (1297) with Edward in Flanders, 156; on truce commission at Groningen Abbey, 156–57; (1298) at Tournai, 157; on embassy to Curia, 159, 164, 167; death of, 171; character of, 164

Household: duties of the knights of the, 39–40; of the Lord

Joinville, Geoffrey de: (1299) on embassy to Montreuil, 173; (1300) on embassy to Curia, 180; (1308) at Curia, 242

Joinville, Jean de, 9

Joppa, emir of, 28

Jorz, Thomas, Cardinal of Sta. Sabina: (1305–6) on embassy to Curia, 207, 208; (1308) in charge of English affairs at Curia, 224

Joux, Abbaye de (Vaud): 36; papal grants to, at Othon's request, 211, 229–30

Joux, Jean de, 151

Kilfeakle (Tipperary), 111

Kilsheelan (Tipperary), manor of, 111

Kirkham, church of, 90

Kublai, the Great Khan, 26

Lacedaemon, Ebal de Grandson, bishop of, 12

Lacy, Henry de. See Lincoln, Henry

Lajazzo: (1294) battle of, 133

La Lance, Chartreuse de (Vaud): (1308) Othon given papal permission to found it, 230; (1318) lands for its foundation granted and cornerstone laid, 258–59

Lancaster, Red Rose of, 75

Lancaster, Thomas, earl of: (1300) asks favor from king through Othon, 182; (1316) leader of baronial party, 256; mentioned, 221

Lancaster and Leicester, Edmund, earl of: (1253) Sicilian crown offered to, 4, 7, 21; (1268) takes Cross, 16; (1272) at Acre, 30; (1275) marries queen of Navarre, 60; (1276) suggested as substitute for Edward on crusade, 61; (1278) his protection asked by Jacques

and Henri de Grandson, 69; (1283) letter to Edward, requesting the loan of Othon, 75; (1293–94) his unsuccessful mission to Paris, 136–37; adopts *Rosa gallica* as his emblem, 75: his character, 137; his cook, 66

Lanercost, chronicler of, 120–21

Langtoft, Piers: his opinion of Welsh climate, 49; quoted, 137, 142

Langton, John, bishop of Chichester: (1300) audits Walter Langton's accounts, 183; mentioned, 134, 135

Langton, Walter, bishop of Coventry and Lichfield: (1296) heads embassy to Empire, 142; on embassy to Cambrai, 143; empowered to treat for armistice, 146; consecrated, 148; (1296–97) on King's Council at Cambrai, 148–49; 152; (1300) his accounts audited, 182–83; (1301) on embassy to Paris, 187; (1301–2) on embassy to Curia, 187–88; (1303) named to head embassy to Benedict XI, 205; attacked by Winchelsey, 204–5; (1305) on embassy to Clement V on his election, 205; named collector of tenth in England, 203; (1305–6) heads embassy to Curia, 207, 208; (1307) at Parliament of Carlisle, 214; appointed on embassy to France, 215; imprisoned by Edward II, 221; his position at court, 192, 204

Laon, bishops of. See Helinand; Grandson, Barthélemy de

Laporte, Guitard de, 197

La Tour, "Perrod" de, Lord of Châtillon, 268

Laupen (Bern): (1310) Henry VII grants castle and town to Othon, 237; (1324) Othon

transfers his rights to "Perrod" de La Tour, 268
Lausanne, bishops of: wars with Savoy, 35. *See also* Cossonay, Jean de; Champvent, Guillaume de; Champvent, Othon de; Oron, Pierre de; Vuippens, Girard de
Lausanne, cathedral of: (1275) consecrated, 67; altar-frontal for, 124–25; mentioned, 88
Lausanne, citizens of: (1281–84) at war with Guillaume de Champvent, 68
LeBlund, William, 14, 74
Leisseth, Robert, constable of Bordeaux, 196
Le Marchant, Jean, bailiff of Channel Islands, 266
Leo IX (Bruno), pope (1049–54), 11
Lewes: (1265) battle of, 14
Libre de Fine, 246
Liège, Tealdo Visconti, archdeacon of. *See* Gregory X
Liège, Thibaut de Bar, bishop of, 148
Limoges, Cahors, and Périguex, seneschal of, 48
Lincoln, Henry de Lacy, earl of: (1277) Othon serves under, in First Welsh War, 50; (1278) swears to marriage contract between Margaret of England and Jean of Brabant, 52; (1287) at Oloron, 93; (1289) in Gascony, 97; (1299) on embassy to Montreuil, 173; (1300) on embassy to Curia, 181; (1301) on embassy to Paris, 187; (1303) in Gascony, 189; on embassy to Paris, 189; draws up Treaty of Paris, 242; takes homage for Gascony in Edward's name, 190; in Gascony, 191; named to head embassy to Benedict XI, 205; (1304) at Parlement of Toulouse, 198–99; (1305) on embassy to

Clement V on his election, 205; (1305–6) heads embassy to Curia, 207–8; (1307) at Parliament of Carlisle, 214; appointed on embassy to France, 214; embassy to France, 222; mentioned, 66
Lincoln, Parliament of, 178
Llewellyn ap Griffith, Prince of Wales: betrothed to Eleanor de Montfort, 49; (1272–76) refuses homage to Edward, 49; (1276) Edward declares war on, 50; (1277) surrenders, 51; (1278) marries Eleanor de Montfort, 52; (1282) reconciliation with David ap Griffith, and outbreak of Second Welsh War, 70; defeat and death of, 70; mentioned, 64
Lombardy, Iron Crown of, 233, 238
London, bishop of. *See* Baldock
Lord Edward. *See* Edward I
Loreto, Holy House of, 127
Loria, Ruggiero da: (1283) captures Charles of Salerno, 80; (1287) captures Guy de Montfort, 93; (1289) in command at siege of Gaeta, 102; (1301) witnesses marriage of Isabelle of Villehardouin and Philippe of Savoy, 185; mentioned, 86
Lorraine, Ferri, duke of, 148
Louis IV, Holy Roman Emperor (1314–47), 267
Louis IX, king of France (1226–70): (1269) advances money to Edward for crusading expenses, 17; (1270) at crusade of Tunis, and death of, 18, 19; mentioned, 5, 9
Louis X, king of France (1314–16), 253
Lovetot, Sir John, 204–5
Lucca, bankers of, 83. *See also* Ballardi; "Luke de Luk"
Lucca, Ptolemy of, 30
"Luke de Luk," Italian banker, 57

Lull, Raymond, 246
Lusignan, Amaury of: (1290–91) commander of Cypriots at siege of Acre, 118
Lusignan, Henry of. *See* Henry II, king of Cyprus
Lusignan, Hugh of, count of La Marche, 7
Lusignan, Hugh of, king of Cyprus. *See* Hugh III
Luxemburg, Henry of. *See* Henry VII
Luxury, increase of, in early fourteenth century, 219–20
Lyons, 236
Lyons: (1274) Council of, 51, 63
Lyons, Pierre of Savoy, archbishop of, 236

Malik el-Aschraf, sultan of Egypt (1290–93): (1290) sends embassy to Acre, 117–18; (1291) second embassy to Acre, 118; siege of Acre, 121; letters to king of Armenia, 127–28; (1293) assassinated, 128
Manfred, king of Sicily (1255–61), 4, 5, 21
Margaret, daughter of Edward I: (1278) betrothed to Jean of Brabant, 52; (1290) marries Jean, 112–13
Margaret, queen of Norway, 58
Margaret, queen of Scotland, 58
Margaret, "The Maid of Norway," queen of Scotland: (1289) receives dispensation for marriage to Edward of Carnarvon, 103
Margaret of France, queen of England: (1298) betrothed to Edward I, 170, 173; (1299) marries Edward, 176; (1300) asks favor of him through Othon, 182; mentioned, 177
Margaret of Provence, queen of France: (1275) arranges marriage of Edmund of Lancaster

to queen of Navarre, 60; (1276) plans marriage of Joan of Acre to Hartmann of Habsburg, 59–60; (1281–82) and Habsburg-Savoyard war, 67; her hatred of Charles I, 21, 58, 76; her homage to emperor for Provence, 59; her opinion of Jean de Grailly, 110
Maria of Hungary, queen of Sicily, 97
Marsan, Constance de Béarn, vicomtesse de: wife of Henry of Almain, 32; (1304) received back into Edward's grace, 199; (1309) death of, 254; mentioned, 198
Martel, Philip: (1305–6) on embassy to Curia, 207, 208; (1306) appointed to settle Gascon claims, 210
Martin IV (Simon de Brie), pope (1281–85): (1281) elected through Angevin influence, 63; and Edward's crusading plans, 63; (1283) declares Aragon forfeit and offers Sicilian crown to Charles of Valois, 81; and English crusading tenth, 82; (1285) death of, 82; mentioned, 76
Mauléon, castle of, 214–15, 223
Meillan (Lot-et-Garonne), castle of, 209
Mente, Desirata de, town crier of Bayonne, 40
Mézières, Philippe de, 132
Michael Paleologus, emperor of Constantinople (1259–82), 18
Middleton, William, bishop of Norwich, 66
Molay, Jacques de, Master of the Temple: grants annuity to Othon, 57, 227; (1291) succeeds Guillaume de Beaujeu, 128; at coronation of Hayton of Armenia, 128; (1314) burnt at the stake, 219, 252
Monreale, Giovanni Boccamazzo, archbishop of: (1286) papal

legate in War of Sicilian Vespers, 92; (1288) at Canfranc, 95

Monte Canisio, Dionisia de: (the elder), 66; (the younger), 159

Montfaucon, Gautier de: (1297) ally of Edward, 151; (1297–1300) ally of Guillaume de Champvent, 152, 182; (1298) on embassy to Curia, 163

Montfavres, priory of, 184

Montferrat, Guglielmo Spadalunga, marquis of, 97

Montfort, Amaury de: (1271) bedridden at Padua, 65; (1276) captured and imprisoned in England, 50, 64; and claims to Leicester lands, 60

Montfort, Eleanor de: betrothed to Llewellyn ap Griffith, 49; (1276) captured on way to Wales, 50; (1278) marries Llewellyn, 52; mentioned, 64

Montfort, Guy de: Angevin vicar of Tuscany, 32; (1271) assassinates Henry of Almain, 33; (1273) excommunicated, 34; (1281) forbidden to return to England, 64–65; (1287) defeated and captured by Loria, 93; his claims to Leicester lands, 60

Montfort, Jean de, 65

Montfort, Simon de: earl of Leicester, 8, 14; (the younger), 33

Monthermer, Ralph, 151

Montreuil, Process of, 210

Montreuil, Treaty of. See Anglo-French War

Mont-St.-Michel, abbot of, 265–66

Morat (Bern), 67

Moudon (Vaud), 13

Mozzi, bankers of Florence: (1305) attempt to defraud Othon, 195; mentioned, 194

Muntaner, Ramon: quoted, 92

Murimuth, Adam: quoted, 221–22, 254

Murlens, Oger de, miller of Bayonne, 40

Namur, Jean de: (1298) on Flemish embassy to Curia, 166–68, 170–71

Narbonne, Gilles Aycelin, archbishop of: (1298) on French embassy to Curia, 162; (1305) with Clement V at Bordeaux, 201; (1311) and settlement of Treaty of Paris (1303), 242

Nassau, Adolf of. See Adolf

Navarre, Blanche, queen of, 60

Nazareth, 28, 127

Neocastro, Bartolomeo di: (1286) Sicilian ambassador to Curia, 86; mentioned, 101

Neuchâtel, Cathérine de, 257–58

Neuchâtel, counts of: relations with lords of Grandson, 257

Neuchâtel, Raoûl, count of, 257, 258

Newerk, Henry, 144

Nicholas III (Giovanni Caetani), pope (1277–80), 61

Nicholas IV (Girolamo Masci), pope (1288–92): (1288) abrogates Treaty of Oloron, 94; (1289) abrogates Treaty of Canfranc, excommunicates Alfonso, grants tenth to Philip for Aragonese war, and crowns Charles II, 99; refuses dispensation for marriage of Eleanor and Alfonso but grants one for marriage of Edward of Carnarvon and Margaret of Scotland, 103; (1289–90) and crusade, 99, 103–4, 116

Nogaret, Guillaume de: (1303) arrests Boniface VIII, 200; (1311) prosecutor at posthumous trial of Boniface, 245; and project for crusade, 212; mentioned, 160

Norwich, bishops of. See Middleton; Salmon

Novara, bishop of, 239

"Oheny" (Ireland), 111
Oloron. *See* Sicilian Vespers
Orewin's Bridge: (1272) battle of, 70
Orleton, Adam, 244
Oron, Amphélisie d', 188
Oron, Girard d': (1282) sells properties to Othon, 68; (1290) heir to Pierre de Vuippens, 112; (1320) appointed subwarden of Channel Islands, 266; (1321-23) in Channel Islands, 266-67; (1323) appointed on commission of inquiry to Islands, 266; (1323) mission to Empire, 267
Oron, Girard d' (cleric), 88
Oron, Guillemette d', 188
Oron, Pierre d', bishop of Lausanne: (1312-16) at war with Louis II of Vaud, 247-48; mentioned, 104
Oron, Rodolphe d', 88
Osgodby, Adam, 230
Osman I, 9
Othon IV, Holy Roman Emperor (1198-1212), 3, 4
Othon IV, count of Burgundy. *See* Burgundy
Ottaker II, king of Bohemia (1253-78), 67

Palermo, 22-24
Palestrina, Simon Beaulieu, bishop of: (1295) papal legate to France, England, and the Empire, 141-46 *passim*
Palud, Aymon de la: (1312) attacks Othon and is excommunicated, 247; as husband of Marguerite de Cossonay, 249
Paris, Matthew, 12
Paris, Treaty of: (1259), 48, 84; (1303), 190. *See also* Anglo-French War
Parlement of Paris, 48, 112, 136. *See also* Gascony
Parliament: (1292) meets at

Othon's house, 136; of Carlisle (1307), 214-16; of Lincoln (1301), 178; of Westminster (1294), 137; of Westminster (1295), 141; of Westminster (1305), 206
Parma, bishop of, 248
Payerne (Vaud): granted to Pierre of Savoy by Richard of Cornwall, 67; (1283) falls to Imperial troops, 68
Peckham, John, archbishop of Canterbury: (1282) his quarrel with Henri de Grandson, 87-88; (1283) his opposition to Edward, 82; (1290) Othon takes Cross from, 113; and liberation of Amaury de Montfort, 64; his opinion of Wales, 93; his relations with Edward, 87-88; mentioned, 202
Pecorara, Cardinal, 203, 212
Pembroke, Aymer of Valence, earl of: (1296) heads embassy to Cambrai, 143; (1297) on truce commission at Groningen Abbey, 156-57; (1298) at Tournai, 157; on embassy to Curia, 159; (1299) on embassy to Montreuil, 173; (1303) draws up Treaty of Paris, 242; (1307) commander in Scotland, 216; on embassy to France, 222; (1317) on embassy to Curia, 255
Pembroke, William of Valence, earl of: (1272) named executor of Edward's will, 31; (1287) at Oloron, 93; (1289) with Edward in Gascony, 97; mentioned, 66
Penchester, Stephen, Warden of the Cinque Ports, 49
Peter III, king of Aragon (1276-85), king of Sicily (1282-85): as husband of Constance of Hohenstaufen, 21, 60; (1281) his foreign and domestic difficulties, 76-77; (1282) invades Sicily, 77-78; (1283)

308

St.-Eutrope (Saintes, Charente-In-
férieure), prior of, 96
St.-Jean d'Acre. *See* Acre
St.-Laurent (Ain), priory of, 105
St. Louis. *See* Louis IX
St. Mary of the Germans (Teutonic
Knights), Commander of the
Order of, 118
St.-Maurice (Valais): (1273) for
which Philippe of Savoy does
homage to Edward, 34, 47;
mentioned, 38
St.-Pol, Guy, count of: (1298) on
embassy to Curia, 162; named
to administer Gascony pending
final decision, 169
St.-Sever, Pierre Aimeri de, 180
St. Thomas, Commander of Order
of, 118
Salerno, Charles of. *See* Charles II
Salins (Jura): and revenues raised
on salterns of, 105, 113–14
Salisbury, Simon of Ghent, bishop
of, 173
Salmon, John, bishop of Norwich:
(1287) heads commission that
sentenced Jean de Grailly,
110; at Oloron, 93; (1307) on
embassy to France, 222;
(1310) on mission to France,
241–42; (1317) on embassy
to Curia, 255
Sanchia of Provence, queen of the
Romans, 58
Sancho IV, king of Castile (1284–
95), 92
Sanudo, Marino: quoted, 123
Sapiti: Andrea, Edward's proctor
at Curia, 224; Filippo, his son,
229
Sauma, Rabban, 108
Sautier, Jean, castellan of Grandson: taken prisoner by Savoyards, 186; (1310) takes homage of Laupen for Othon, 237
Savelli, Pandolfo de', Senator of
Rome, 84
Savoy, Agnès de, daughter of
Amedée, 160–61

Savoy, Amedée, The Great, count
of: (1291) and payment to
Othon for crusading expenses,
114; (1294) first wife dies,
149; (1295) appointed to
meet with papal legates, 142;
on embassy to Empire, 142;
on embassy to Cambrai, 143;
at Roxborough with Edward,
145; empowered to treat for
armistice, 146; (1296–97) on
King's Council at Cambrai,
148–49; (1297) arbitrates
truce between Guillaume de
Champvent and Louis I of
Vaud, 152; and projected marriage with Joan of Acre, 149;
on truce commission at Groningen Abbey, 156–57; (1298)
at Tournai, 157; on embassy
to Curia, 159, 164, 167–68,
170–71; (1299) on mission to
Paris, 172; witnesses liberation
of Balliol, 177; as proxy at
Montreuil for betrothal of Edward and Margaret of France,
173; (1300) on embassy to
Curia, 181; arbitrates treaty
between Guillaume de Champvent and Louis I of Vaud,
186; (1301) appointed on embassy to Curia but refuses to
go, 187; on embassy to Paris,
187; (1303) in Gascony, 189;
on embassy to Paris, 189;
takes seizin of restored Gascon
towns for Edward, 191; (1303–
6) at war with dauphin of
Vienne, 193; (1304) at Parlement of Toulouse, 198–99;
(1306) truce in war with dauphin, 211; granted permission
to build chapel at La Tour-de-
Peilz, 211–12; (1308) at Edward II's coronation, 222;
(1309) on Imperial embassy
to Curia, 233–34; arbitrates
truce between Girard de Vuippens and Louis II of Vaud,

Soe, Guillaume de: (1303) Edward's debts to, 192–93; (1309) appointed governor of Viterbo, 225

Solens, Hamo de, 91

Sowin, Edward's groom, 20, 23

Suchy (Vaud), 177

Surrey, William of Warenne, earl of: (1271) at consecration of Vale Royal Abbey, 51

Swabia, Philip of, 3, 4

℟ agliacozzo: (1268) battle of, 5

Temple, Masters of the Order of the. *See* Beaujeu, Guillaume de; Bérard; Molay

Temple, Order of the: (1307) arrest of the Templars, 219; (1312) suppression of the Order, 244, 245; their goods granted to Hospitallers, 245; mentioned, 24

Testa, Guillaume de, archdeacon of Aran: (1306) appointed papal collector in England, 212; (1307) excommunicates Bruce, 214

Thanney, Luc de, seneschal of Gascony, 48, 49

Thibaut II, king of Navarre (1253–70), 20, 31

Thiette, Philippe de: (1298) on Flemish embassy to Curia, 166–68, 170–71

Thoros, king of Armenia, 128

Thors (Aube), Templars' house at: (1308) its revenues granted to Othon, 230

Tiepolo, Giacomo, 117

Tilbury, Denis of, 112

Tipperary (Ireland): county of, granted to Othon, 75: vill of, 111

Torre, Guido della, Captain of Milan, 238

Toulouse, Pierre de la Chapele Taillefer, archbishop of, 169

(La) Tour-de-Peilz (Vaud), 212

Tournai, truce of. *See* Anglo-French War

Travel: by land, 41–43, 98; by sea, 43–44; in Holy Land, 126–27

Trent, Henry, bishop of, 238

Tripoli, 16, 103

Troyes, Guichard, bishop of, 219

Tunis: 19–20; emir of, 18

Turweston (Buckinghamshire), manor of, 126

Tusculum, Ordoño Alurz, bishop of, 88

Tybetot, Robert: (1272) named executor of Edward's will, 31; (1277) at consecration of Vale Royal Abbey, 51; peace commissioner in First Welsh War, 51; mentioned, 66

Tyngewick, Nicholas, Edward's doctor, 213

"℧lmeto," Lady of, 223–24

Ulster, Richard de Burgh, earl of, 111

Unam Sanctam, 188, 226

Urban IV (Jacques Pantaléon), pope (1261–64), 4

Utrecht, Jean de Syrick, bishop of, 148

Valence, Aymer of (cleric), 88

Valence: Aymer of; William of. *See* Pembroke

Vale Royal Abbey (Cheshire): (1277) consecrated, 50–51; (1286) grateful for papal favors granted through Othon, 89–90

Valley, priory of (Channel Islands), 265

Valois, Charles of: (1283) Sicilian crown offered to, 81; (1300) occupies Douai, 179; (1305) with Clement V at Bordeaux, 201; injured at Clement's coronation, 207; (1308) at coronation of Edward II, 221; as